GENERATIVE ARTIFICIAL INTELLIGENCE EMPOWERED LEARNING

This book explores the integration of Generative Artificial Intelligence (GenAI), such as ChatGPT, into educational practices and research methodologies. With the potential to transform traditional learning environments, this book addresses both the opportunities and challenges that come with leveraging GenAI for enhancing teaching and learning experiences.

This comprehensive guide delves into multiple aspects of GenAI in education. It covers critical topics such as project-based learning (PBL), personalized learning through AI, AI-driven student assessment, and the role of AI in special education. Furthermore, it examines ethical considerations, the readiness of students and teachers for AI technologies, and case studies on AI's impact on student outcomes. With insights from educators, researchers, and practitioners from around the globe, the book provides a balanced perspective on both theoretical frameworks and practical implementation of GenAI technologies.

Ideal for educators, researchers, and policymakers, this book serves as a practical resource for those looking to effectively integrate AI into their pedagogical and research efforts. It is an essential reference for anyone interested in staying at the forefront of educational innovation and exploring the future possibilities of AI-empowered learning.

Mahmoud Elkhodr is a lecturer at Central Queensland University, Australia, specializing in cybersecurity, IoT, ehealth, and GenAI educational technologies. He developed the semantic obfuscation technique and has published widely on IoT and cybersecurity, significantly contributing to research on GenAI's role in education.

Ergun Gide is a professor and distinguished educator at Central Queensland University, Australia, specializing in intelligent systems and emerging digital technologies. A recipient of multiple Australian learning and teaching and research supervision awards, he has extensively published research in GenAI, intelligent systems, emerging digital technologies, and educational innovation.

GENERATIVE ARTIFICIAL INTELLIGENCE EMPOWERED LEARNING

A New Frontier in Educational Technology

Edited by Mahmoud Elkhodr and Ergun Gide

CRC Press
Taylor & Francis Group
Boca Raton London New York

CRC Press is an imprint of the
Taylor & Francis Group, an **Informa** business

A CHAPMAN & HALL BOOK

Designed cover image: Getty Images

First edition published 2025
by CRC Press
2385 NW Executive Center Drive, Suite 320, Boca Raton FL 33431

and by CRC Press
4 Park Square, Milton Park, Abingdon, Oxon, OX14 4RN

CRC Press is an imprint of Taylor & Francis Group, LLC

© 2025 selection and editorial matter, Mahmoud Elkhodr and Ergun Gide; individual chapters, the contributors

Library of Congress Cataloging-in-Publication Data
Names: Elkhodr, Mahmoud, author. | Gide, Ergun, author.
Title: Generative artificial intelligence empowered learning : a new frontier in educational technology / edited by Mahmoud Elkhodr and Ergun Gide.
Description: First edition. | Boca Raton, FL : CRC Press, 2025. | Includes bibliographical references and index.
Identifiers: LCCN 2024057842 (print) | LCCN 2024057843 (ebook) | ISBN 9781032727523 (hbk) | ISBN 9781032727516 (pbk) | ISBN 9781003422433 (ebk)
Subjects: LCSH: Artificial intelligence—Educational applications—Case studies.
Classification: LCC LB1028.43 .G475 2025 (print) | LCC LB1028.43 (ebook) | DDC 371.33/463—dc23/eng/20250211
LC record available at https://lccn.loc.gov/2024057842
LC ebook record available at https://lccn.loc.gov/2024057843

ISBN: 978-1-032-72752-3 (hbk)
ISBN: 978-1-032-72751-6 (pbk)
ISBN: 978-1-003-42243-3 (ebk)

DOI: 10.1201/9781003422433

Typeset in Sabon
by Apex CoVantage, LLC

CONTENTS

NOTES ON CONTRIBUTORS

Ashutosh Adhikari is a final-year student pursuing Bachelor of Technology with Honors degree in artificial intelligence at Narsee Monjee Institute of Management Studies (NMIMS), India. Adhikari has developed technical skills through diverse projects in generative AI and sustainable AI solutions, with research interests in educational applications of AI.

Teresa Aires is an organizational psychologist pursuing a PhD in management at Nova School of Business and Economics. Aires' research centers on remote work, sleep, negotiations, and well-being. Her recent projects include collaborations with companies to optimize organizational dynamics through AI-driven strategies.

Ayeshah A. Alazmi is an associate professor in the Department of Educational Administration in Kuwait University's College of Education. A graduate of Virginia Tech, Dr. Alazmi has authored numerous papers on educational leadership and educational law and is active in academic committees and associations.

Huda S. Alazmi is an associate professor of curriculum and instruction at Kuwait University. With a PhD in curriculum and instruction specializing in social studies education from Virginia Tech University, Dr. Alazmi's research covers citizenship education, technology integration in classrooms, and teacher education.

Daryl Ann Borel, EdD, is an assistant professor at Lamar University in Beaumont, Texas, with over 30 years of experience in technology-enhanced teaching, learning, and innovation. Dr. Borel's research focuses on artificial intelligence in higher education. Holding an EdD in educational leadership with a focus on e-learning, an MEd in supervision with a concentration in computer science, and a BS in mathematics, Dr. Borel is a leading educator in AI's ethical applications in academia.

Ananya Datta is a final-year student pursuing Bachelor of Technology degree in artificial intelligence at NMIMS, India, with a keen focus on data science and machine learning.

G. S. Divya is an assistant professor in the Department of Automobile Engineering at Dayananda Sagar College of Engineering, Bangalore, India. With a PhD in production engineering and management, Dr. Divya has over 11 years of experience in teaching and research, focusing on personalized learning and skill development in education.

Yusufu Gambo is a lecturer in the Department of Computer Science at Adamawa State University in Mubi, Nigeria. Focusing on human-centered computing and applied AI, Gambo's research investigates ethical, practical, and societal implications of AI in educational and human-centered applications.

T. K. Jijeesh is an English faculty associate in the Department of Artificial Intelligence at Amrita Vishwa Vidyapeetham, Coimbatore, India. Jijeesh is pursuing a PhD on the intersection of English and AI education, and he has published several books and research papers on cross-disciplinary collaborations.

Newman Lau specializes in interaction design, applying cross-disciplinary concepts in research that centers on user behavior, motivation, and user-centric analysis.

Yuanyuan Li is a professor in the Music College of Capital Normal University in Beijing, China, specializing in vocal education and advancing music pedagogy within inclusive education. A distinguished member of various music associations, Professor Li has led significant educational projects recognized by China's Ministry of Education.

Xi Liu is a PhD candidate at the Hong Kong Polytechnic University School of Design, focusing on learning experience design for children with special educational needs (SEN).

Ying Liu is a lecturer at the London School of Science and Technology, UK, where Dr. Liu actively supports disadvantaged communities. With a PhD, MBA, and PGCert-HE, as well as a fellowship from the Advanced Higher Education Academy, Dr. Liu also serves as an international project advisor for China's education ministry and country director of international higher education teaching and learning.

Tulio Maximo is an assistant professor at the Hong Kong Polytechnic University School of Design. Dr. Maximo's research covers intergenerational and inclusive design, social entrepreneurship, and healthcare services, with a focus on improving society through design-led initiatives.

Ami Munshi is an assistant professor in the Artificial Intelligence Department at NMIMS University, India. With over 16 years in academia, Dr. Munshi specializes in deep learning, natural language processing (NLP), and generative AI. He has earned an MTech and a PhD in AI and electronics.

Harshith B. Nair is a postgraduate scholar in the Department of Education, Regional Institute of Education (NCERT), Mysuru, India. Nair's research explores intersections of education, technology, and psychology, with extensive publications on educational reform and the effective integration of technology into teaching.

Smita Sail is an assistant professor and the chair of the Department of English at the Amrita School of Engineering, Bangalore, India. With a PhD focusing on postcolonial literature, Dr. Sail supervises research in English and AI and has published widely on educational technology and literary studies.

Jeff Schatten, PhD, is an associate professor of business administration at Washington and Lee University. He specializes in artificial intelligence and organizational behavior. With a PhD in managerial sciences from Georgia State University, Dr. Schatten's interdisciplinary research explores AI's impact on work and society, merging philosophy with business insights.

Ting Zhao is a principal lecturer and scholar in early years music education at Beijing Youth and Politics Vocational College, China. With over a decade of experience, Zhao focuses on integrating traditional and contemporary pedagogy, child development, and technology in music education.

PREFACE

Generative Artificial Intelligence (GenAI) represents an unprecedented frontier in educational technology, poised to reshape the way students learn, educators teach, and researchers conduct inquiries across diverse academic landscapes. *Generative Artificial Intelligence Empowered Learning: A New Frontier in Educational Technology* offers a critical and comprehensive exploration of how GenAI tools, such as ChatGPT, are being integrated into educational environments worldwide. Edited by Mahmoud Elkhodr and Ergun Gide from Central Queensland University, this work brings together a diverse group of scholars, educators, and practitioners to examine the transformative potential of GenAI technologies within both traditional and innovative educational frameworks.

The chapters in this book are structured to provide a balanced view of the theoretical, practical, and ethical considerations surrounding GenAI in education. From ethical complexities in academic research to practical applications in the classroom, this work addresses the nuances and challenges educators face when they incorporate GenAI tools responsibly and effectively.

In Chapter 1, Daryl Ann Borel discusses the ethical complexities of using GenAI in academic research. Topics include issues such as validity, originality, intellectual property rights, and academic integrity, emphasizing the need for clear guidelines and regulatory frameworks. Insights are drawn from experiences in an online graduate educational research methods course, where students engaged with GenAI as a research assistant, illustrating both the potential and the challenges of integrating AI into academic settings.

Chapter 2, co-authored by Ying Liu, Yuanyuan Li, and Ting Zhao, presents the LivePBL DEEP method – a systematic approach for incorporating project-based learning (PBL) with GenAI in music education. This method integrates direction, education, event, and project phases, offering educators a cohesive framework to overcome the fragmented use of GenAI tools and enhance learning outcomes, particularly in underrepresented educational contexts.

In Chapter 3, Teresa Aires and Jeff Schatten delve into the potential of AI to cultivate curiosity and growth mindsets among learners. The research combines cognitive development theories with immersive AI-driven learning strategies in K-12 and higher education, providing actionable recommendations for educators, parents, and policymakers to leverage AI in fostering curiosity and engagement.

Chapter 4, authored by Yusufu Gambo, presents a case study from Nigeria on students' readiness to adopt GenAI tools in academic settings. Using a mixed-methods approach, the chapter highlights both the enthusiasm and apprehensions of students regarding AI. Key concerns, such as data privacy and critical thinking, are addressed, with recommendations for structured policies and training to better equip students for AI integration in their learning processes.

In Chapter 5, Huda S. Alazmi and Ayeshah A. Alazmi examine the perspectives of students and teachers at Kuwait University on the ethical and responsible use of GenAI. This comparative study sheds light on the importance of understanding cultural contexts when developing AI-related educational policies, offering nuanced insights into how GenAI can be ethically implemented in academic environments.

Chapter 6 by T. K. Jijeesh and Smita Sail explores the role of AI in personalized learning. The research addresses how AI can enhance language learning through cross-disciplinary collaboration, integrating GenAI with English education to support differentiated instruction and improve student engagement.

In Chapter 7, G. S. Divya examines the impacts of GenAI on student outcomes, emphasizing individualized learning, adaptive assessments, and the fostering of creativity. By leveraging GenAI to provide real-time feedback and promote critical thinking, this chapter highlights how AI-driven tools can support both academic and social-emotional development, equipping students with essential skills for lifelong learning.

Chapter 8, authored by Ashutosh Adhikari, Ananya Datta, and Ami Munshi, focuses on the role of AI-driven summarization techniques in streamlining knowledge acquisition. Using quantized large language models (LLMs) and advanced evaluation metrics, this chapter illustrates how AI can expedite content processing for students, educators, and researchers, enhancing educational efficiency and accessibility.

In Chapter 9, Harshith B. Nair introduces a framework for building teacher capacity in integrating GenAI into classrooms. This framework, grounded in TPACK and social learning theory, includes an eight-week training course that emphasizes GenAI literacy, ethics, and practical application, providing educators with the foundational knowledge needed to foster innovative and effective AI-integrated teaching practices.

Chapter 10 examines GenAI's role in special education, presented by Xi Liu, Newman Lau, and Tulio Maximo. This chapter highlights a case study from Hong Kong, where students in special education settings engage with GenAI tools. The findings reveal positive responses from students, teachers, and social workers and unique challenges that come with using GenAI in specialized educational contexts. Recommendations are provided for implementing GenAI tools that support inclusive and accessible learning.

Together, the chapters in this book illustrate a holistic view of GenAI in education, addressing the technological, ethical, and pedagogical dimensions of AI integration. Through practical frameworks, case studies, and policy recommendations, this work is intended to guide educators, researchers, and policymakers in harnessing GenAI to create inclusive, innovative, and responsible learning environments. As the educational sector continues to evolve alongside advancements in AI, this book aims to serve as a foundational resource, inspiring further exploration and fostering informed discussions on the responsible use of AI in education.

1

ETHICAL COMPLEXITIES AND EDUCATIONAL CHALLENGES FOR GENERATIVE AI IN ACADEMIC RESEARCH

Balancing Innovation and Responsibility in Education

Daryl Ann Borel

1.1 Introduction

Since its launch in November 2022, Generative Artificial Intelligence (GenAI), a disruptive technology, offers transformative capabilities and immense implications across various domains, including the potential to streamline the aspects of academic research. But researchers must be aware of the strengths, limitations, and ethical implications of these tools. An exponential amount of information is being created worldwide, and it is estimated that 80% of information is textual (Anawis, 2014). According to Mysore et al. (2023), the academic landscape is undergoing a significant increase in the number of scholarly publications. This proliferation is particularly impactful in the field of academic research, as artificial intelligence (AI) can assist in generating novel research, especially when it comes to analyzing large volumes of textual information. Through online tools and free or fee-based apps, everyone can now take advantage of the capability to generate new ideas from prior knowledge, perhaps connected in unexpected new ways.

The use of GenAI in academic research presents both opportunities and challenges. Hsu (2023) and Van der Maden et al. (2023) highlighted its potential to generate research questions, locate and summarize articles, facilitate literature reviews, optimize research design, analyze data, and streamline the writing process. However, they cautioned that critical thinking and ethical considerations are crucial in ensuring accuracy and preserving scholarly standards. Platt and Platt (2023) found that GenAI can effectively perform content analysis with moderate accuracy. Kunda (2023) further emphasized the need for regulation in the use of GenAI tools, particularly in academic

DOI: 10.1201/9781003422433-1

research, to address concerns about academic honesty and intellectual property rights. Moya (2023) underscored the importance of integrating GenAI tools use with integrity, suggesting the need for specific and practical guidance, support for educational stakeholders, and an equity, diversity, and inclusion lens.

In this chapter, I want to take you on an excursion through how GenAI is transforming academic research, as well as sharing perspectives from students who had the option of using GenAI tools in a graduate online research methods course. The excursion will begin with a comparison of how academic research was typically done 30 years ago and how the process has evolved with the integration of digital resources, online databases, and advanced technology tools such as AI. As we proceed, we will explore the ethical considerations of using GenAI in research and the use of GenAI as a research assistant in the research process. I come to the task of writing this chapter from a combination of vantage points. I am an online professor in the Educational Leadership department at a regional Southeast Texas University. As part of my responsibilities I develop online curriculum, help faculty incorporate new technologies into their teaching, teach a graduate research course where we use GenAI tools, and conduct research that has prepared me to write this chapter. In addition to my perspective, I have also drawn on the experiences of colleagues with experience in GenAI tools. Many of the examples in this chapter are from my university's fully online Educational Administration Master's program.

1.2 Academic Research – Then and Now

Let's begin our excursion with a look at what academic research looked like about 30 years ago. Before the widespread adoption of digital resources and online databases, conducting academic research involved predominantly manual methods that were labor-intensive and required the user's physical presence in the library and a great deal of patience and organization. Libraries primarily used card catalogs, which were physical files of indexed cards with information about the library's collections. Some libraries in the early 1990s had begun to implement early digital card catalogs known as Online Public Access Catalogs (OPACs). These systems allowed library users to search for books, journals, and other materials electronically by keyword, author, title, or subject rather than using the traditional physical card catalogs (Greenberg, 2020). However, the process still necessitated the user's physical presence in the library and was labor-intensive.

I think back to when I first started doing research as a graduate student in the early 90s and as a beginning faculty member. Before heading to the library, I would identify a research topic, formulate research questions, and keywords related to the research topic. I would manually flip through the card catalog or scroll through the OPAC to search for relevant entries, manually writing down call numbers and other details needed to locate materials. With the call numbers, I would navigate the library stacks, microfiche, or microfilm to obtain the books, periodicals, newspapers, etc. If the needed books or articles were not available in the library, I used the interlibrary loan service to borrow them from other libraries. After securing the necessary books and articles, I would manually take detailed notes or use a copy machine with rolls of quarters to make copies. This labor-intensive process required my physical presence in the library many days. Finally, I would compile massive notebooks that I would bring back and forth to the library that included bibliographic information, quotes, summaries, synthesized information, identification of key themes, and connections between sources.

To write an academic research paper, I would use a basic word processor. I would prepare the literature review from the information in my notebooks. Depending on the research methodology, data collection could involve surveys, interviews, experiments, or observations. I would design and conduct these activities manually without the aid of digital tools. The collected data would be analyzed using manual methods or basic statistical tools available at the time. This could involve calculations by hand or using simple statistical software on computers. After analyzing the data, findings, conclusions, and the remainder of the research paper would be written following the conventions of academic writing. The entire process required careful attention to detail to ensure accuracy and was significantly slower than modern digital research. The advent of early digital catalog systems and personal computers began to streamline some tasks, but the core research activities remained largely manual and hands-on. Additionally, having to be physically present in the library could be an issue for those far from major research libraries and access to resources were limited to what the library had in its physical collection without requesting the resource through interlibrary loan.

The academic research process has evolved significantly with the integration of digital resources, online databases, and advanced technology tools such as AI. Researchers now have access to a vast amount of information at their fingertips from their desk whether at work or at home, enabling them to conduct more efficient and thorough research compared to traditional manual methods. This transformation has revolutionized how researchers get information, sort information, analyze, conduct their investigations, collaborate with peers, and disseminate their findings with very little cost.

When conducting academic research today, researchers often start by utilizing online library databases and catalogs. These digital platforms provide access to a wide range of scholarly articles, journals, books, and other resources that can be searched and accessed remotely. Instead of physically visiting a library and sorting through physical materials, researchers can now conduct searches using keywords, authors, titles, or subjects to quickly locate relevant information. With the emergence of GenAI tools, researchers have access to powerful AI algorithms that can assist in various stages of the research process. GenAI tools can help researchers brainstorm topic formation, refine research questions, perform literature reviews, analyze large datasets, identify patterns and trends, generate insights, and even suggest new research directions. These tools can automate repetitive tasks, such as data cleaning and analysis, freeing up researchers to focus on higher-level thinking and interpretation of results (Velazquez, 2024). The academic research process today is characterized by increased efficiency, accessibility, and collaboration. Researchers can leverage digital resources and GenAI tools to streamline their workflow, discover new connections between ideas, and conduct high-quality research much faster.

1.3   Ethical Considerations, Challenges, and Limitations of Using GenAI in Research

GenAI is a powerful technology that employs algorithms to identify patterns in large datasets and makes use of these patterns to generate new content in a range of formats. However, as we integrate GenAI in education, it is important for researchers to understand the ethical considerations, challenges, and limitations of these tools. Ethical considerations are paramount in academic research, ensuring integrity, trust, and innovation; they safeguard participants, uphold credibility, and shape a foundation for socially responsible advancements. In a recent study, Law (2024) found that more than half of the papers in their literature review study related to GenAI mentioned ethical considerations, including plagiarism, biases, educational inequality (i.e., the GenAI program may create disparities among students due to unequal accessibility to and proficiency in using the tool), copyright issues, and learner motivation impairment (i.e., ChatGPT produces writing without students putting in significant effort).

The other important aspects of ethical concerns and limitations include hallucinations – generating fictious information presented as factual or accurate – or misinformation, bias and discrimination, and data privacy and security. AI systems are trained on data, and if the training data are biased or reflect societal prejudices, the AI models can perpetuate those biases. The major argument is that since AI-powered chatbots collect and analyze data to provide personalized learning experiences, there is a need to ensure that personal information is protected and handled in a secure manner. Also, AI-powered chatbots, such as ChatGPT, may produce correct-sounding but logically incorrect results (Dwivedi et al., 2023; National Academic Integrity Network, 2023).

Additionally, chatbots may generate a response with in-text citations but does not necessarily include the citations in the references (Hsu, 2023).

The nature of GenAI models, particularly when given simple prompts, can be very reductive, resulting in content that is over-simplified, low quality, or very generic. Due to their fundamental structure, as well as regularly released newer versions, content from many GenAI models can be difficult to reproduce consistently. This is particularly problematic in research and academia where reproducibility is a cornerstone of establishing credibility. Many GenAI models are trained on data with cutoff dates, resulting in outdated information or the inability to provide answers about current information and events. In some cases, the data cutoff date is not made explicitly clear to the user. Finally, it is crucial to maintain transparency in the use of GenAI tools, disclosing any automated processes and ensuring accountability for their outcomes.

1.3.1 Actual Case Example – Ethical Use

Graduate Educational Administration students enrolled in my Educational Leadership five-week online Research Methods course during Spring 2024 were given the option of using GenAI tools to complete a research proposal that was due in week five. The use of GenAI tools to assist with the research process, including ethical use, was introduced during a synchronous web conference during week one. Additionally, there were videos in the blackboard shell demonstrating various GenAI tools. In week five, students were asked to complete an end-of-course reflection. Below are final reflective responses related to their perceptions related to the ethical use of GenAI tools.

Question 1: How comfortable are you with the ethical implications of using GenAI tools in academic research? (1 = not comfortable at all and 7 = extremely comfortable)

Mean (n = 370): 4.36

Question 2: What concerns, if any, do you have about the ethical use of GenAI tools in research? (Select all that apply.)

Summary of results (n = 370):

Concern	Frequency	Percentage
Plagiarism and originality	221	59.7
Accuracy of information	195	52.7
Dependency on technology	147	39.7
Biases	82	22.1
No concern	45	12.1
Privacy issues	22	5.9
Other	10	2.7

Question 3: Please share any experiences where you felt the use of a GenAI tool was particularly ethical or unethical in the context of academic research.

Sample student responses:

Student 1: "I feel the AI tools are ethical as long as the student is transparent about the use of AI tools in research. Clearly disclose when AI tools are used, what kind of data is being processed, and how the tools influence the research process."

Student 2: "AI was helpful in generating ideas and I would not consider that unethical."

Student 3: "Ethically you can utilize generative AI tools by creating synthetic data for algorithm testing or model validation while maintaining privacy and confidentiality. Unethical use happens when data is fabricated in order to manipulate findings, jeopardizing the validity of research findings."

Student 4: "AI tools can give you a plethora of information, however, it is up to the user to ensure that data is ethical and does not include any biases. Personally, I do not simply take AI's information at face value. It can be used as a guide but one must make one's own inferences."

Student 5: "In my experience, the use of Generative AI tools can be considered ethical when they are employed to enhance productivity and efficiency in academic research, such as automating tedious tasks like data analysis or summarization. However, it may be deemed unethical if these tools are used to plagiarize or fabricate content without proper attribution or validation, undermining academic integrity and originality."

Student 6: "I previously felt AI was unethical in the context of student work. However, within this course and through instruction by Dr. Borel, I felt it was more ethical and helpful if used appropriately to aid learning."

1.3.2 Discussion of Results

The end-of-course reflection survey revealed varied perceptions among students regarding the ethical use of GenAI tools in academic research. Data from 370 students showed a mean comfort level of 4.36 on a scale of 1 to 7, indicating a moderate level of comfort. This suggests that while many students are somewhat comfortable with the ethical use of GenAI tools, a significant number of students still have reservations or require further guidance. The most common concern, cited by 59.7% of students, was the potential for GenAI tools to facilitate plagiarism or undermine originality. Over half of the students (52.7%) were concerned about the accuracy of information generated by these tools, highlighting the need for critical evaluation of AI-generated content. Additionally, 39.7% of students expressed concerns about becoming overly reliant on technology, which could diminish their own analytical and critical thinking skills. Biases in AI-generated outputs were a concern for 22.1% of students, while 12.1% indicated they had no concerns about the ethical use of GenAI tools.

Students also shared specific experiences and perspectives on the ethical use of GenAI tools. Many emphasized the importance of transparency and clear disclosure when using AI tools in research, suggesting that ethical use is achievable with proper acknowledgment of the tools' influence. Some students found AI tools ethically helpful in generating ideas, viewing them as a means to enhance creativity without compromising ethical standards. Students highlighted the need for users to critically evaluate AI-generated information and ensure it is free from bias and ethical issues. Many appreciated the productivity and efficiency gains offered by AI tools, considering them ethical when used to streamline tasks like data analysis and summarization. Some students reported a shift in their perception of AI tools from unethical to ethical when used appropriately and with proper guidance, indicating the value of education and training in fostering ethical use. However, concerns were raised about the unethical use of AI tools to fabricate data or manipulate findings, which could compromise the validity and integrity of research.

Overall, the survey results underscore the importance of education and clear guidelines in addressing students' concerns about the ethical use of GenAI tools. While many students see the potential benefits of these tools, ensuring transparency, accuracy, and critical evaluation is essential to maintaining academic integrity and trust in AI-assisted research.

1.4   GenAI as a Research Assistant

The next stop on our excursion will be a discussion of how GenAI can be used as a research assistant. GenAI tools can be a valuable resource to help researchers with topic formulation, refining the research questions, developing the literature review, selecting the methodology based on research questions and data collected, crafting the research instrument, analyzing and visualizing the data, drafting conclusions and recommendations, as well as writing, editing, and providing feedback on the document.

1.4.1   Brainstorming Topic Formulation

The first decision, and one of the most important steps, for any educational research study is to determine exactly *what* to study – the topic formulation.

GenAI tools, such as ChatGPT, can help brainstorm ideas, explore facets, and aggregate information about a research topic. For example, ChatGPT can generate a diversity of ideas that may not have been considered, which can lead to a more creative and innovation research topic. GenAI tools can significantly enrich brainstorming processes by providing insights derived from current trends, historical data, and cross-disciplinary studies. The tools are more efficient than traditional brainstorming methods, allowing for more ideas generated in less time and can help refine ideas by providing feedback and suggestions based on the information provided. Additionally, there is also the collaborative potential, allowing multiple people to contribute to the brainstorming process simultaneously. Finally, GenAI tools can help properly size the topic, which usually needs to be reduced – or occasionally expanded – in scope.

The quality and relevance of the AI's responses are greatly influenced by how the prompts are framed. Crafting prompts that elicit useful responses requires practice, utilizing a technique called "iterative refinement," where you provide feedback on the AI's responses and ask it to improve them. Many prompt sessions evolve into lengthy dialogues. Mollick (2023) recommends the following:

> The best way to use AI systems is not to craft the perfect prompt, but rather to use it interactively. Try asking for something. Then ask the AI to modify or adjust its output. Work with the AI, rather than trying to issue a single command that does everything you want. The more you experiment, the better off you are.

There are numerous prompt frameworks that can be used to improve the results of prompts. Table 1.1 represents a framework that ensures that prompts are clear, informative, and effective. This framework defines the specific role or perspective that a GenAI tool, such as ChatGPT, should adopt, the task or objectives, the specific requirements, and the output or format of the response.

1.4.1.1 ChatGPT, CoPilot, Gemini, or Claude Prompts

Example 1

Act as Bobby Flay, the chef, generate an amazing recipe using ingredients I have in my fridge and pantry. Start asking me what ingredients I have available. Do not use all the ingredients – only use what you need for the dish. List the measurement in imperial system units. Give me a recipe title, a 100-word paragraph describing the dish, a list of ingredients, and simple-to-follow steps. Write in plain English without jargon.

TABLE 1.1 Prompting Framework – RTRO

Role (Act as)	Task (Create a)	Requirements (Be sure to)	Output (Turn into)
• Instructor/Teacher	• Research Question	• Include	• Plain text
• Learning Designer	• Thesis Statement	• Exclude	• Paragraph
• Researcher	• Grant Proposal	• Number	• Summary
• Graduate Student	• Lesson	• Length	• Bulleted list
• Project Manager	• Essay	• Steps	• Concept map
• Committee Chair	• Summary	• Formal Tone	• Table
• Facilitator	• Abstract	• Conversational	• Questionnaire
• Presenter	• Analysis	Tone	• Spreadsheet
• First Author	• Citation	• Inclusive	• Graph
• Senior Author	• Introduction		• Ordered List
• Peer Reviewer	• Conclusion		• Unordered List
• Editor	• Topic Sentence		• Slides
• PhD Student	• Blog Draft		• Code
• Chef	• Outline		• APA Style
• Domestic Engineer	• Proposal		• MLA Style
	• Video Script		
	• Letter of rec		
	• Email		

Example 2

Imagine you are an expert in *[specific issue or subject]* and generate ideas for a research topic about this *[specific issue or subject]*. Include current trends, challenges, and potential areas of innovation within this *[specific issue or subject]*. Your response should be a detailed thought-provoking list to guide further exploration and development of the research topic.

1.4.1.2   Recommendations

To maximize the benefits of GenAI tools for topic formulation or idea generation, it is recommended that researchers begin by brainstorming potential topics with peers, mentors, or within the research community. This can provide valuable feedback. Then conduct a preliminary search to gauge the feasibility of topics. This involves doing basic keyword searches in academic databases and reading the literature before turning to GenAI tools. After completing a preliminary search, leverage GenAI tools to combine one or more of the topics, suggest new topic ideas, mine for patterns or identify emerging trends, or size the topic. GenAI tools can be used as a thesaurus to help researchers find more creative words and phrases. Also, utilize GenAI tools to facilitate collaborative brainstorming sessions, enhancing the diversity and creativity of ideas.

1.4.2 Refining the Research Question

Once a topic has been identified and sufficiently sized, the next step is to develop the problem statement and research questions. GenAI tools can assist with this endeavor and with providing a list of keywords or search terms that will be useful in research searches and generating a list of title suggestions. When using GenAI tools to assist with research questions, large language models may introduce or perpetuate biases. It is critical to assess and mitigate potential biases in AI-generated research questions. Also, it is essential that the researcher ensure that research questions are novel or original and they contribute meaningfully to the field.

1.4.2.1 Example ChatGPT, CoPilot, Gemini, or Claude Prompt

Example 1

Assume the role of a researcher, suggest titles and a research question for an academic research paper on the following topic: A research study about the effects of integrating iPads into instruction on student engagement and attitude toward learning social studies among fifth-grade students. Write in plain English without jargon.

Example 2

Assume the role of a researcher, develop a research question for an academic paper on *[problem statement]*, ensuring it is clear and focused. Your response should be one sentence, beginning with "What" or "How." Clearly indicate "what" the research is about, including the problem and intervention; should include "who" the participants are in the study, and "where" the study takes place (such as high school, elementary, and grade level). Avoid describing the results. Write in plain English without jargon.

Follow-up prompt: Identify five additional questions.

1.4.2.2 Actual Case Example

Graduate Educational Administration students enrolled in my Educational Leadership five-week online Research Methods course during Spring 2024 were given the option of using GenAI tools to assist with the development of their research proposal that was due in week five. The use of GenAI tools to assist with brainstorming a research topic and generating research questions was introduced during a synchronous web conference during week one. Additionally, there were videos in the blackboard shell demonstrating various GenAI tools. In week five, students were asked to complete an end-of-course reflection. Below are final reflective responses related to their perceptions of using GenAI tools to develop their research topic and research questions.

Question 1: Please specify which GenAI tool(s), if any, you utilized for developing your research question(s)? (Select all that apply.)

Summary of results (n = 369):

Tool	Frequency	Percentage
ChatGPT	175	47.4
CoPilot	6	1.6
Elicit	55	14.9
Grammarly	86	23.3
Other (please specify)	30	8.1
NA – did not use GenAI tools to develop my research question(s)	93	25.2

Question 2: How did the GenAI tool(s) influence the quality and specificity of your research question(s)? (Select all that apply.)

Summary of results (n = 370):

Tool Use	Frequency	Percentage
Enhanced clarity and specificity	195	52.7
Provided novel perspectives or angles	32	8.6
Assisted in narrowing down broad topics into focused research question(s)	123	33.2
Assisted in drafting research question(s)	118	31.9
Other (please specify)	9	2.4
NA – did not use GenAI tools to develop my research question(s)	104	28.1

Question 3: To what extent did the use of GenAI tools influence the development and formulation of your research question(s)? (1 = not at all useful or did not use and 7 = extremely useful)

Mean (n = 370): 3.48

Question 4: Please provide any specific examples or instances where the GenAI tools were particularly helpful in shaping your research question(s) (open-ended).

Sample student responses:

Student 1: "While addressing my discussion questions, I received constructive feedback from some of my cohorts indicating that my questions were overly broad and potentially encompassed multiple research problems. To refine and focus my inquiries, I leveraged AI tools to assist in narrowing down my questions."

Student 2: "Generative AI tools played a significant role in shaping my research questions by assisting in the exploration of diverse perspectives and identifying emerging trends or areas of interest within the field. For instance, they helped generate potential research questions by analyzing existing literature and highlighting relevant topics or gaps in knowledge, ultimately guiding the formulation of focused and relevant research inquiries."

Student 3: "It helped my shaped my research questions by helping me use more precise academic language when writing them."

Student 4: "I had a broad idea about what I wanted to research but was unable to determine exactly how to say it. I used AI to help rewrite it several times to give me ideas about how I liked it best and actually used a blend of several responses to 'Frankenstein' my final question."

Student 5: "I used the video tutorial provided to generate my research question in Week 1, *Using generative AI to develop your research questions*. It was easy to follow the steps, pause the video, and work through constructing an effective research question. It helped me make my question more efficient and clearer to my chosen topic."

Student 6: "Since I've never created a research question before, using GenAI allowed me to see ideas and helped me create different options to arrive at my final question."

Student 7: "With Chat GPT It helped me gain clarity on what exactly I needed to write about and how to clarify what research question I am trying to answer. I had an issue I knew I wanted to write about I just did not know how to format it as a research question, so Chat GPT helped guide me to do that."

Student 8: "With Chat GPT It helped me gain clarity on what exactly I needed to write about and how to clarify what research question I am trying to answer. I had an issue I knew I wanted to write about I just did not know how to format it as a research question so Chat GPT helped guide me to do that."

Student 9: "It helped me come up with a draft of one question and spark my thought process."

Student 10: "When I gave it the topic, it gave me some good feedback on the questions. It framed it the way I wanted to say everything and helped me realize if the question did not work the way I intended. I ended up putting three different ones together to make the final draft."

1.4.2.3 Discussion of Results

During Spring 2024, in a five-week online Research Methods course, 369 Graduate Educational Administration students were given the option to use GenAI tools to assist with developing their research proposals. The use of these tools was introduced through a synchronous web conference in week one, supplemented by instructional videos in the course shell. At the end of the course, students reflected on their experiences using GenAI tools for brainstorming research topics and generating research questions.

Among the students who responded, 47.4% used ChatGPT, 14.9% used Elicit, 23.3% used Grammarly, 1.6% used CoPilot, and 8.1% used other tools. Notably, 25.2% of students did not use any GenAI tools. Regarding the influence of these tools on the quality and specificity of their research questions, 52.7% of students reported enhanced clarity and specificity, 33.2% mentioned assistance in narrowing down broad topics, and 31.9% found the tools helpful in drafting their research questions. The mean usefulness score was 3.48 out of 7, indicating a moderate impact.

Students provided specific examples of how GenAI tools were helpful. Some received constructive feedback that helped refine overly broad questions. Others appreciated how AI tools helped explore diverse perspectives and identify emerging trends, guiding the formulation of focused research questions. Several students found the tools helpful in using precise academic language, while others utilized AI to refine and merge multiple suggestions into a coherent final question. The tools were particularly useful for those who followed video tutorials to construct effective research questions. Students who were new to creating research questions found GenAI tools beneficial in generating ideas and clarifying their questions. Overall, the use of GenAI tools facilitated the research process by providing clarity, refining questions, and offering diverse perspectives, highlighting their potential in academic research development.

1.4.2.4   Recommendations

To effectively use GenAI tools for refining research questions, researchers should adopt a systematic approach. The process of refining research questions should be iterative, utilizing specific prompt to guide the AI in refining the research questions. Starting with a broad research question, researchers can use GenAI tools to suggest refinements, making the question more specific and focused. This iterative refinement helps ensure clarity and precision. Ask the AI to develop a clear and focused research question based on a given problem statement. Follow-up prompts can help generate additional questions, providing a comprehensive set of refined research questions. Use GenAI tools to suggest unique angles or perspectives on a given topic that may not have been previously considered. Comparing proposed research questions with existing ones helps ensure they are distinct and add value to the academic discourse. GenAI tools can be used to enhance the clarity and specificity of research questions, making them more actionable and focused. Researchers should use AI tools to break down complex questions into more manageable sub-questions, ensuring that each one is clear and specific. The research question should clearly indicate what the research is about, including the problem, intervention, participants, and setting. GenAI tools can provide up-to-date information on current trends, challenges, and developments within the field, helping frame research questions in a way that aligns with contemporary issues and priorities, thus ensuring contextualization and relevance.

1.4.3   The Literature Review

The literature review phase of a research study poses significant challenges to many novice researchers. Literature reviews help identify research gaps, determine the scope of a discipline, and can synthesize evidence to answer research questions. GenAI tools can support literature topics and expedite the steps of the literature review process (Atkinson, 2024; Wagner et al., 2022). However, gathering and integrating relevant literature on a specific topic is not always straightforward. The amount of published research literature continues to expand exponentially, accelerating with technology advances (Fire & Guestrin, 2019; Mysore et al., 2023). With the proliferation of the literature, utilizing GenAI tools can keep track of vastly more information than any person and may find connections that might be missed entirely by humans by being able to retrieve, synthesize, visualize, and summarize massive amounts of information (Wagner et al., 2022).

The ethical use of GenAI tools in the literature review process includes transparency, bias mitigation, complementarity, and copyright issues. Researchers should be transparent, clearly disclose the use of GenAI tools used to select and analyze the literature including algorithms, databases, and criteria used; critically assess and adjust outputs to ensure a balanced and inclusive review of the available literature to mitigate bias; and use GenAI tools as a complement to, rather than a replacement for, human judgment and expertise. And, most importantly, ensure that AI-assisted literature reviews respect intellectual property rights.

1.4.3.1   GenAI Tools to Assist with Developing a Literature Review

Table 1.2 presents an overview of various GenAI tools that can assist in literature review processes, categorized by their primary functions: outlining, searching, understanding, and writing.

1.4.3.2   Prompts

Example 1. Create an Outline – ChatGPT, CoPilot, Gemini, or Claude Prompts

Create a literature review outline for a research study about Hispanic students' perceptions of factors that make academic success more difficult.

TABLE 1.2 Helpful GenAI Literature Review Tools

Outline	*Search*	*Understand*	*Write*
ChatGPT 4o	Connected Papers	docAnalyzer	Jenni
Claude.ai	Consensus	Explain Paper	Yomu
CoPilot	Elicit		
Gemini	Litmaps		
	Research Rabbit		
	Scite		

- Custom GPTs
- Custom GPT – MixerBox Scholar
- Custom GPT – Science
- Custom GPT – Scholar AI
- Custom GPT – Vector

Example 2. Search for Literature – Elicit

What are middle school Hispanic students' perceptions of factors that make academic success more difficult?

Example 3. Understand a Paper – Explain Paper

[upload a paper, or part of a paper, highlight confusing text]

Example 4. Write/Edit – Jenni

[Input what you are writing about, will also build an outline, helps with writers' block]

1.4.3.3 Actual Case Example

Graduate Educational Administration students enrolled in my Educational Leadership five-week online Research Methods course during Spring 2024 were given the option of using GenAI tools to assist with the development of their research proposal. The use of GenAI tools to assist with the literature review was introduced during a synchronous web conference. Additionally, there were videos in the blackboard shell demonstrating various GenAI tools. In week five, students were asked to complete an end-of-course reflection. Below are final reflective responses related to their perceptions of using GenAI tools to develop their literature review.

Question 1: Please specify which GenAI tool(s), if any, you utilized for developing your literature review?

Summary of results ($n = 368$):

Tool	Frequency	Percentage
ChatGPT	167	45.4
CoPilot	7	1.9
Elicit	68	18.5
Grammarly	69	18.7
Scite	18	4.9
Research Rabbit	15	4.1
Consensus	11	3.0
SciSpace	2	0.5
Connected Papers	4	1.1
Other (please specify)	3	0.8
NA – did not use GenAI tools to develop my literature review	108	29.3

Question 2: To what extent did the use of GenAI tools influence the development and formulation of your literature review? (1 = not at all useful or did not use and 7 = extremely useful)

Mean (n = 367) : 3.46

Question 3: Please provide any specific examples or instances where the GenAI tools were particularly helpful in developing your literature review (open-ended).

Student 1: "Generative AI tools were particularly useful in compiling sources and drafting an outline for my literature review."

Student 2: "Although I did not like to use Generative AI tools, they were helpful in looking at key themes when developing my literature review."

Student 3: "The Generative AI tools helped me find articles to include in my literature review."

Student 4: "AI was helpful in organizing my thoughts and helping to get them to be more cohesive."

Student 5: "Using the AI tools to search article data bases was a wonderful experience that took the stress out of looking through databases."

Student 6: "It was useful in helping find the exact articles that were significant to my problem statements. Therefore, it helped guide me to the articles and the conclusions that the articles made helped shape my literature review."

Student 7: "The Generative AI tools helped me summarize so that I could understand in simpler language."

Student 8: "The generative AI tool was helpful to me when I had to consult a doubt about a particular piece of information I had. I just wanted to have a different perspective or find out what 'others' were thinking."

Student 9: "Generative AI tools helped with looking up articles for my literature review. It was useful with finding the key points of my articles to help me establish the gateway to finding the right information."

Student 10: "They pinpointed key research themes and summarized complex information. They helped me streamline my research and enhanced its quality."

1.4.3.4   Discussion of Results

During Spring 2024, Graduate Educational Administration students enrolled in an Educational Leadership five-week online Research Methods course were given the option to use GenAI tools to assist with developing their research proposals. The introduction to GenAI tools for literature review was conducted during a synchronous web conference and additional instructional videos were provided. At the end of the course, students reflected on their experiences with these tools.

Among the 368 students who responded, 45.4% used ChatGPT, 18.7% used Grammarly, 18.5% used Elicit, 4.9% used Scite, 4.1% used Research Rabbit, 3.0% used Consensus, 1.9% used CoPilot, 1.1% used Connected Papers, 0.5% used SciSpace, and 0.8% used other tools. Notably, 29.3% of students did not use any GenAI tools. The mean usefulness score for the influence of GenAI tools on the development and formulation of the literature review was 3.46 out of 7, indicating a moderate impact.

Students provided specific examples of how GenAI tools were beneficial. Many found the tools particularly useful for compiling sources and drafting outlines for their literature reviews. Some students, despite initial reservations, acknowledged that the tools helped identify key themes and organize their thoughts cohesively. The AI tools facilitated easier searches through article databases, reducing the stress of manually sifting through numerous sources. They also helped students find articles that were significant to their research problems, aiding in shaping their literature reviews by guiding them to relevant articles and conclusions.

Several students appreciated the AI tools for summarizing complex information into simpler language, which enhanced their understanding and the overall quality of their literature reviews. The tools also provided different perspectives and helped clarify doubts by offering insights from various angles. Overall, the use of GenAI tools streamlined the research process, making it more efficient and improving the quality of the literature reviews by pinpointing key research themes and summarizing complex information. In summary, the integration of GenAI tools into the literature review process proved to be beneficial for many students, providing clarity, efficiency, and enhanced quality in their research efforts.

1.4.3.5 Recommendations

To maximize the benefits of GenAI tools in the literature review process, researchers should adopt a systematic approach that leverages the unique capabilities of these tools while maintaining rigorous academic standards. Recommendations are as follows:

1. Use GenAI tools to generate comprehensive lists of keywords and search terms and create an outline or bullet points about the topic. By inputting broad and specific terms related to their research topic, researchers can expand the scope of their literature search and ensure a thorough exploration of existing research. It is important to regularly update and refine the keyword list as new insights are gained during the literature review process.
2. Streamline the retrieval and organization of literature using AI-powered search engines and databases to quickly find relevant articles, books, and papers and categorize and summarize them for easier identification of key themes and gaps. Utilizing AI-driven databases and search engines such as Elicit and Consensus and employing AI tools to create summaries and abstracts for quick reference and comparison can greatly enhance efficiency.
3. GenAI tools can assist in identifying and summarizing the literature; however, it is crucial to critically evaluate the AI-generated outputs to ensure quality and relevance. Manually reviewing AI-generated summaries and abstracts to confirm their accuracy and relevance, cross-checking references and citations for completeness and correctness, and being vigilant about potential biases in AI-generated outputs are the essential steps in maintaining academic integrity.
4. Use GenAI tools to synthesize the literature and identify thematic connections. By analyzing large volumes of text, AI can highlight patterns, trends, and emerging themes within the literature. Tools such as Connected Papers and Research Rabbit can be used to visualize connections between different pieces of literature, and AI-driven thematic analysis tools can help identify and synthesize key themes and patterns across the literature.
5. Integrating AI-generated insights into the literature review requires careful attention to maintain academic integrity. Using AI tools for drafting and refining sections of the literature review, ensuring AI-generated content is clearly marked and appropriately cited, and combining AI-generated insights with manual analysis can produce a cohesive and comprehensive literature review. Ensuring that all sources are correctly attributed and transparently acknowledging AI-generated contributions are essential.

1.4.4 Selecting the Methodology and Crafting the Research Instrument

The data requirements for research questions determine the methodology and in turn the methodology determines the type of research instrument. AI optimizes experimental designs, suggesting appropriate sample sizes and statistical methods for more accurate results.

Using the RTRO framework described in Section 1.4.1, ChatGPT, Claude, CoPilot, or Gemini will assist with selecting an appropriate research methodology based on the research question and quickly draft research instruments. The more robust and detailed the prompt, the better and more accurate is the response received. Of course, the researcher must make sure that the information is accurate.

The ethical use of GenAI tools in selecting methodology and crafting a research instrument involves informed consent. If GenAI is used to craft the research instrument, participants should be informed, particularly if it influenced the nature of the questions and how the data were collected and used. The researcher should ensure that data collection tools comply with data privacy and security regulations. To ensure reliability and validity of the instrument, rigorous testing, such as pilot studies, expert reviews, and statistical analyses, should be conducted. All questions used should be ethically sound, respect the dignity and rights of the participants, and relevant to the research objectives. These issues can be included in the "consent statement" that participants agree to when completing the research instrument. Oftentimes, there is a link provided with additional details.

1.4.4.1 Prompt Using the RTRO Framework

Role (Act as): You are a researcher with expertise in educational technology, interested in understanding perceptions and implications of integrating AI into K12 education. Your focus is on the use of AI to augment traditional teaching methods, including ethical considerations, best practices, assessment, and student feedback.

Task (Create a): Develop a survey instrument specifically designed to measure the perceptions and implications of teachers toward integrating AI into K12 education. This survey should explore various dimensions of perceptions and attitudes, including ethical considerations, best practices, assessment, and student feedback.

Requirement (Be sure to):

1. Ensure the survey contains 20 Likert scale questions. Each question should allow respondents to rate their level of agreement or disagreement on a scale (e.g., Strongly agree, Agree, Neutral, Disagree, Strongly disagree)

2. Cover a range of topics related to the integration of AI into K12 education.

Output (Turn into): The output should be a table-formatted survey with directions, grouped by topic.

Follow-up prompt: Export to CSV so the survey can be downloaded for editing and then uploaded to Qualtrics or any other survey maker tool.

1.4.4.2 Hypothetical Case Examples

Example 1. Kristen is about to begin field work on her qualitative research study. She plans to complete semi-structured interviews with six participants. To protect the participants' privacy and anonymity, Kristen uses GenAI to create a list of pseudonyms for her participants to choose from. Ashley always keeps a record of her prompts and the output provided by GenAI, in case she needs to disclose this use in the future.

This is an appropriate use of GenAI. Kristen kept a record of the prompt and will acknowledge the use of GenAI.

Example 2. Joshua wants to include an image in his survey instrument about a novel virus, but his original image is fuzzy and doesn't clearly represent the virus. He is unable to replicate the image as the electron microscope is being serviced. Instead of using the real image from the electron microscope, Joshua uses an AI generator to create an image for his survey instrument.

This is an inappropriate use of GenAI, Joshua's image is fraudulent. This is an example of research misconduct.

1.4.4.3 Recommendations

To effectively utilize GenAI tools in selecting the research methodology and crafting the research instrument, researchers should follow a structured approach that ensures accuracy, ethical compliance, and relevance. The RTRO framework can be particularly useful in this regard, guiding the development of prompts that yield detailed and precise outputs.

Researchers should provide robust and detailed prompts to GenAI tools like ChatGPT, Claude, CoPilot, or Gemini. The specificity of the prompt directly influences the quality and accuracy of the response. For instance, when developing a survey instrument, researchers should clearly outline the objectives, the dimensions to be explored, and the desired format of the output. For example, defining the role might involve instructing the AI to act as an educational researcher, while the task could involve creating a survey instrument to measure teachers' perceptions of AI integration in K12 education. The requirements should specify elements like including 20 Likert scale questions covering various topics, and the output should be a table-formatted survey grouped by topic. Using prompts that specify the role, task, requirements, and output can help in creating comprehensive and tailored research instruments.

Ethical considerations must be at the forefront when using GenAI tools for methodology selection and instrument crafting. Researchers must ensure informed consent from participants, particularly if GenAI tools influence the nature of the questions or data collection methods. Participants should be informed about how the data will be collected, used, and stored, and data collection tools must comply with privacy and security regulations.

To ensure the reliability and validity of the instruments crafted with the assistance of GenAI tools, researchers should conduct rigorous testing. This includes pilot studies, expert reviews, and statistical analyses to refine the instruments. It is crucial that all questions respect the dignity and rights of the participants and are relevant to the research objectives. Including these details in the consent statement and providing additional information through links can enhance transparency and ethical compliance. For instance, a researcher with expertise in educational technology might use a prompt to develop a survey instrument measuring teachers' perceptions of integrating AI into K12 education. The prompt should ensure that the survey includes an appropriate number of Likert scale questions covering various aspects such as ethical considerations, best practices, assessment, and student feedback. The output should be a well-structured, table-formatted survey ready for further editing and uploading to survey platforms such as Qualtrics.

1.5 Data Analysis, Findings, and Visualization

Data analysis in research uses relevant techniques to evaluate data to find meaning. Statistical techniques are required for quantitative data and there are various techniques used to identify patterns and themes for qualitative data. Utilizing GenAI tools for data analysis, findings and visualization, particularly text-based data, can be a game-changer. GenAI tools sifts through data, spots patterns, and serves up the analysis at lighting speed. Before the advent of GenAI tools, conducting data analyses required a researcher to possess expertise in programming and statistical methods. Now with deep learning models and neural networks, such specialized knowledge is no longer essential (George, 2023). When using GenAI tools for data analysis, privacy, security, and ethical implications must be at the forefront. The researcher must keep the data's integrity intact and always respect the ethical boundaries that govern the use of the data. For data analysis, Ijaz (2024) recommends using custom GPTs or plugins because these technologies ensure the accuracy and reliability of data analysis through its advance anti-hallucination technology. This technology creates a context boundary around the data, which acts as a protective layer, ensuring that the chatbot generates responses based solely on the provided data, eliminating the risk of bias and inaccuracies.

The ethical use of GenAI tools in the data analysis process includes data privacy and confidentiality, interpretation and contextualization, account-ability for AI-assisted findings, and use of predictive analytics. Strict adher-ence to human subjects' data privacy and confidentiality must be managed to safeguard participant data against unauthorized access or misuse. While AI can identify patterns and correlations, the interpretation requires human judgment, particularly in contextualizing results within the broader research framework and existing literature. Researchers must retain ultimate account-ability and responsibility for conclusions drawn. It is unethical to attribute errors or controversial findings to AI systems. Predictive models should be used responsibly, with consideration for the potential social, psychological, and ethical impacts of their predictions.

1.5.1 Example of GenAI Tools to Analyze and Visualize Data

- Use a CSV file generated from ChatGPT, CoPilot, Gemini, or Claude
- Use Data Analyst ChatGPT plugin to perform an initial scan of the dataset structure (powered by Julius.ai):

  - Suggests next steps and confirms whether to move forward.
  - Summarizes main data and ideas for broad analysis.
  - Provides conclusions.
  - Performs analysis steps.
  - Provides ideas and suggestions for further examination.
  - Provides visualizations.
  - Performs refinements/corrections as needed across these steps.

1.5.2 Hypothetical Case Examples

Example 1. Latoya has completed her data collection for her research study. She uses a mixed-methods approach and needs to conduct both statisti-cal analysis and textual analysis. She has been trained on using both Stata and SPSS for statistical analysis but has decided to use a GenAI tool for her text-based analysis as she feels this will be more time effective and give deeper meaning to her data. Without removing any identifying information or sensi-tive information, she uploads her interview transcripts into the GenAI tool and prompts it to identify the emergent themes.

This is an inappropriate use of GenAI. Latoya breached the participants' privacy and confidentiality. She failed to disclose her use of GenAI and did not disclose to her participants any planned use of participant data with GenAI in the consent form.

Example 2. Joseph has collected a large set of quantitative data for a project he is working on. He now needs to analyze and interpret the data using statistical modelling. To do this, Joseph is using some advanced Excel functionalities, including complex formulas. Joseph uses GenAI to provide him with step-by-step instructions on how to do some of the technical skills he is unsure of, and the GenAI tool is also able to provide him with the formulas he needs. Joseph always keeps a record of his prompts and the output from the GenAI, in case he needs to disclose this in the future.

> This is an appropriate use of GenAI. Joseph kept a record of the prompt and will acknowledge the use of GenAI.

1.5.3   Recommendations

Ensuring the integrity of the data and respecting ethical boundaries is crucial. Researchers should adhere to strict data privacy and confidentiality protocols to safeguard participant information against unauthorized access or misuse. Tools like custom GPTs or plugins, recommended by Ijaz (2024), can enhance the accuracy and reliability of data analysis by using advanced anti-hallucination technology. This technology creates a protective context boundary around the data, ensuring that the AI-generated responses are based solely on the provided data, thereby eliminating the risk of bias and inaccuracies.

Ethical use of GenAI tools in data analysis involves several key considerations. Researchers must manage data privacy and confidentiality to protect human subjects. While AI can efficiently identify patterns and correlations, interpreting these results requires human judgment to contextualize findings within the broader research framework and existing literature. Researchers must retain ultimate accountability for their conclusions and avoid attributing errors or controversial findings solely to AI systems. Predictive models should be used responsibly, with careful consideration of their social, psychological, and ethical impacts. For example, researchers can use a CSV file generated from GenAI tools like ChatGPT, CoPilot, Gemini, or Claude and employ the Data Analyst ChatGPT plugin, powered by Julius.ai, to perform an initial scan of the dataset structure. This tool can suggest next steps, summarize main data, provide broad analysis ideas, draw conclusions, perform analysis steps, offer further examination suggestions, and provide visualizations. Refinements and corrections can be made as needed throughout these steps to ensure a thorough and accurate analysis.

1.6   Drafting Conclusions and Recommendations

AI can play a critical role in enhancing the quality and efficiency of creating and organizing research content. GenAI tools excel in assisting the writing process through expanding text, offering predictive text capabilities and providing autocompletion features, significantly aiding in the drafting process. Utilizing GenAI tools for drafting conclusions and recommendations can significantly streamline the research process, allowing researchers to generate well-structured and concise summaries of their findings. After inputting the main points and findings, GenAI tools can generate a concise well-structured draft of conclusions and recommendations that align with the content and tone of the paper. This ensures that the conclusions are both comprehensive and coherent, providing a clear reflection of the research conducted.

1.6.1 Example Prompt to Generate a Draft of Conclusions and Recommendations

Original Prompt using ChatGPT, MS CoPilot, Gemini, or Claude
Using the following manuscript identify and explain the conclusions and recommendations in an academic tone.
Modified Prompt using PromptPerfect

Identify and explain the conclusions and recommendations from the following manuscript using an academic tone. Your response should provide a detailed analysis of the conclusions drawn from the manuscript, highlighting the key findings and implications. Additionally, you should offer well-founded recommendations based on the conclusions, considering the broader context and potential future research directions, as well as discussing how the conclusions relate to the literature cited in the literature review. Please ensure that your explanations are presented in a scholarly manner, using formal language, and referencing the academic literature or theories where applicable.

1.6.2 Hypothetical Case Example

Example 1. Marisol is a graduate student who is completing a research project for a research methods course. This is the first time she has written an academic research paper. Writing is not one of her strengths and English is not her first language. She has found that using a GenAI tool helps her with copyediting. She uses it to check for spelling and grammatical errors and reviews the feedback regarding strengths and weaknesses. She makes sure she abides by all copyright and intellectual property rights. She acknowledges the use of this tool in her paper and confirms with her instructor to ensure that the use of the tool is permissible. Marisol always keeps a record of her prompts and the output from the GenAI, in case she needs to disclose this in the future.

This is an appropriate use of GenAI. Marisol kept a record of the prompt and will acknowledge the use of GenAI.

1.6.3 Recommendations

AI tools can suggest extensions to preliminary findings and discussion sections, helping researchers articulate complex data in a more understandable manner in drafting conclusions and recommendations. Predictive text capabilities are particularly useful in academic writing, where AI can anticipate and suggest technical terms streamlining the writing process. However, caution should be considered about the potential misuse of AI in generating fraudulent information, highlighting the need for vigilance in maintaining academic integrity. AI tools can streamline the content development process; however, it is essential to maintain transparency in AI usage to uphold the credibility and integrity of academic writing. Additionally, it is important to remember that the content entered in GenAI tools could potentially be discoverable. Therefore, researchers must avoid including any identifiable information or intellectual property in these tools. Always maintain confidentiality and ensure compliance with ethical guidelines when using GenAI for drafting conclusions and recommendations.

1.7 Tools, Strategies, and Examples

The last stop on our excursion will be to summarize and review some of the tools available for conducting academic research. The emergence of new GenAI tools at our disposal to assist with academic research show how GenAI opens new creative modalities and opportunities for exploration, and therefore new opportunities for academic research. For example, tools such as Thesify.ai and Trinka.ai provide feedback, highlighting strengths and weaknesses and spelling and grammatical errors in a manuscript. The tools listed in Table 1.3 are intended to be a representative list of tools that can be used to assist with the academic research process. This list is not meant to be all inclusive, as new tools are being introduced daily!

1.8 Summary of Recommendations/Insights

To maximize the benefits of GenAI tools in academic research, it is essential to follow structured and systematic approaches at each stage of the research process. When formulating research topics, researchers should start by brainstorming with peers and conducting preliminary searches in academic databases before leveraging GenAI tools. These tools can then be used to refine topics, suggest new ideas, and identify emerging trends. Utilizing GenAI tools as a thesaurus can enhance the creativity and diversity of brainstorming sessions, facilitating collaborative efforts and generating comprehensive lists of keywords and search terms.

TABLE 1.3 Tools to Assist with the Academic Research Process

Tool	Description	Suggested Use in Research
ChatGPT 4o	Open AI's generative AI Model	Useful for brainstorming, topic/problem formulation, summarizing, extracting data, finding papers, and much more
Claude.ai	Anthropic's generative AI model	Useful for brainstorming, topic/problem formulation, summarizing, extracting data, finding papers, and much more
CoPilot	Microsoft's generative AI model	Useful for brainstorming, topic/problem formulation, summarizing, extracting data, finding papers, and much more
Copy.ai	Writing tool	Writing and editing
Connected Papers	Find and explore papers relevant to a field of work in a visual way	Topic/problem formulation and literature review
Consensus	Search engine for research	Topic/problem formulation and literature review
Custom GPT – AI Data Analyst	Designed to guide user through data cleaning, data analysis, statistical analysis, and visualization	Data analysis and visualization
Custom GPT – Critical-Scholarly-Analysis	Acts as an expert reviewer for academic papers, providing critical, scholarly analysis.	Writing and editing
Custom GPT – Data Analysis and Report AI	Limitless, detailed scientific data analysis and reporting	Data analysis
Custom GPT – Data Analysis Pro	Multidimensional data analysis tool to simplify the analysis and analytical process, with automated chart creation	Data analysis
Custom GPT – Data Analysis - SPSS	Statistical analysis and SPSS, including what statistical test to use for hypothesis	Data analysis

Custom GPT – MixerBox Scholar	ChatGPT plugin designed to streamline the academic research process and provides fast and accurate access to a plethora of academic documents, research reports, theses, and other scholarly resources	Literature review
Custom GPT – Qualitative Data Analysis	An expert tool in thematic analysis that identifies themes in transcripts and provides detailed theme information	Data analysis
Custom GPT – Science	Searches over 250M academic papers, specializing in open access	Literature review
Custom GPT – Scholar AI	Searches over 200M+ peer-reviewed articles	Literature review
Custom GPT – Statistics and Data Analysis	Assists with queries regarding statistics and data analysis	Data analysis
Custom GPT – Vector	Finds relevant papers with unprecedented accuracy using vector embeddings of paper titles and abstracts	Data analysis
DALL-E 3	Text-to-image generator	Images and presentation
docAnalyzer	Acts as a conversational interface for PDFs, providing real-time pinpointed answers to context-specific questions about a research document	Literature review and editing
Elicit	Visualizes relationships between topics and sources	Literature review
Explain Paper	Allows users to highlight confusing sections of a paper and receive simplified explanations of the key concepts	Writing, editing, and literature review
Gemini	Google's generative AI model	Useful for brainstorming, summarizing, extracting data, finding papers, and much more
Grammarly	Paraphrase, word choice, and sentence structure	Writing, fixing grammatical errors, and editing

(Continued)

TABLE 1.3 (Continued)

Tool	Description	Suggested Use in Research
Jenni	An AI text editor tool	Useful for writing, fixing grammatical errors, editing, adding citations, and crafting draft opposing argument
Julius.ai	Data analysis	Data analysis
Litmaps	Find relevant papers, related articles, and organize research articles; search by title, keyword, DOI, or author	Literature review
Midjourney	Generates images	Create images for research dissemination
myessayfeedback.ai	AI-powered formative feedback	Editing and writing
Perplexity.ai	Answers queries	Brainstorming and refining a paper
Prompt Perfect	Assists with improving the quality of prompts	Prompt assistance
QuillBot	AI paraphrasing tool	Paraphrasing – editing and writing
Rephrase	Paraphrasing tool	Paraphrasing – editing and writing
Research Rabbit	Citation-based interactive literature maps	Literature review
SciSpace	Explore and explain papers	Literature review
Scite	Scans relevant publications and produces summary with citations and bibliography	Literature review
Stability	Generates images	Images and presentation
Scribbr	Paraphrasing tool	Paraphrasing – editing and writing
Synthesia	Creates videos	Videos and presentation
Trinka	Writing, editing, and proofreading	Editing and writing
thesify	Personal AI research assistant, which can review an essay, a report, or a manuscript and provide instant feedback	Editing and writing
Wordtune	AI writing tool and grammar checker	Editing and writing
Yomu	Brainstorming and refining a paper	Brainstorming and refining a paper

GenAI tools can provide unique perspectives, ensure clarity and specificity, and suggest current trends and challenges within the field to align research questions with contemporary issues. For refining research questions, an iterative approach is recommended. Researchers should use specific prompts to guide the AI in refining questions, starting with broad queries and gradually making them more focused and actionable. Regularly refine and adjust prompts to improve the quality and relevance of AI-generated outputs. This iterative refinement process ensures that research questions are precise, relevant, and add value to the academic discourse.

During the literature review process, GenAI tools should be used to generate extensive keyword lists, streamline the retrieval and organization of the literature, and synthesize the findings. Researchers must critically evaluate AI-generated outputs to maintain quality and relevance, manually reviewing summaries and cross-checking references. AI-driven thematic analysis tools can help identify key themes and patterns, and integrating these insights into the literature review while maintaining academic integrity is crucial. Clear attribution and transparency about AI-generated contributions are essential for a cohesive and comprehensive review.

In selecting the research methodology and crafting research instruments, detailed and robust prompts should be used to ensure accuracy and relevance. Researchers must ensure informed consent from participants and comply with privacy and security regulations. Rigorous testing, including pilot studies and expert reviews, is necessary to validate the instruments crafted with GenAI tools. Providing clear instructions and maintaining transparency in the development process enhances ethical compliance and the reliability of research instruments.

Data analysis and reporting findings using GenAI tools requires strict adherence to data privacy and confidentiality protocols. Researchers must manage the ethical implications of AI-generated findings, ensuring accurate interpretation within the broader research framework. Tools like custom GPTs or plugins enhance the accuracy of data analysis using advanced anti-hallucination technology, eliminating biases and inaccuracies. Researchers should remain accountable for their conclusions and use predictive models responsibly, considering their social, psychological, and ethical impacts.

When drafting conclusions and recommendations, as well as composing the report, AI tools can streamline the writing process, but researchers must maintain transparency to uphold academic integrity and avoid including identifiable information.

AI technology continues to evolve; researchers should stay informed about the latest developments and continuously adapt their use of GenAI tools. Regularly updating their knowledge of new AI tools and features, participating in training and workshops to improve proficiency in using AI, and sharing the best practices and insights with the academic community can foster collaborative learning and improvement. Invest time in learning effective prompt engineering techniques to harness the full potential of GenAI tools. Finally, always acknowledge the use of GenAI tools in any published work, ensuring ethical standards are maintained.

Following these structured approaches and maintaining ethical standards, researchers can effectively utilize GenAI tools to enhance the academic research process.

1.9 Conclusion

Concluding our excursion to facilitate the use of GenAI in academic research more effectively, educators and researchers must acknowledge that the integration is not without challenges. According to Velazquez (2024), "the integration of AI into educational research will enable the transcendence of boundaries, moving from a few textual data to massive corpora, thereby enhancing collaborative research." Thus, the impact of AI on research methodology cannot be underestimated. Although the robustness of quantitative and qualitative approaches with software was already significant, patterns that the human eye cannot detect immediately will be discerned by AI vision. Ethical considerations emerge to the forefront, particularly regarding data privacy, bias, and authenticity. A mere test of how ChatGPT invents non-existent sources for citation reveals that their current algorithms are not immune to bias and could fall into pseudo-analysis. Therefore, the ethical landscape also requires development to ensure that the use of AI in research adheres to clear guidelines and strict ethical principles.

It is imperative to acknowledge that entrusting total responsibility to AI and its artificial neural network is not yet feasible. This is because AI does not obviate the necessity for researchers to engage in reflective thinking to attain a profound understanding of the texts analyzed. Consequently, AI does not supplant humans in research; rather, it transforms into a supportive tool designed to enhance and expedite the processes of data analysis and systematization, ensuring a meticulous and efficient exploration of information. Navigating through the opportunities and challenges presented by AI in academic research necessitates a balanced approach (Hsu, 2023). According to Chiang et al. (2024), "by actively involving students in the learning process and utilizing AI tools to facilitate various stages of the learning cycle, we can promote a deeper understanding of the subject matter and foster active engagement" (p. 360). The integration of AI tools into academia promises a future characterized by advanced research capabilities, data-driven pedagogical strategies, and the advancement of academic research that is both technologically advanced and ethically sound. Educational leaders and researchers are encouraged to positively accept new technologies, actively adapt to new challenges, consciously cope with new changes, and embed the innovation and development of GenAI tools in academic research.

I expound on the theory that educational leaders should listen to our students. The final reflective question the graduate students in my Research Methods course responded to was, "In what ways did AI tools you used during this course enhance your research process?" I conclude this chapter with a few of their responses. It is my hope we listen to our students!

Student 1: "It made my work process much faster because the information was easily summarized and categorized, allowing me to focus on my topic and expand my learning."

Student 2: "AI was helpful because it helped me build on my own ideas and allowed me to look at things from more than one perspective."

Student 3: "AI tools enhanced my research process. I was able to formulate my ideas into writing when I was stuck. I was able to also create strong research questions, develop outlines, and complete a quality review of the literature."

Student 4: "AI tools only enhanced my research process by providing guidance and making things clearer and more understandable."

References

Anawis, M. (2014). *Text mining: The next frontier*. Research & Development World. https://www.rdworldonline.com/text-mining-the-next-data-frontier/.

Atkinson, C. (2024). Cheap, quick, and rigorous: Artificial intelligence and the systematic literature review. *Social Science Computer Review*, 42(2), 376–393. https://dor.org/10.1177/08944393231196281.

Chiang, Y. V., Chang, M., & Chen, N.-S. (2024). Can generative AI help realize the shift from an outcome-oriented to a process-outcome-balanced educational practice? *Educational Technology & Society*, 27(2), 347–385. https://doi.org/10.30191/ETS.202404_27(2).TP04.

Dwivedi, Y. K., Kshetri, N., Hughes, L., Slade, E. L., Jeyaraj, A., Kar, A. K., Baabdullah, A. M., Koohang, A., Raghavan, V., Ahuja, M., Albanna, H., Albashrawi, M. A., Al-Busaidi, A. S., Balakrishnan, J., Barlette, Y., Basu, S., Bose, I., Brooks, L., Buhalis, D., . . . Wright, R. (2023). Opinion paper: "So what if ChatGPT wrote it?" Multidisciplinary perspectives on opportunities, challenges and implications of generative conversational AI for research, practice and policy. *International Journal of Information Management*, 71, 102642. https://doi.org/10.1016/j.ijinfomgt.2023.102642.

Fire, M., & Guestrin, C. (2019). Over-optimization of academic publishing metrics: Observing Goodhart's Law in action. *GigaScience*, 8, 1–20. https://doi.org/10.1093/gigascience/giz053.

George, A. S. (2023). The potential of generative AI to reform graduate education. *Partners Universal Internal Research Journal*, 2(4), 36–50. https://doi.org/10.5281/zenodo.10421475.

Greenberg, S. (2020). *Card tricks: The decline & fall of a bibliographic tool*. National Library of Medicine. https://circulatingnow.nlm.nih.gov/2020/02/06/card-tricks-the-decline-fall-of-a-bibliographic-tool/.

Hsu, H.-P. (2023). Can generative artificial intelligence write an academic journal article? Opportunities, challenges, and implications. *Irish Journal of Technology Enhanced Learning*, 7(2), 158–171. https://doi.org/10.22554/ijtel.v7i2.152.

Ijaz, H. (2024). The role of custom GPTs and plugins in enhancing data analysis accuracy. *Journal of Artificial Intelligence Research*, 15(3), 123–145. https://doi.org/10.1234/jair.2024.5678.

Kunda, I. (2023). Regulating the use of generative AI in academic research and publications. *PUBMET*. https://doi.org/10.15291/pubmet.4274.

Law, L. (2024). Application of generative artificial intelligence (GenAI) in language teaching and learning: A scoping literature review. *Computers and Education Open*, 6. https://doi.org/10.1016/j.caeo.2024.100174.

Mollick, E. (2023). A guide to prompting AI (for what it is worth). *One Useful Thing*. https://www.oneusefulthing.org/p/a-guide-to-prompting-ai-for-what.

Moya, B.A., & Eaton, S.E. (2023). Examining recommendations for artificial intelligence use with integrity from a scholarship of teaching and learning lens. *RELIEVE*, 29(2). https://doi.org/10.30827/relieve.v29i2.29295.

Mysore, S., Jasim, M., Song, H., Akbar, S., Randal, A. K. C., & Mahyar, N. (2023). How data scientists review the scholarly literature. In *Proceedings of the 2023 conference on human information interaction*, 137–152. https://doi.org/10.1145/3576840.

National Academic Integrity Network. (2023). *NAIN generative AI guidelines for educators*. https://www.qqi.ie/news/nain-publishes-new-genai-guidelines-for-educators.

Platt, M., & Platt, D. (2023). Effectiveness of generative artificial intelligence for scientific content analysis. In *2023 IEEE 17th international conference on application of information and communication technologies (AICT)*, 1–4. https://doi.org/10.1109/AICT59525.2023.10313167.

Van der Maden, W., Van Beck, E., Nicenboim, I., Van der Burg, V., Kun, P., Lomas, D., & Kang, E. (2023). Towards a design (research) framework with Generative AI. In *Designing interactive systems conference (Dis'23 companion): Companion publication of the 2023 ACM designing interactive systems conference,* 107–109. https://doi.org/10.1145/3563703.3591453.

Velazquez, U. A. D. (2024). Artificial intelligence in educational research. In Y. Rybarczyk (Ed.), *Research advances in data mining techniques and applications*. IntechOpen. https://doi.org/10.5772/intechopen.113844.

Wagner, G., Lukyanenko, R., & Pare, G. (2022). Artificial intelligence and the conduct of literature review. *Journal of Information Technology*, 37(2), 209–226. https://doi.org/10.1177/02683962211048201.

2

INTEGRATING WEAK GENERATIVE AI WITH PROJECT-BASED LEARNING

The LivePBL DEEP Method in Hybrid Music Education

Ying Liu, Yuanyuan Li, and Ting Zhao

2.1 Introduction

Generative Artificial Intelligence (GenAI) has been rapidly applied (Klein, 2023a) through the advancement of large language models (LLMs), which can generate text, images, or even music by learning from large datasets to answer natural language inquiries (Minaee et al., 2024; Zhao et al., 2024). At the application layer, GenAI produces novel outputs based on algorithms that learn patterns and information, enabling tasks such as language translation and content creation. GenAI tools have been spanning content creation across diverse contexts through the further layered GenAI development on "user" interfaces through ICT APPs (Information Communication Technology Applications, for example, Apps on a desktop, web, mobile, and/or enterprise resources platform). This has led to its growing use in education (Springs, 2024). Figure 2.1 shows the evolution of such AI era.

The current research has applied GenAI innovatively across various educational levels (Jin et al., 2024; Kasneci et al., 2023), for example, facilitating academic study such as extracting relevant information, aiding in literature reviews or supporting an educational organization, creating customized educational resources, supporting curriculum planning, streamlining administrative tasks, assisting in generating exam questions and marking student work, to name but a few.

However, although many GenAI technologies seem to be powerful, the implementations of the applications are diverse and fragmented. We argue that they significantly lack design orientation for "end-users," thereby making these applications in a teaching and learning environment more challenging to scale and apply systematically (Kasneci et al., 2023). Teachers

DOI: 10.1201/9781003422433-2

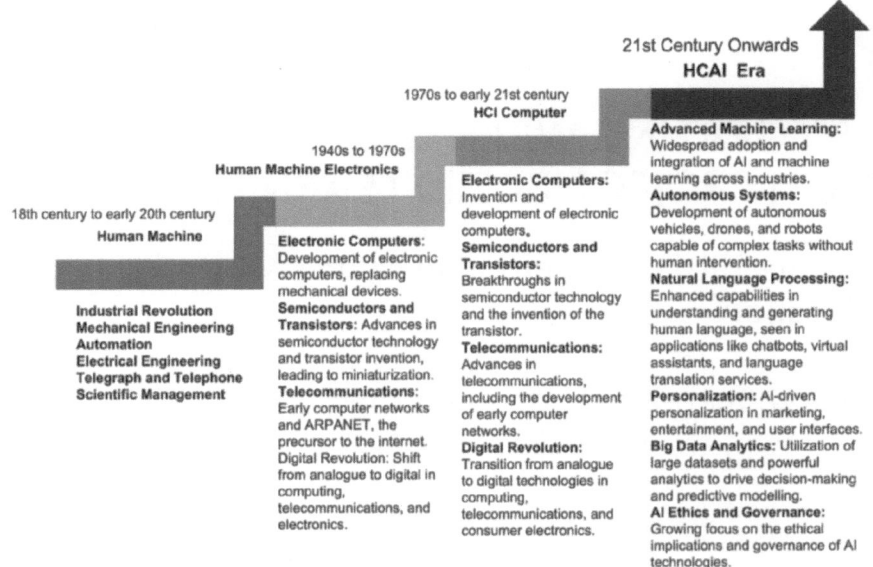

FIGURE 2.1 Evolution of the AI era.

and learners are "end-users"; they also need practical navigation in using a GenAI tool (Fischer, 2023) to design their teaching and learning.

To enable the full potential of GenAI in education, there is a critical need for a design method to *orientate* in:

1. Bridging Theory and Practice: Connecting relevant theories with practical applications of GenAI in educational settings.
2. Educational Contexts: Understanding the different learning environments and needs of stakeholders versus users.
3. Human-Centered Interactive Communication: Impacting interactions of collective experience and skill communication in learning activities.
4. Hybrid Learning Environments: Navigating and optimizing teaching and learning in blended physical and digital spaces.

From a philosophical standpoint, "orientation" in design is a multifaceted concept encompassing the cognitive structures that guide the design process.

In designing a teaching environment, orientation involves creating systematic, conscious, and object-oriented activities (Torvinen, 2017). It navigates using instructional tools and methods to connect learners with the core principles of the subject matter. By incorporating real-world scenarios (Stuedahl, 2015), engaging students actively, and structuring learning progressively, teachers can design environments that foster meaningful learning. Most recently, in particular, to meet growing employability demands, it is beneficial that GenAI can be aligned with professional practices and lifelong learning skill development. Design orientation is foundational to how individuals navigate and make sense of their ideas within a complex and ever-changing reality (Wilson, 2008). The broader importance of orientation in design, as a fundamental concept in various fields, highlights its role in ensuring effective learning, clear communication, and efficient operation across different domains. Unclear orientation in GenAI development can lead to confusion and inefficiencies (Zirar et al., 2023).

We present a design method called the "LivePBL DEEP Method" (the DEEP method), which aims to empower the use of GenAI in hybrid teaching and learning practices through the following four phases (Figure 2.2 shows the direction, education, event, project (DEEP) method which aligns with the design of PBL in principles):

1. Direction: Orientate in setting what personalized learning goals are – what to achieve.
2. Education: Orientate in setting a dedicated educational domain – what to learn.
3. Event: Foster interactive activities with real-world learning experiences – how to learn.
4. Project: Construct collaborative stakeholder engagement – how to achieve.

This method has evolved through our research and development since the beginning of COVID-19. In this chapter, we discuss how the method can be applied to integrate ChatGPT into a dedicated educational domain called

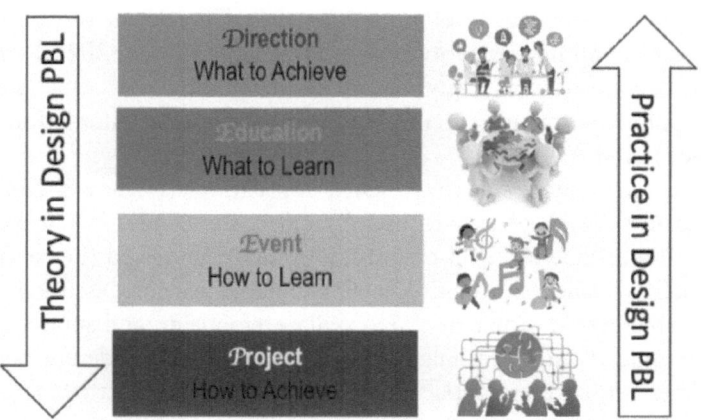

FIGURE 2.2 The DEEP method.

project-based learning (PBL). Before introducing the method further, it is essential to understand the fundamental design boundaries in question.

2.1.1 The Design Orientation in Weak GenAI

There has been extensive research in design thinking and design philosophies that underpin GenAI development. While this chapter does not comprehensively discuss these topics, it is important to navigate the spectrum between Strong GenAI (S-GenAI) and Weak GenAI (W-GenAI) (Flowers, 2019). S-GenAI embeds human-like cognitive abilities, enabling autonomous reasoning and problem-solving with advanced technologies such as deep learning and large language models (LLMs). However, social intelligence is crucial and drives a paradigm shift in AI (Dautenhahn, 2008). Therefore, in contrast, W-GenAI is designed for specific tasks, facilitating content generation and enhancing human interactions through predetermined algorithms and tools (OpenAI, 2023a, 2023b).

Our research has found that many design methods are unclear about whether they aim to model a generic application of GenAI for developers to implement computationally or to only guide end-users, leaving them to integrate GenAI within their application domains. Consequently, a vast and diverse range of GenAI models are seemingly complex and lack the cost-effectiveness to guide actual end-users. This raises the next design boundary we consider in constructing our method, opting for a W-GenAI rather than an S-GenAI approach.

2.1.2 The Design Orientation in ChatGPT Dynamic Roles in HCI and HCAI

Another justification for developing our method to root in W-GenAI is that, as W-GenAI continues to evolve (Gabriels, 2018; Kumar, 2025), design orientation becomes increasingly crucial to navigating the convergence of a GenAI application from conventional human–computer interaction (HCI) to human-centered AI (HCAI).

In the current digital sphere of GenAI applications (Fischer, 2023), even the term "learner" is too generic to usefully reflect the "end-user" in educational contexts. Take ChatGPT as a case study. Many overviewed (Lee et al., 2024) that ChatGPT facilitates adaptive or differentiated learning, assists in cognitive critical or real-world problem-solving skill development, and supports collaborative learning, sharing learning experiences, and team co-design both online and offline. Yet, all these applications involve highly contextual, situated, and dynamically changing human roles. To overcome such complexity, a design method can loosely couple (Grinshtain et al., 2023) ChatGPT digitally and intelligently to the specific needs and context of the application being designed.

2.1.3 The Design Orientation in Project-Based Learning as an Educational Domain

Introducing PBL as an educational domain, this flexibility in loose coupling allows ChatGPT to transition between various human roles based on the needs. Given the diverse range of design approaches in education, we adopted PBL as an application domain for piloting and testing our method (Tang et al., 2024). This choice is driven by PBL's emphasis on active, real-world learning, which aligns well with the adaptive and responsive nature of Chat-GPT. By focusing on PBL, we aim to illustrate ChatGPT's dynamic roles and how it can be integrated to address practical challenges in teaching and learning environments (Ng, 2024).

Significant research on PBL (Bradley-Levine & Mosier, 2024) reports that students learn better by actively engaging personally in the real world and in meaningful projects over a period of time. Learners work on projects involving complex questions, problems, or challenges, often with multiple steps and a practical outcome or final product (Smith, 2024). Despite PBL's advantages, its practical application faces significant limitations in fostering engagement and practical knowledge application. These challenges include high resource intensity, complex assessments, varying teacher skills, student readiness, and scalability issues (Xu, 2023). How can we design a PBL that applies ChatGPT to overcome these limitations and streamline the resource-intensive nature of PBL? The rest of this chapter is organized as follows.

2.1.4 Chapter Overview

Section 2.2 reviews the literature to establish a conceptual framework underpinning the DEEP method construction. It clarifies the concept of design orientation and the application of W-GenAI in educational contexts. The section explores PBL as a dedicated application domain in education and addresses the lack of holistic integration and system efficiency in current W-GenAI applications. It reviews ChatGPT's generic functions and defines the concepts of loose coupling and dynamic roles to scale the use of Chat-GPT in PBL. By leveraging ChatGPT's flexible and context-sensitive roles, the review discusses how the DEEP method can orientate a ChatGPT application development to meet practical challenges in PBL.

Section 2.3 outlines the research methodology. We introduce the research setting, which includes the LivePBL collaborative initiatives involving university faculty, school headteachers, and community leaders. We discuss a case-based study approach, piloting the DEEP method to integrate ChatGPT into the co-design of PBL and HCI. This involved applying ChatGPT in various educational settings through hybrid teaching and learning environments. We developed templates followed by CPD Certification standards to deliver

PBL sessions with ChatGPT, and so we have realized personalized learning and transformed teaching practices.

Section 2.4 provides a practical demonstration of the LivePBL DEEP method in action. It describes a specific pilot project that implemented the method, including detailed examples of how ChatGPT was used to enhance personalized learning experiences, facilitate interactive sessions, and promote collaborative stakeholder co-design engagement, situational awareness, skill development, and family involvement in learning processes.

Finally, Sections 2.5–2.8 conclude this chapter by summarizing the key points discussed, reaffirming the significance of the LivePBL DEEP method. It highlights the main contributions to ChatGPT applications and the potential of W-GenAI to transform educational practices through PBL, enhancing adaptability and responsiveness in teaching and learning. The section also outlines the limitations of our research and suggests directions for future studies.

2.2   Foundation of the DEEP Method

To establish a foundation for the LivePBL DEEP method in question, this section combine various relevant and critical design issues (Figure 2.3 shows the conceptual map that guides the foundational development). It's important to note that "methodology" refers to the systematic analysis of the methods used within a field, whereas "method" describes specific procedures or sets of procedures designed to accomplish tasks (Gericke et al., 2024). Although

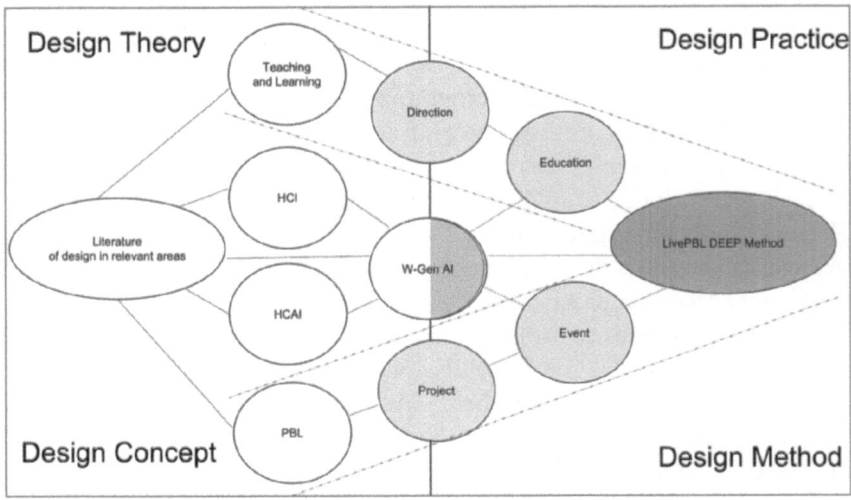

FIGURE 2.3   Conceptual map of the DEEP method.

these terms have distinct meanings, we will use them interchangeably in this chapter for the sake of simplicity. We begin clarifying what we mean by "design orientation" in a GenAI application.

2.2.1 The Design Orientation in Weak GenAI

From a philosophical standpoint, orientation involves successfully navigating and understanding a new situation. Werner Stegmaier explores the concept of orientation and argues that "the processes and structures involved in orientation come before all our thinking, perceiving, and acting. By becoming aware of these structures, we can gain a more realistic understanding of our complex and ever-changing world" (Stegmaier, 2019). In this context, a design orientation is a process of developing or even innovating a structure or mechanism that underpins a designer's thoughts, perceptions, and actions.

The orientation in the design of GenAI applications has a clear boundary between S-GenAI and W-GenAI, reflecting varied design aspirations and methodologies. Table 2.1 provides Strong GenAI and Weak GenAI definitions.

For example, Ghaffarzadegan et al. (2023) introduced generative agent-based modelling, which merges mechanistic models with GenAI to expose the dynamics within social systems. Their approach, which simulates human behaviors and societal interactions through advanced AI systems, pushes toward a form of S-GenAI, demonstrating potential in areas traditionally reserved for human expertise. Greenstein and Labovich's (2023) insights into the evolving applications of GenAI possibly hint at a progression toward expanding and automating AI's capabilities. Kelly (2005) suggests that S-GenAI's ability to mimic complex human cognitive processes, such as creativity, is indeed advancing significantly.

However, Dautenhahn (2008) highlights the importance of social intelligence in chatbots, proposing that AI systems should not only execute tasks requiring intellect but also engage socially with, not replaced by, humans. More recently, Fischer (2023) advocates for a synergy between AI and humans

TABLE 2.1 Strong GenAI and Weak GenAI Definitions

Strong GenAI or Weak GenAI in Layers of LLMs

Large Language Models (LLMs)
Input Layer: Takes in the raw text data.
Embedding Layer: Converts words into dense vectors that represent their semantic meaning.
Attention Layers: Multiple transformer layers that apply self-attention mechanisms to capture relationships between words.
Feedforward Layers: Dense layers that process the output of the attention layers.

(*Continued*)

TABLE 2.1 (Continued)

Strong GenAI or Weak GenAI in Layers of LLMs

Strong GenAI

Definition: Strong GenAI refers to AI systems with generalized cognitive abilities akin to human intelligence. They can understand, learn, and apply knowledge across a wide range of tasks.

Goal in LLM Context: To create a model that not only understands and generates language but can also perform reasoning, problem-solving, and possess self-awareness.

Coupling LLM Strategies

Cognitive Modules: Each cognitive function (e.g., memory, reasoning, and perception) can be developed as a loosely coupled module, integrated into the LLM framework. This allows for independent development and optimization.

Inter-layer Communication: Loose coupling can be applied between layers to allow flexibility. For instance, the attention mechanism can be decoupled to allow different attention strategies for different tasks.

Scalability: By loosely coupling the layers, the system can scale different parts independently. For example, the reasoning module can be scaled separately from the language generation module.

Safety and Robustness: Loose coupling ensures that updates or failures in one module do not cascade through the entire system, enhancing the overall safety and robustness.

Summary

Goal: Achieve general cognitive abilities

Layers: Loosely coupled cognitive modules within the LLM framework

Benefits: Scalability, safety, and independent development of cognitive functions

Weak GenAI

Definition: Weak AI, in this context, refers to AI systems specialized in specific tasks, but when combined, they give an impression of general intelligence. They do not possess true general cognitive abilities.

Goal in LLM Context: To create specialized models that perform exceptionally well in specific tasks and can be integrated to mimic general capabilities.

Specialized Modules: Each layer or a set of layers in the LLM can be specialized for a particular task, such as text generation, sentiment analysis, or translation. These modules can be loosely coupled to form a cohesive system.

Independent Upgrades: Loose coupling allows for individual components (e.g., embedding layers for different languages) to be updated or replaced without affecting the entire model.

Integration of External Tools: Weak AI systems often integrate external tools or APIs. Loose coupling enables seamless integration and interaction with these tools, enhancing functionality without tightly binding the components.

Modularity in Layers: Layers in an LLM can be designed to be modular. For instance, attention layers can be modified independently to improve performance for specific tasks without altering the feedforward layers.

Goal: Perform specialized tasks effectively, creating an illusion of general intelligence

Layers: Specialized and modular layers within the LLM

Benefits: Flexibility, ease of integration, and independent upgrades rather than competition, which is more indicative of W-GenAI. Design orientation can gravitate toward W-GenAI so as to focus on enhancing tasks in an actual workplace environment through a smart, responsive design in a soft system learning for action (Checkland & Scholes, 1990).

W-GenAI refers to being designed to perform specific tasks by responding to inputs using pre-programmed algorithms and patterns learned from vast datasets. For example, Fischer's viewpoint orientates the AI design role as a supporter of human activity, enhancing rather than replicating human cognitive functions, thus ensuring that AI remains a tool rather than a replacement. Schmidt et al. (2024) explored how simulations of human thinking can be integrated into human-centered design using ChatGPT. This design orientates AI's interactive ability to facilitate certain human cognitive processes rather than completely embodying human intelligence.

2.2.2   ChatGPT Design Orientation in Learning: Dynamic Roles, HCI, and HCAI

There has been a rapid and volatile increase in research and experimentation with ChatGPT in educational contexts. To provide an overview, we established the W-GenAI design orientation to distinguish and apply the Design Concept, Design Model, Design Method, and Design Theory. These definitions are provided in Table 2.2. We distinguish the concept between ChatGPT Generic Functions and ChatGPT Application Domains. We reviewed the current research and application development of ChatGPT in education. In this section, we present our key findings. The critical gaps also exist across different design orientations that cover the spectrum spanning from:

1. the initial idea (design concept),
2. the actual execution and application in real-world scenarios (design practice),
3. the specific techniques used to realize the idea (design method), and
4. through the theoretical underpinnings (design theory).

A significant array of research efforts has been devoted to constructing design frameworks, guidelines, or principles for the design of ChatGPT workflows. See Ray (2023), Leora et al. (2024), and the literature review references therein. All these developments are involved in designing ChatGPT "end-users." We can conclude that the current crafting of effective natural language prompts is insufficient, so in-context learning is integrated to meet the needs of dynamic roles in our project (Table 2.3 shows some examples of such dynamic roles).

There seem to be only guidelines that have been developed for specific user groups, for example, including older adults, courseware users, individuals

TABLE 2.2 Definitions of Design Concept, Design Theory, Design Method, and Design Practice

Design Concept	*Design Theory*
A design concept refers to a foundational idea or vision that underpins a particular design project or approach. In the context of educational technology, it represents the overarching goals that guide a development. For example, a design concept might focus on creating a ChatGPT application that can provide personalized learning experiences or facilitate interactive learning. The concept serves as the initial inspiration and direction for further development.	Design theory encompasses the theoretical frameworks and principles that inform the design process. It includes the study of design principles, user behavior, and the impact of design decisions on user experience. In educational contexts, design theory might explore how students interact with AI tools, the cognitive processes involved in learning with AI, and how different design elements can enhance educational outcomes. Design theory provides a structured approach to understanding and improving design practices based on empirical research and theoretical insights.
Design Method	**Design Practice**
Design method refers to the specific procedures and techniques used to create and implement a design. It involves the practical steps taken to translate a design concept and theory into a tangible product or solution. In the development of educational technologies like ChatGPT, design methods might include user-centered design, iterative prototyping, usability testing, and data-driven refinement. These methods ensure that the final product effectively meets the needs of its users and adheres to the guiding principles established by the design concept and theory.	Design practice is the actual application of design concepts, theories, and methods in real-world settings. It involves the day-to-day activities of designers and developers as they create, test, and refine educational tools. Design practice encompasses everything from brainstorming sessions and wireframing to coding and user testing. In the context of ChatGPT, design practice includes the practical challenges and solutions encountered when integrating the AI into classrooms, gathering user feedback, and making iterative improvements based on that feedback. It represents the hands-on work of bringing a design from concept to implementation and ensuring its success in practice.

from diverse cultural backgrounds, people with disabilities, and those with varying literacy levels, the use of mobile Apps, and ethical concerns such as privacy. The current "end-users" are insufficiently specialized by the generic functions. Table 2.4 lists ChatGPT generic functional roles.

It is understandable that the aim of GenAI enterprise design is to promote the rise of widespread commercial use of Apps and App stores. To orientate

TABLE 2.3 Examples of the Dynamic Roles in the Project

ChatGPT Dynamic Roles in Piloting LivePBL DEEP Method

Student music role
Music students who are trained to become teachers interact with ChatGPT to enhance their understanding of PBL methodologies and to get ideas on structuring engaging and educational music lessons for children. They use ChatGPT to:

• Generate ideas for music projects that align with children's interests and learning levels.
• Develop lesson plans incorporating interactive activities, such as creating simple musical instruments from household items or composing short pieces of music.
• Receive feedback on their proposed plans to ensure they are age-appropriate and pedagogically sound.

Teacher music role
Experienced music teachers oversee the co-design process using ChatGPT to:

• Provide personalized guidance to music students, helping them refine their lesson plans.
• Find and integrate additional resources, such as instructional videos, sheet music, and interactive software.
• Facilitate discussions with music students and families to tailor the learning experience based on feedback and ongoing assessment of the children's progress.

Family role
Families participate actively in the learning process, supported by ChatGPT to:
• Understand the goals and activities of the PBL project.
• Find funny family-friendly music activities that they can do together at home.
• Communicate with music students and teachers through the platform to provide feedback on what activities their children enjoyed the most and what challenges they faced.

TABLE 2.4 ChatGPT Generic Functional Roles

Application Flexibility:
• ChatGPT's functions are not fixed but can change dynamically according to the context and requirements of the application domain.
• It can switch between roles such as a tutor, content creator, data analyst, or project manager based on user interactions and specific tasks.

Application Context-Sensitivity:
• The design method ensures ChatGPT understands the context in which it is operating, enabling it to provide relevant and appropriate responses and actions.
• For example, in an educational domain, ChatGPT might provide personalized tutoring for one user while generating lesson plans for another.

Role Assignment:
• Roles are assigned based on predefined parameters and real-time data, allowing ChatGPT to adapt to new tasks and responsibilities as they arise.
• Dynamic role assignment can be influenced by user inputs, application needs, and ongoing interactions.

(*Continued*)

TABLE 2.4 (Continued)

Integration with Domain-Specific Tools:

- ChatGPT can integrate with various domain-specific tools and platforms, leveraging their capabilities to enhance its own functionality.
- For example, in a project management context, ChatGPT might integrate with scheduling tools to help manage timelines and deliverables.

User-Centric Experiences and Feedback:

- The dynamic role concept is designed with the end-user in mind, ensuring that ChatGPT's functionalities are directly aligned with user needs and enhance their experience.
- User feedback and interactions continuously refine and adapt the roles ChatGPT assumes.

Roles in Academic Study:

- Content Generation: Creates study materials, summaries, and notes, helping students grasp complex concepts more easily.
- Personalized Learning: Adapts learning resources and pathways to individual student needs, optimizing the learning process.
- Tutoring and Assistance: Provides on-demand help and explanations, acting as a virtual tutor for students needing extra support.
- Language Translation: Makes academic content accessible in multiple languages, supporting international students.
- Automated Feedback and Assessment: Offers instant feedback on assignments and quizzes, helping students learn from their mistakes and improve.
- Interactive Learning Tools: Develops interactive simulations and educational games that enhance understanding through hands-on experience.

Roles in Academic Research:

- Literature Review: Automates the process of reviewing and summarizing existing research, saving time and ensuring comprehensive coverage of relevant studies.
- Data Analysis: Assists in analyzing large datasets, identifying patterns, and generating insights that might be missed by human researchers.
- Hypothesis Generation: Suggests new hypotheses and research directions based on existing data and trends, fostering innovation.
- Writing Assistance: Aids in drafting research papers, reports, and grant proposals, ensuring clarity and coherence in academic writing.
- Collaboration Tools: Facilitates collaboration among researchers through AI-powered communication and project management tools.
- Experimentation and Simulation: Helps design and simulate experiments, providing preliminary results and refining experimental setups.

a ChatGPT system development, there must be "application developers." This is "raising questions on appropriate types of controlling LLMs at contextual levels of algorithmic transparency, perceiving user awareness of how the algorithms work and how to develop ChatGPT apps effectively" (Alvarado & Waern, 2018). Therefore, these designs for the generic functions are rooted in S-GenAI (not in W-GenAI).

Therefore, the design orientation for using ChatGPT could have been clearer; that should have received more meaningful and impactful attention in the navigation of current actual practices. Education cannot be treated as an independent singular application domain, nor as a mere component of a large model or architecture with diverse contexts that lack a design method to integrate individuals or organizations in education. We conclude the following four challenging research areas.

2.2.2.1 Personalized Learning Experiences with ChatGPT

ChatGPT demonstrates the concept of personalized learning by leveraging NLP to create tailored educational experiences. ChatGPT's interactive capability is limited to conversational exchanges. It currently lacks the ability to navigate students' communicative learning in a subject area through collaborative experiences and experimentation. A design method in W-GenAI can enhance this adaptability, ensuring that explanations are matched to the student's level of experience and interests, which is crucial for engagement and retention. Furthermore, tracking student progress with ChatGPT offers a dynamic, collaborative, and social learning path, thereby realizing the ultimate design potential of personalized education to meet individual needs.

2.2.2.2 Adapting Learning Materials to Individual Student Needs

The adaptability of ChatGPT in customizing learning materials to individual student needs highlights a critical educational design principle that requires a method, not just an abstract concept. By analyzing student behavior and preferences, teachers and learners need a method to effectively use ChatGPT to tailor content, providing diagrams for visual learners and detailed texts for those who prefer written explanations. This method must be designed to implement a responsive and adaptive learning environment, ultimately enhancing adaptive and inclusive learning outcomes.

2.2.2.3 Transformative Impacts on Teaching

Much of the research on ChatGPT aims to integrate its use into teaching practices, which only represent a practical application of a design concept. To embody a forward-thinking educational design in theory, however, a design method in W-GenAI is essential for curriculum development, grading automation, and feedback provision. A design approach addresses significant teaching challenges, allowing teachers to focus on personalized instruction. Specifically, the ability to manage hybrid classes effectively connects developing countries to solutions that mitigate teacher shortages and resource constraints, thus enhancing educational quality and efficiency across both formal and non-formal education.

2.2.2.4 Revolutionizing Learning Efficacy and Accessibility

Much current ChatGPT research aims to address the design concept of improving learning efficacy and accessibility. A design method in W-GenAI is needed to personalize educational content, enhance relevance and retention, and democratize education by providing high-quality support to students who lack resources. Implementing this scalable integration into educational systems requires designing how ChatGPT can transform traditional learning models, offering personalized support and thereby achieving the ultimate goal of making education more inclusive and effective.

2.2.3 Adopting Project-Based Learning through Design

Education has its own design disciplines (Zakaria et al., 2019), and education through design represents a methodological paradigm. Our case study focuses on the design of PBL as an application domain within teaching and learning environments. Du and Han (2016) reviewed the literature concerning the definitions of PBL; they concluded the following:

1. "Projects are central, not peripheral to the curriculum."
2. "Projects are focused on questions or problems that 'drive' students to encounter (and struggle with) the central concepts and principles of the discipline."
3. "Projects involve students in a constructive investigation."
4. "Projects are student-driven to some significant degree."
5. "Projects are realistic, not school-like."

The design orientation in PBL is linked with learning objects, where learners use various tools and models to conceptualize and understand the object of the study (Lloyd & Bohemia, 2013; Razali et al., 2022; Tan, 2017). This involves active engagement and helping learners recognize and outline the core aspects of the object, leading to a detailed and justified understanding over time. PBL opens many opportunities for understanding multidisciplinary knowledge from various educational areas and institutions to address complex problems.

PBL can be a holistic approach that makes design a powerful methodology for educational practices, fostering systems thinking and integrating technology into learner-centered approaches aligning with the multifaceted and dynamic nature of learning (Warr et al., 2022). Effective PBL design must address the diverse needs of learners, adapt to changing societal and technological landscapes, and prepare students for real-world challenges (Warr et al., 2020). However, PBL has been overlooked in practice. Poorly designed and executed projects can lead to wasted time, misguided efforts, and unmet learning objectives (Larmer et al., 2021). It is crucial to ensure the adoption of best PBL practices through an educational design. For example, García-Martín and Pérez-Martínez (2021) emphasized the need for a teaching style that focuses on developing student competencies, noting that while teachers find PBL attractive, they often fail to use PBL and help new teachers overcome practical challenges.

The role of AI in enhancing PBL has been explored in recent literature, aiming to suggest iterative improvements and simulate real-world outcomes, as examined by Chen et al. (2020). Danielescu (2023) investigated how interacting with AI during projects can help students develop technical skills and critical thinking. Smith (2024) highlighted integrating AI into PBL to offer deeper analytical engagement and adaptive feedback, fostering a personalized and effective learning environment.

However, as we discussed earlier, ChatGPT struggles with providing fully contextualized learning experiences aligned with an educational domain, as well as individual interests and contexts of collaborative social learning (Klein, 2023a, 2023b; Labadze et al., 2023). ChatGPT lacks situational awareness and tailored interactions, which can result in disjointed and impersonal learning processes, impacting cognitive development and student engagement.

PBL can effectively loosely couple ChatGPT between HCI and HCAI and involve teachers, learners, and other stakeholders. HCI digital technologies focus on creating intuitive and engaging interfaces between users and digital tools (Dautenhahn, 2008). In PBL, these technologies make learning more interactive and collaborative (Nurhidayah et al., 2021), fostering creativity. Mucundanyi and Woodley (2021) explored interactive digital tools like smartboards and tablets to facilitate real-time data sessions, allowing students to visualize ideas and organize information effectively. Digital collaboration platforms enable virtual participation, enhancing document sharing, task management, and communication (Fischer, 2023; Klein, 2023b). Digital Learning Journals (Zhorova et al., 2022) is another case that serves as HCI, providing digital tools for reflective writing that encourage learners to record their thoughts and insights on their learning experiences.

2.3 Research Methodology

We adopted a case-based study approach, piloting the DEEP method to integrate ChatGPT into the co-design of PBL. This involved deploying ChatGPT in various educational settings in music education through hybrid teaching environments using co-designed templates. These templates follow CPD Certification standards and deliver PBL sessions to achieve personalized learning, adapt materials, and transform teaching practices. The research setting is based on the LivePBL model, shown in Figure 2.4, including a collaborative

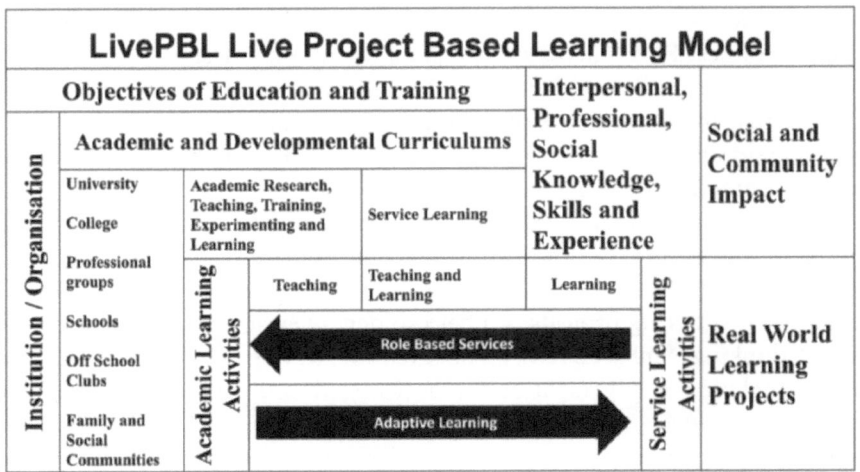

FIGURE 2.4 LivePBL model in education domains.

effort involving Music College, Capital Normal University in Beijing, China, as well as school headteachers, families, and communities across the UK, Nepal, and China, supported by digital platforms and a Learning Management System.

The Sino-International Seminar LivePBL focuses on music education, co-designing PBL through virtual social projects with international music teachers and student teachers. One specific use case demonstrates the ChatGPT's role in facilitating personalized learning for children in a family learning program, enhancing creativity, content personalization, and dynamic curriculum adjustments.

2.3.1 Research Setting

Our research setting used ChatGPT 3.5 in the co-design of PBL and HCI Digital Learning Journals. The LivePBL program operates through a hybrid PBL model, functioning as an effective research and development framework with stakeholders. This program, initiated during COVID-19, involves university faculty, school headteachers, and community leaders from the Dalian Shuxiang social community, spanning the UK, Nepal, and China. This diverse collaboration includes the following:

- University and college students guided by academic faculty.
- Children in schools and clubs led by headteachers.
- Families engaged through community-based learning initiatives.

See LivePBL publications (Liu et al., 2022; Wang et al., 2020; Zhang et al., 2022; Zhou et al., 2023).

In China, undergraduate education heavily relies on exam preparation, limiting skill development beyond memorization. Capital Normal University, focused on training future teachers, faces challenges in providing practical teaching experiences due to limited mobility and resources. Additionally, teacher training programs often lack international exposure, restricting the adoption of innovative teaching strategies. Implementing the LivePBL DEEP method with ChatGPT in non-formal educational settings addresses these challenges by preparing students for the complexities of modern education, ensuring adaptability, cultural awareness, and proficiency in essential 21st-century skills.

Supported by digital platforms like Zoom and an LMS operated by The Support School in Liverpool, UK, this approach views PBL through sociocultural activities, making it a ground for testing new educational strategies and technologies. Feedback is systematically collected from participants through structured interviews, surveys, and direct observations.

2.3.2 Pilot Programme: Sino-International Seminar LivePBL Liking Vocal Education through Project-Based Learning

In 2023, this hybrid program was relaunched for a 12-week PBL session, following CPD certification to navigate design principles in constructing teaching and learning environments. It provided unique opportunities to explore ChatGPT for Sino-international music teachers, student teachers, and local community schoolteachers. PBL was co-designed through virtual social project practices, with participants benefiting from macro-teaching seminars, micro-teaching workshops, and cross-international cultural teamwork via a digital LMS platform, HCI Digital Learning Journals with ChatGPT inquiries and feedback, guided participants who shared valuable teaching and learning experiences. Students evaluated their outcomes by publishing papers at the 2023 London International Conference on Education and the 2024 International Society of Music Education annual conference. The collected data are analyzed to assess the DEEP method's effectiveness in achieving educational goals and identifying the areas for improvement. Evaluation reports summarize key findings, lessons learned, and recommendations for future implementations. Figure 2.5 illustrates the design of a teaching and learning environment.

2.3.3 The Use Case

In this use case, ChatGPT is utilized to facilitate personalized learning in music education for children participating in an online family learning program. The project involves music students, teachers, and families collaboratively

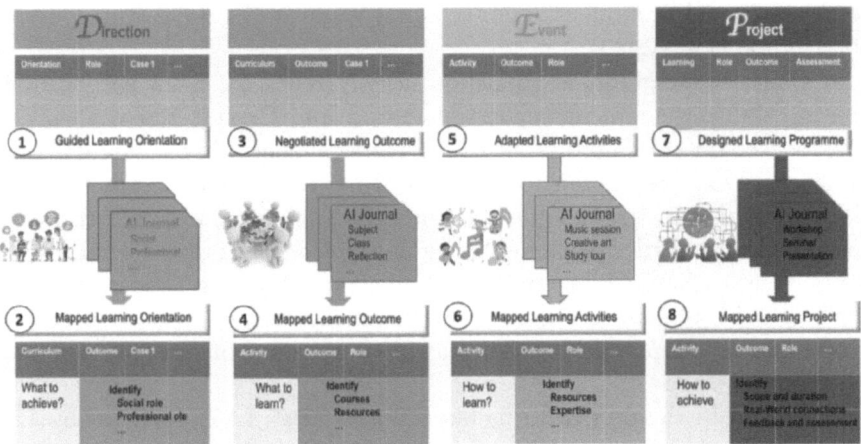

FIGURE 2.5 LivePBL DEEP method design of a teaching and learning environment.

designing and implementing a PBL curriculum. Table 2.3 lists the dynamic roles of ChatGPT, which are discussed in detail in Section 2.2:

- Music student's role
- Music teacher's role
- Family role

The data collected throughout the pilot were structured in several key areas where ChatGPT empowered the PBL process. Data collection particularly focused on how ChatGPT enhanced creativity and direction setting by helping generate and refine project ideas, ensuring clear and engaging directions for PBL activities. ChatGPT supported the creation of personalized, high-quality educational content tailored to students' learning styles and interests, leading to high engagement levels. Data were collected interactively and from real-time support during sessions, maintaining participation and addressing immediate learning challenges. The continuous feedback loop facilitated by ChatGPT enabled dynamic adjustments to the curriculum, ensuring that the learning experience remained relevant and effective. Examples of the DEEP method, as referenced in Figure 2.4, are provided in Appendices I, II, III, and IV, covering Direction, Education, Event, and Project, respectively.

2.4 Discussions

In piloting the use of ChatGPT for personalized learning in music education, the DEEP method provided a structured navigation that guided the process using ChatGPT and HCI Digital Learning Journals from the initial direction setting to the final project reflections. Data collection and analysis were integral to understanding the impact of ChatGPT on facilitating the co-design of PBL converging teaching and learning.

2.4.1 Using the Method in the Dimension of Direction

The DEEP method began with initial brainstorming sessions where music students and teachers utilized ChatGPT to generate project ideas. In one session, music students proposed a theme, "Music Around the World," and ChatGPT suggested structuring the project by focusing on different cultures each week. Teachers provided feedback, emphasizing the need for age-appropriate activities. For example, individual music students used ChatGPT to explore various cultural songs and instruments, which were then presented to the team. Teachers offered insights on which activities might be too complex for younger children. This collaborative effort, facilitated by ChatGPT, ensured that the learning process was co-designed, allowing for personalization with a clear and engaging focus from the start. The data collected from these sessions included brainstorming transcripts and feedback from teachers, which demonstrated how ChatGPT significantly enhanced the creative process and helped set a clear direction for the PBL activities.

2.4.2 Using the Method in the Dimension of Education

As the project progressed into the education phase, music students developed detailed lesson plans with instructions for each activity, supported by ChatGPT. For instance, music students created a lesson plan and discussed the plan with parents. They used ChatGPT to find interactive online rhythm games and tutorials on making simple drums from household items. Teachers also have reviewed these plans, providing feedback through ChatGPT.

A music teacher noted that the activities were highly engaging but suggested adding a section on the history of the Chinese song to give children more context. Families also used ChatGPT to understand the project goals and activities, asking questions and suggesting additional activities that could be performed at home.

A family suggested teaching children a song through a ChatGPT exploration to improve children's and families' digital literacy as a weekend activity. The data collected included lesson plans, compiled resources, and feedback from both teachers and families. This phase demonstrated that ChatGPT effectively assisted in developing high-quality educational materials tailored to the children's learning styles and interests.

2.4.3 Using the Method in the Dimension of Event

The implementation phase saw the project come to life through weekly online sessions. ChatGPT assisted in scheduling and sending reminders to families.

During these sessions, families used ChatGPT to ask questions. When their children struggled with keeping rhythm, ChatGPT suggested alternative practice methods and provided links to online rhythm games.

Teachers and music students monitored these interactions, making real-time adjustments as needed. The project culminated in a virtual workshop where children showcased what they had learned. ChatGPT helped organize the event by scheduling performances and providing tips on making the presentations engaging. The data collected included attendance records, participation rates, and observational feedback from the virtual concert. For instance, a family noted that their son was more motivated to learn after receiving real-time support from ChatGPT during practice sessions. This phase highlighted the importance of interactive and real-time support in maintaining high levels of engagement in PBL activities.

2.4.4 Using the Method in the Dimension of Project

Throughout the project, continuous feedback was collected from families through ChatGPT. Each week, families shared their experiences and challenges, such as difficulties in understanding certain musical concepts. ChatGPT facilitated reflective Digital Learning Sessions, where music students and teachers discussed this feedback. For example, based on a family's feedback, music students adjusted their lesson plan to include simpler explanations of musical notes. Teachers praised this adaptability and noted the improved engagement in subsequent sessions. The project culminated in reflective sessions where music students and teachers used ChatGPT to discuss successes and areas for improvement.

2.5 Summary of Critically Addressed Research Areas

In this section, we highlight the key points discussed in the chapter, reaffirming the significance of the LivePBL DEEP method.

Lack of Clear Design Orientation for W-GenAI in Educational Theory. We have emphasized the need for a structured design method to bridge the gap between theoretical concepts and practical applications of W-GenAI in education. It argues that traditional learning theories and fragmented applications of W-GenAI fail to systematically align AI tools with educational objectives, necessitating a robust framework like the DEEP method.

Challenges in ChatGPT Application Design for HCI and HCAI in PBL. We have identified a critical need to integrate ChatGPT with HCI and HCAI in the design of PBL. This involves creating more intuitive, engaging, and ethically aligned interactions that cater to diverse educational needs and improve the overall learning experience.

Scalability and Adaptability Issues. The scalability of the DEEP method is questioned, particularly its reliance on technological infrastructure, which might not be available in resource-poor settings. The adaptability of the method across different educational contexts and its ability to cater to varied learning environments are other significant concerns.

Teacher Training and Acceptance. Effective implementation of the DEEP method requires extensive teacher training and professional development. The text highlights potential resistance from less tech-savvy educators, which could hinder the adoption and efficacy of the method.

Continuous Evaluation and Feedback Mechanisms. The need for robust, ongoing evaluation and feedback mechanisms is highlighted to ensure the DEEP method's continuous improvement and alignment with educational goals. The resource-intensive nature of this requirement is also noted as a potential challenge.

2.6   Contributions

Our Design Orientation of W-GenAI in Theory. The LivePBL DEEP method, constructed through the phases of Direction, Education, Event, and Project, serves as a novel design framework for integrating W-GenAI with PBL. It addresses the limitations of traditional learning theories and fragmented W-GenAI applications by providing a structured, user-centric, and ethically aligned approach tailored to educational goals. This method ensures that W-GenAI tools are systematically and effectively applied, aligning with educational objectives to enhance the learning process. Our research strengthens the theoretical foundation of W-GenAI in education, showcasing how these tools can create personalized, engaging, and effective learning experiences.

ChatGPT Application Design with HCI and HCAI in PBL. The DEEP method enhances traditional PBL by integrating ChatGPT, making the learning process more adaptive and responsive to diverse educational needs. This integration improves human–computer interaction interfaces by creating more intuitive and engaging interactions between users and AI tools. Additionally, it ensures ethical and user-centered AI design in human-centered AI. The phased approach facilitates comprehensive learning experiences, from setting personalized goals to delivering interactive and practical activities and fostering continuous improvement through feedback. Our research demonstrates how ChatGPT can effectively support co-design in PBL, providing valuable insights into the practical applications of AI in educational settings.

ChatGPT Loosely Coupling an Educational Domain. The pilot project in hybrid and non-formal music education showcased the DEEP method's practical application. The method facilitates the co-design of PBL through ChatGPT, providing personalized support and enriched learning experiences. Students observed innovative teaching methods and participated in hybrid learning models, boosting skills and confidence through interactive ChatGPT activities and virtual exchanges. Family involvement fostered a community-based learning approach, supporting children's educational journeys. The DEEP method contributes to ChatGPT application development by motivating music and art learning, cultural appreciation, improved social skills, reflective thinking, and a broader global perspective. Participation in this multicultural project prepared students for inclusive and cooperative global engagements, fostering a holistic educational experience. Overall, the DEEP method represents a significant advancement in ChatGPT application design orientation, offering a valuable framework for future educational initiatives.

2.7 Limitations and Future Research

While the DEEP method showcases considerable promise, several limitations must be acknowledged. The method's reliance on W-GenAI tools poses a challenge, especially in educational settings with limited technological infrastructure. This dependence could exacerbate existing educational inequalities between resource-rich and resource-poor environments. Scalability is another challenge, as implementing this comprehensive approach requires substantial investment in training and technology. Teacher training and acceptance are crucial; teachers must be proficient with W-GenAI tools, necessitating extensive professional development. Resistance from less tech-savvy teachers could hinder adoption. Ethical and privacy concerns are paramount, requiring stringent guidelines to ensure ethical use and protect student privacy. The method's adaptability to different cultural and educational contexts adds complexity, necessitating customization to fit local needs and values. Continuous evaluation and feedback are critical but can be resource-intensive, complicating the method's implementation.

Several pilot projects are underway to further scale the DEEP method, integrating PBL with W-GenAI. In classrooms with mixed-ability students, the DEEP method can provide adaptive learning pathways that adjust in real time, ensuring every student remains engaged and challenged. This promotes continuous progress and caters to individual learning speeds. Inclusivity is also addressed by offering tools that support diverse learning needs, such as W-GenAI-driven language translation and speech-to-text technologies, which help non-native speakers and students with disabilities access course materials. The method also assists teachers in creating inclusive lesson plans that accommodate various learning styles.

Connecting classroom learning with practical applications is another focus. The DEEP method can bridge this gap by providing hands-on learning opportunities through real-world scenarios. For instance, in a business course, W-GenAI can power simulations, allowing students to manage a virtual company and see the consequences of their decisions. This experiential learning approach helps students understand the practical implications of theoretical concepts, preparing them for real-world challenges and enhancing their problem-solving skills.

2.8 Conclusions

The LivePBL DEEP method represents a significant advancement in the integration of W-GenAI into educational frameworks, particularly through problem-based learning (PBL). This novel design framework offers a structured, user-centric approach to aligning W-GenAI tools with educational objectives, overcoming the shortcomings of traditional learning theories and fragmented GenAI applications. Our research highlights the potential of ChatGPT to enhance PBL by creating adaptive, responsive, and engaging learning experiences. By piloting through hybrid and non-formal music education, the DEEP method has demonstrated its ability to provide personalized support and enriched learning experiences, fostering community-based learning and supporting students in social practices.

However, scalability remains a concern due to reliance on technological infrastructure, which may not be readily available in resource-poor settings. Furthermore, the method's adaptability across diverse educational contexts and its ability to cater to varied learning environments require further exploration. The effective implementation of the DEEP method is contingent upon comprehensive teacher training and professional development. Resistance from less tech-savvy educators could hinder adoption and efficacy, underscoring the need for targeted training programs.

Ongoing projects aim to extend the DEEP method's reach by integrating PBL with W-GenAI in various classroom settings, focusing on adaptive learning pathways, inclusivity, and real-world applications to prepare students for real-world challenges and enhance problem-solving skills. In summary, while the DEEP method holds substantial promise for enhancing educational experiences through W-GenAI integration, addressing its limitations and refining the method through continued research and pilot projects is essential for achieving broader adoption and success.

Appendix I: Samples of the Design on Direction

Samples of Using LivePBL DEEP Method to Design

Direction – What to Achieve

Involves setting clear goals, objectives, and guidelines for the project. It ensures all activities align with the project's vision and desired outcomes. Use ChatGPT to brainstorm and refine specific objectives for the project.

Objectives

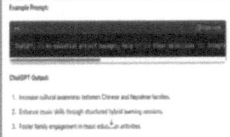

Increase cultural awareness between Chinese and Nepalese families.

Enhance music skills through structured hybrid learning sessions.

Foster family engagement in music education activities.

Role Assignment and Persona Development: Create detailed personas for different stakeholders involved in the project.

Learner's Roles

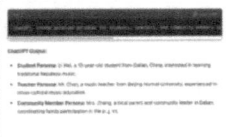

Student Persona: Li Wei, a 10-year-old student from Dalian, China, is interested in learning traditional Nepalese music.

Teacher Persona: Mr. Chen, a music teacher from Beijing Normal University, is experienced in cross-cultural music education.

Community Member Persona: Mrs. Zhang, a local parent and community leader in Dalian, coordinating family participation in the project.

Guided Learning Journals

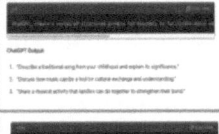

Describe a traditional song from your childhood and explain its significance.

Discuss how music can be a tool for cultural exchange and understanding.

Share a musical activity that families can do together.

What are the current practices of music education in Chinese and Nepalese families?

How does music facilitate intergenerational learning in both cultures?

What are the challenges and benefits of hybrid music education?

How can we measure the impact of cultural exchange through music education?

Feedback Procedures

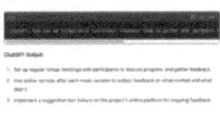

Set up regular virtual meetings with participants to discuss progress and gather feedback.

Use online surveys after each music session to collect feedback on what worked and what didn't.

Implement a suggestion box feature on the project's online platform for ongoing feedback.

Appendix II: Samples of the Design on Education

Education - What to Learn

Brainstorm and refine a hybrid curriculum integrating one or more modules in music education; develop innovative instructional methods to enhance the learning experience; develop one or more specific music skills among learners.

Modules

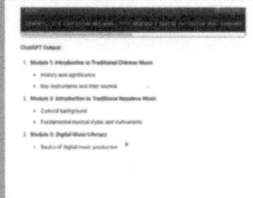

Module 1: Introduction to Traditional Chinese Music
- History and significance
- Key instruments and their sounds

Module 2: Introduction to Traditional Nepalese Music
- Cultural background
- Fundamental musical styles and instruments

Module 3: Digital Music Literacy
- Basics of digital music production
- Integrating traditional music with digital tools

Module 4: Bilingual Music Education
- Learning music terminology in both Chinese and English
- Exercises to practice bilingual communication through music

Instruction

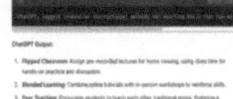

Flipped Classroom: Assign pre-recorded lectures for home viewing, using class time for hands-on practice and discussion.

Blended Learning: Combine online tutorials with in-person workshops to reinforce skills.

Peer Teaching: Encourage students to teach each other traditional songs, fostering a collaborative learning environment.

Bilingual Instruction: Conduct sessions in both Chinese and Nepalese, alternating languages to enhance bilingual skills.

Skills

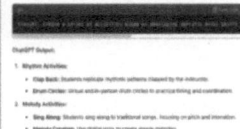

Learners are able to:
- Replicate rhythmic patterns clapped by the instructor.
- Play virtual and in-person drum circles to practice timing and coordination.
- Sing Along to traditional songs, focusing on pitch and intonation.
- Work in groups to prepare and perform a piece of music.
- Communicate with each other from different cultures and work together to create a group journal, present and performance.

Appendix III: Samples of the Design on Event

Event – How to Learn

Define specific objectives for action-based and individual preferred activities; align each activity with the project's educational and cultural goals as an event; create a festival to celebrate and promote the culture of China and Nepal through music at home online; provide educational workshops on traditional music, and to foster a sense of community and mutual appreciation among participants.

Engaging Strategies

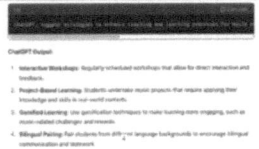

Use interactive storytelling to explain the origins of the music.

Include hands-on activities where children can try playing the instruments.

Organize simple rhythm games and sing-along sessions.

Provide colourful, informative materials about the instruments and their cultural significance.

Event Promotion Plan

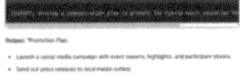

Promotion Plan:
- Launch a social media campaign with event teasers, highlights, and participant stories.
- Send out press releases to local media outlets.
- Collaborate with local influencers to share event information.
- Use email newsletters to keep registered participants informed and engaged.

Rhythm Activities:
- Clap Back: Students replicate rhythmic patterns clapped by the instructor.
- Drum Circles: Virtual and in-person drum circles to practice timing and coordination.

Harmony Activities:
- Choral Practice: Group singing sessions to practice harmonizing.
- Digital Harmony: Use music software to experiment with harmonic combinations.

Teamwork Activities:
- Group Performances: Students work in groups to prepare and perform a piece of music.
- Collaborative Projects: Joint projects where students from different cultures work together to create a musical composition.

Bilingual Communication Activities:
- Language Exchange Sessions: Students practice explaining musical concepts in both Chinese and Nepalese.
- Bilingual Songwriting: Collaborative songwriting sessions where lyrics are written in both languages.

Fusion Performance
- Duration: 45 minutes
- Performers: A mix of Chinese and Nepalese musicians

Post-Event Evaluation

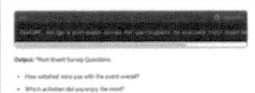

Post-Event Survey Questions:
- How satisfied were you with the event overall?
- Which activities did you enjoy the most?
- Do you feel the event helped you learn more about Chinese and Nepalese music?
- What suggestions do you have for future events?
- Would you participate in similar events in the future?

Appendix IV: Samples of the Design on Project

Project – How to Achieve

Outlining, planning, and executing the integration of the other three dimensions (Direction, Education, Event) into a cohesive project-based learning (PBL) framework. It involves formulating learning processes, setting goals, designing activities, and ensuring that the project is manageable and effective.

LivePBL Project

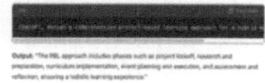

The objectives are to promote cultural exchange through music, develop musical and bilingual communication skills, and foster collaborative learning among participants

Instructive Sessions

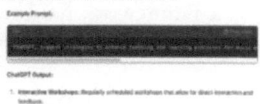

Interactive Workshops: Regularly scheduled workshops that allow for direct interaction and feedback.

Project-Based Learning: Students undertake music projects that require applying their knowledge and skills in real-world contexts.

Reflective Learning: Use journaling techniques to make learning more engaging, such as music-related challenges and rewards.

Bilingual Pairing: Pair students from different language backgrounds to encourage bilingual communication and teamwork.

References

Alvarado, O., & Waern, A. (2018). *Towards Algorithmic Experience: Initial Efforts for Social Media Contexts*. Proceedings of the 2018 CHI Conference on Human Factors in Computing Systems.

Bradley-Levine, J., & Mosier, G. (2024). *Literature Review on Project-Based Learning*. University of Indianapolis Center of Excellence in Leadership of Learning. https://journals.sagepub.com/doi/abs/10.1177/1365480216659733.

Checkland, P. B., & Scholes, J. (1990). *Soft Systems Methodology in Action*. John Wiley & Sons, Inc., New York.

Chen, L., Chen, P., & Lin, Z. (2020). Artificial Intelligence in Education: A Review. *IEEE Access, 8*, 15.

Danielescu, A. (2023). *AI-Ecology*. Proceedings of the 2023 CHI Conference on Human Factors in Computing Systems, Hamburg, Germany.

Dautenhahn, K. (2008). A Paradigm Shift in Artificial Intelligence: Why Social Intelligence Matters in the Design and Development of Robots with Human-Like Intelligence. In M. Lungarella, F. Iida, J. Bongard, & R. Pfeifer (Eds.), *50 Years of AI: Festschrift (Lecture Notes in Artificial Intelligence* (Vol. 4850, pp. 288–302). Springer-Verlag.

Du, X., & Han, J. (2016). A Literature Review on the Definition and Process of Project-Based Learning and Other Relative Studies. *Creative Education, 7*, 1079.

Fischer, G. (2023). AI and Humans not AI versus Humans. *Interaction Design and Architecture(s) Journal (IxD&A), 59*, 19.

Flowers, J. C. (2019). *Strong and Weak AI: Deweyan Considerations*. AAAI Spring Symposium: Towards Conscious AI Systems.

Gabriels, K. (2018). *Addressing the Soft Impacts of Weak AI-Technologies*. Proceedings of the ALIFE 2018: The 2018 Conference on Artificial Life., Tokyo, Japan.

García-Martín, J., & Pérez-Martínez, J. E. (2021). Method to Guide the Design of Project Based Learning Activities Based on Educational Theories. *International Journal of Engineering Education*, 33(3), 20.

Gericke, K., Eckert, C., & Stacey, M. (2024). *What Do We Need to Say About a Design Method?* Proceedings of the 21st International Conference on Engineering Design Theory and Research Methodology, Vancouver, Canada.

Ghaffarzadegan, N., Majumdar, A., Williams, R., & Hosseinichimeh, N. (2023). *Generative Agent-Based Modeling: Unveiling Social System Dynamics through Coupling Mechanistic Models with Generative Artificial Intelligence.* Department of Industrial and Systems Engineering, Virginia Tech, Falls Church, VA.

Greenstein, B., & Labovich, M. (2023). *Patterns of Use Cases: Generative AI, Moving Beyond Use Cases.* https://www.linkedin.com/pulse/patterns-use-cases-generative-ai-moving-beyond-bret-greenstein/.

Grinshtain, Y., Avidov-Ungar, O., Shaked, H., Livneh, I., & Nikritin, D. (2023). "Not Fully Coordinated": The Loosely Coupled Paradigm as a Framework for Understanding Relationships of Educators in Teacher Education Programmes. *Journal of Education for Teaching*, 19.

Jin, Y., Yan, L., Echeverria, V., Gašević, D., & Martinez-Maldonado, R. (2024). *Generative AI in Higher Education: A Global Perspective of Institutional Adoption Policies and Guidelines.* arXiv:2405.11800 [cs.CY], https://arxiv.org/abs/2405.11800.

Kasneci, E., Sessler, K., Küchemann, S., Bannert, M., Dementieva, D., Fischer, F., Gasser, U., Groh, G., Günnemann, S., Hüllermeier, E., Krusche, S., Kutyniok, G., Michaeli, T., Nerdel, C., Pfeffer, J., Poquet, O., Sailer, M., Schmidt, A., Seidel, T., . . . Kasneci, G. (2023). ChatGPT for Good? On Opportunities and Challenges of Large Language Models for Education. *Learning and Individual Differences*, 103.

Kelly, A. J. (2005). Intelligent Design-or Design of Intelligence? *Ethics Education*, 11(2), 3–9. https://acuresearchbank.acu.edu.au/item/8v7zq/intelligent-design-or-design-of-intelligence.

Klein, A. (2023a). *Top 15 Real-Life Use Cases for AI in Educational Industry.* https://redresscompliance.com/top-15-real-life-use-cases-for-ai-in-educational-industry/.

Klein, A. (2023b). *The 3 Capabilities Designers Need to Build for the AI Era.* UX Collective. https://bigmedium.com/ideas/links/the-3-capabilities-designers-need-to-build-for-the.html.

Kumar, A. (2025). Types of AI Explained. https://www.simplilearn.com/tutorials/artificial-intelligence-tutorial/types-of-artificial-intelligence (accessed 04 February 2025).

Labadze, L., Grigolia, M., & Machaidze, L. R. (2023). Role of AI Chatbots in Education: Systematic Literature Review. *International Journal of Educational Technology in Higher Education*, 20, 56.

Larmer, J., Mergendoller, J. R., Boss, S., & Alexandria, V. A. (2021). *Setting the Standard for Project Based Learning: A Proven Approach to Rigorous Classroom Instruction.* ASCD, Alexandria, VA.

Lee, D., Arnold, M., Srivastava, A., Plastow, K., Strelan, P., Ploeckl, F., Lekkas, D., & Palmer, E. (2024). The Impact of Generative AI on Higher Education Learning and Teaching: A Study of Educators' Perspectives. *Computers and Education: Artificial Intelligence*, 6(100215).

Leora, C. A., Karahasanovic, A., Makokha, J., Sebastian, S. N., & Zhao, Y. (2024, June 23–28). *ChatGPT: Mediating Complex Design Processes.* DRS2024: Boston, USA.

Liu, Y., Li, Y., Yang, S., Ren, T., Li, H., Hogg, A., Shah, P., Li, J., Zhang, Y., & Chhetri, A. (2022). A Hybrid and Non-Formal Music Education Connecting China's Local

Family Communities and Cultures with Nepal. *International Journal for Infonomics (IJI)*, *15*(1), 6, 2088–2093.

Lloyd, P., & Bohemia, E. (2013). *New Perspectives in Design Thinking, Teaching, and Learning*. Art, Design, and Communication in Higher Education 2nd International Conference on Design Education Research, Oslo and Akershus University College of Applied Sciences.

Minaee, S., Mikolov, T., Nikzad, N., Chenaghlu, M., Socher, R., Amatriain, X., & Gao, J. (2024). *Large Language Models: A Survey*. arXiv:2402.06196.

Mucundanyi, G., & Woodley, X. (2021). Exploring Free Digital Tools in Education. *International Journal of Education and Development using Information and Communication Technology*, *17*(2), 8.

Ng, D. (2024). Empowering Student Self-Regulated Learning and Science Education through ChatGPT: A Review. *British Journal of Educational Technology*, *55*(1), 17.

Nurhidayah, I. J., Yunita, Y., Juandi, D., & Kusumah, Y. S. (2021). Project Based Learning (PjBL) Learning Model in Science Learning: Literature Review. *Journal of Physics: Conference Series*. https://doi.org/10.1088/1742-6596/2019/1/012043.

OpenAI. (2023a). *GPT-4 is OpenAI's Most Advanced System, Producing Safer and More Useful Responses*. https://openai.com/index/gpt-4/.

OpenAI. (2023b). *Generative Pre-trained Transformer 3 (GPT-3)*. https://openai.com/index/gpt-3-apps/.

Ray, P. P. (2023). ChatGPT: A Comprehensive Review on Background, Applications, Key Challenges, Bias, Ethics, Limitations and Future Scope. *Internet of Things and Cyber-Physical Systems*, *3*, 24.

Razali, N. H., Nik Ali, N. N., Safiyuddin, S. K., & Khalid, F. (2022). Design Thinking Approaches in Education and Their Challenges: A Systematic Literature Review. *Creative Education*, *13*, 11.

Schmidt, A., Elagroudy, P., Draxler, F., Kreuter, F., & Welsch, R. (2024, January–February 8). Simulating the Human in HCD with ChatGPT. *Interactions*, *31*(1), 24–31. https://dl.acm.org/doi/abs/10.1145/3637436.

Smith, J. (2024). PBL and AI: Integrating Artificial Intelligence in Project-Based Learning. *Educational Innovations Journal*, *18*(1), 16, 23–38.

Springs. (2024). *Generative AI In Education: Main Trends For 2024*. Springs.

Stegmaier, W. (2019). *What is Orientation?: A Philosophical Investigation*. De Gruyter.

Stuedahl, D. (2015). Future Orientation in Design, Participation and Learning. *Interaction Design and Architecture(s) Journal - IxD&A*, *26*, 13. https://doi.org/10.55612/s-5002-026-009.

Tan, M. (2017). Design Thinking in Education: A Contemporary Approach. *Journal of Educational Design*, *15*(4), 14.

Tang, X., Ding, X., Ma, X., Zhang, S., & Diao, J. (2024). *An Exploration of Project-Based Learning Supported by Artificial Intelligence*. Proceedings of the 2024 5th International Conference on Big Data and Informatization Education (ICBDIE 2024), Advances in Intelligent Systems Research.

Torvinen, L. T. (2017). *The Concept of Orientation in Teachers' Thinking and Practices in Business Education*. Institute of Education, University of London.

Wang, Y., Liu, X., Zhang, Y., Sang, X., & Wang, M. (2020, March 21–24). *The First Model of Family Education on the Delivery of Bilingual British NCC Digital Literacy Qualifications in Dalian, China – Engaging and Motivating Children'*. Proceedings of the International Conference on Education in Mathematics, Science and Technology (ICEMST), Istanbul, Turkey.

Warr, M., Mishra, P., & Scragg, B. (2020). Designing Theory. *Educational Technology Research and Development*, *68*, 33.

Warr, M., Mishra, P., Scragg, B., & Powers, J. (2022). Complicating Design Thinking in Education: A University-School District Partnership to Design and School for the Future. In K. L. Sanzo & J. P. Scribner (Eds.), *Design Thinking: Research, Innovation, and Implementation*. Information Age Publishing.

Wilson, T. D. (2008). Activity Theory in Information Seeking. *Annual Review of Information Science and Technology, 42*(1), 43.

Xu, X. (2023). *Creating a Conducive Learning Environment for All Students in Higher Education*. University of Groningen. https://doi.org/10.33612/diss.581236834.

Zakaria, M. I., Maat, S. M., & Khalid, F. (2019). A Systematic Review of Problem Based Learning in Education. *Creative Education, 10*(12), 18.

Zhang, L., Ren, T., Xie, Y., Tian, Z., Tang, T., & Li, Y. (2022). Student Choirs and Virtual Social Practices by LivePBL: Linking Vocal Education with Project Based Learning. *Literacy Information and Computer Education Journal, 13*(1), 7.

Zhao, H., Chen, H., Yang, F., Liu, N., Deng, H., Cai, H., Wang, S., Yin, D., & Du, M. (2024). Explainability for Large Language Models: A Survey. *ACM Transactions on Intelligent Systems and Technology, 15*(2), 38.

Zhorova, I., Kokhanovska, O., Khudenko, O., Osypova, N., & Kuzminska, O. (2022). Teachers' Training for the Use of Digital Tools of the Formative Assessment in the Implementation of the Concept of the New Ukrainian School. *Educational Technology Quarterly, 2022*(1), 17.

Zhou, Y., Ren, T., Chen, N., Li, J., Lu, K., Li, Y., Acharya, A., Shah, P., Hogg, A., & Liu, Y. (2023). Student Virtual Social Practices Between China and Nepal. *International Journal of Technology and Inclusive Education, 12*(1), 6.

Zirar, A., Ali, S. I., & Islam, N. (2023). Worker and Workplace Artificial Intelligence (AI) Coexistence: Emerging Themes and Research Agenda. *Technovation, 124*, 102747.

3

CULTIVATING CURIOSITY THROUGH AI

A New Frontier in Personalized and Immersive Education

Teresa Aires and Jeff Schatten

3.1 Introduction

Historically, education has changed little since ancient times, with methods in Egypt, China, India, and Greece all emphasizing memorization and rote learning. The persistence of these age-old techniques across cultures and millennia is remarkable, but it also raises questions about their relevance in our rapidly changing world. While memorization has benefits, including potential cognitive health advantages (Hall et al., 2009), it is insufficient for modern education, particularly when the very things we ask students to memorize can be easily found on the internet. Not only that, but classrooms look the same because rather than having stumbled upon the holy grail of education, we've been stuck in an educational time warp. Though most of us cannot imagine driving a Model T to work every day in 2024 as if we had reached the pinnacle of automotive engineering and stopped there, it is somehow easy to imagine our children "learning" in the same way our great-grandparents did. This stagnation in educational methods is increasingly at odds with our rapidly evolving world. As technology transforms every aspect of our lives, the need for a radical change in education has never been more pressing.

Today's challenges – high dropout rates, ineffective one-size-fits-all approaches, teacher shortage, and student disengagement – stem greatly from outdated methods (UN news, 2024). Despite living in an era where we can video chat with someone on the other side of the planet, our classrooms are stuck in the "sit down, shut up, and memorize" era. They ignore technological advancements and rely on information "injection" rather than application. But AI can turn education from a game of "how much can you

DOI: 10.1201/9781003422433-3

cram into your brain?" into "how creatively can you use what you know?" It presents an opportunity to revolutionize the current educational system, shifting focus from mere memorization to practical knowledge application. However, while AI holds immense potential to revolutionize education, its implementation alone is not a panacea. To truly transform learning, we must also tackle a deeply ingrained problem in our current system: the cultivation of fixed mindsets.

In a twist of ironic misfortune, the very institution meant to cultivate minds seems determined to stunt them instead. The traditional educational setting has long fostered a results-driven approach that inadvertently undermines the development of growth mindsets – the belief that abilities are developed over time through work (Dweck, 2014). Students are often more focused on achieving high grades and meeting specific benchmarks than on the process of learning – and are usually blamed for these issues. This cultivates fixed mindsets, making students believe that abilities work similarly to traits; you either have them or don't (Dweck, 2014). Yet, research has shown that when we teach students to focus on the process and learn from failure – a growth mindset – they are more likely to complete difficult math courses and exhibit superior performance during challenging school transitions (Yeager & Dweck, 2012; Dweck & Yeager, 2019). In adolescents, having a growth mindset results in reduced aggression and stress when facing peer victimization or exclusion (Yeager & Dweck, 2012). Research has shown again and again that to increase resilience (and even test results), we need to equip students with growth mindsets where failure is an opportunity for learning rather than a threat to their intelligence. Still, the current system often reinforces a fixed mindset, where students avoid challenges to maintain their perceived competence seen through grades.

While producing high achievers on paper, the traditional system fails to cultivate true learning and critical thinking skills. It forces students to memorize and forget rather than to process and question, their greatest concern being grades and thus, extrinsic motivation. Alarmingly, the consequences of this educational system may very well exacerbate in an AI-first world, as students can easily access information, scan papers to determine what they ought to memorize and forget it all after the exam, and write articulate papers on subjects they never read about. In a traditional educational system, AI can indeed hurt students a lot faster than the system has until now.

But, before you close this book thinking we've just painted AI as an educational boogeyman out to squeeze children's brains, let us assure you: the story is far more nuanced and, dare we say, exciting. While the integration of AI into traditional educational models poses significant risks, it's crucial to recognize that these dangers stem from the system's inherent flaws rather than AI itself. In fact, when implemented thoughtfully within a reimagined educational framework, AI can address many of these longstanding issues.

With immersion and sensory learning educational systems, AI has the potential to be a powerful force for positive change, offering personalized learning and providing a tool to foster growth mindsets, cultivate curiosity, and develop a culture of lifelong learning. If used for exploration, explanation, and enhancement rather than a shortcut to answers, AI can revolutionize education and encourage students to tackle complex problems. The key may lie in reimagining the educational system to prioritize active learning, critical thinking, and the application of knowledge.

3.2   Rewiring the Brain: AI's Impact on Cognitive Development

As we consider the shortcomings of a broken educational system, it's crucial to understand how learning occurs in the brain. This understanding can guide us in leveraging AI to create more effective educational experiences. The brain's plasticity and its response to different learning environments provide key insights into how we can reshape education for the better.

The frontal lobe, particularly the prefrontal cortex, plays a crucial role in higher-order cognitive functions such as decision-making, planning, and complex problem-solving and executive functions such as self-regulation and social behavior (Chayer & Freedman, 2001). In children, the frontal lobe is even more important as it undergoes significant development, which also makes it more vulnerable to damage – early frontal lobe injury in children is worse than in adults with similar injuries (Kolb et al., 2013). And, throughout life, the brain follows a "use it or lose it" principle as it optimizes its function based on usage and need (Kolk & Rakic, 2022).

As AI becomes increasingly integrated into educational settings, its influence on frontal lobe plasticity may vary significantly based on individual learning styles and motivations. For some efficiency-driven learners, AI may primarily serve as a tool for quick information retrieval and task completion. These individuals might use AI to swiftly finish assignments, freeing up time for other activities they deem more important or enjoyable. In this scenario, the frontal lobe might adapt to prioritize rapid decision-making and efficient task management.

Conversely, curiosity-driven learners might leverage AI as a springboard for deeper exploration and connection of ideas. For these individuals, AI could become a catalyst for curiosity-driven learning, prompting them to ask more complex questions and seek out connections between diverse concepts. This approach could foster frontal lobe plasticity that enhances cognitive flexibility, analytical thinking, and the ability to synthesize information across disciplines (Chayer & Freedman, 2001).

Ultimately, AI does not need to inherently dictate the path of cognitive development. Rather, it serves to amplify and accelerate existing tendencies in learning approaches. While learners across the spectrum may achieve correct answers using AI, the cognitive processes involved and the resulting frontal lobe plasticity can differ significantly. Some may develop enhanced efficiency in information processing, while others might cultivate more robust analytical and creative thinking skills.

Whichever the case may be, the use of AI could incite lifelong learning if learners are deeply engaged in AI-enhanced environments that consistently spark curiosity and provide context for exploration. This hinges largely on the concepts of immersion and sensory learning as environments that facilitate a continuous AI conversation in a feedback loop of curiosity and discovery rather than a way out of thinking.

3.3   Immersion and Sensory Learning: A Promising Solution

While AI has the potential to significantly impact cognitive development, its effectiveness may be maximized when combined with immersive and sensory learning experiences. These approaches provide the context and lived experiences necessary for AI to truly enhance the learning outcomes.

3.3.1   Benefits of Immersion and Sensory Learning

With over 25 years of experience as a pedagogue and psychologist, Margarida Rodrigues advocates for educational programs that prioritize literacy through immersion, enabling learners to internalize concepts until they become second nature. To illustrate this in her training sessions with teachers, she usually presents a thought experiment involving "Tumyri," a fictional word she invented. Since she does not provide them with more information, teachers usually try to google it unsuccessfully. When asked to imagine spending two weeks in Tumyri, teachers respond with diverse interpretations – some envision a country to explore, others a spaceship for interstellar travel, and some picture a beach paradise. Then, Rodrigues tells them that's what learning without immersion feels like; even with tools like Google or AI at our disposal, learning remains superficial without lived experience.

The lack of contextual understanding limits teachers' ability to ask meaningful questions or gain deep insights about Tumyri. They struggle to determine whether to inquire about its geography, culture, or mode of transportation because they lack the foundational knowledge that comes from lived experience. This scenario vividly contrasts the depth of understanding gained through immersion with the shallow knowledge often acquired in traditional educational settings. Research has shown that experience shapes cognitive abilities in the way it forms and removes synapses – tiny gaps between neurons where signals are transmitted and which are fundamental to brain function – in the brain (Kolk & Rakic, 2022; Gelfo, 2019). Immersion provides lived experience, fostering a level of in-depth knowledge and nuanced understanding that conventional education systems frequently fail to achieve. As the pedagogue succinctly put it, "lived experience is fundamental for the detail with which you ask questions."

3.3.2 AI's Role in Enhancing Immersion and Sensory Learning

In immersive learning programs, AI is not a threat but a catalyst for deeper exploration. It can provide instant information, offer new perspectives, and suggest avenues of inquiry – all grounded in students' genuine curiosity. Rather than thwarting critical thinking, AI can propel it in programs where students have lived experiences and thus question AI outputs and use them for further investigation.

The concept of immersive learning, rooted in John Dewey's educational philosophy, emphasizes that literacy must be lived, not merely taught. Dewey advocated for hands-on, experiential education where students engage directly with their environment, arguing that learning occurs through doing (Dewey, 1938). This approach remains highly relevant in the age of AI, where students are active participants of the world they live in. When immersed in a field, students gain firsthand experience and deep understanding and are better equipped to utilize AI as a powerful learning tool. After immersion, AI becomes a useful resource because students can formulate meaningful queries based on their lived experiences. In immersion programs inspired by Dewey's ideas, AI is not a threat to but a catalyst for deeper exploration. The same rationale follows for AI's impact on creativity.

Margarida Rodrigues explains that, in immersive and sensory educational systems, creativity emerges as a natural consequence of experience and learning. She explains that creative breakthroughs often follow periods of apparent mental emptiness, occurring after deep immersion in a subject. This underscores the crucial role of lived experience in fostering creativity. Unlike rote knowledge, creativity can't be directly taught; it must be cultivated through rich, diverse experiences. In this context, AI serves not only as a replacement for creative thinking but also as a tool for enhancing the immersive experiences that fuel creativity. By providing access to vast information and freeing cognitive resources from routine tasks, AI can potentially create more space for the reflective pauses and connections that lead to creative insights. Table 3.1 illustrates the opportunities in immersion and sensory educational programs compared to traditional programs.

TABLE 3.1 Immersion and Sensory Learning Opportunities Compared to Traditional Models

	Traditional Models	*Immersion and Sensory Learning*
Student Engagement	Limited hands-on experience	Active participation in lived experiences
Knowledge Retention	Often short-term (for a class's duration) with subsequent forgetting accepted	Long-term comprehension and application through multiple cognitive pathways
Skill Development	Focus on memorization and basic skills	Emphasis on higher-order thinking, pattern recognition, and creative problem-solving
AI Integration	Limited or no integration and incentives to cheat	AI used as a catalyst for deeper exploration and creativity
Practical Application	Often lacks real-world context	Learning through doing, direct engagement with the environment
Critical Thinking	Limited by rote learning approaches	Enhanced through questioning AI outputs and using them for further investigation
Creativity	Often not directly addressed	Naturally emerges through experience and learning
Curriculum Design	Often focused on standardized content	Reimagined to prioritize experience and application of concepts
Learning Assessment	Often exam-based, focused on short-term recall and fixed mindset	Measured by long-term comprehension and application, focused on growth mindset

3.3.3 Challenges in Implementing Immersion and Sensory Learning

Besides the need for immersion, Rodrigues believes AI will prompt a redefinition of learning. Currently, we often consider knowledge retained for about three months (or a class's duration) as evidence of learning, accepting subsequent forgetting as normal. However, this raises questions about the true nature of learning. Does it mean knowing, using, or surpassing a concept? If learning implies application and advancement, then forgetting after three months wouldn't qualify. But if an exam defines learning, forgetting might be acceptable. AI challenges these notions, potentially shifting focus toward sensory learning – utilizing the five senses to experience and explore the world – an aspect AI doesn't yet replicate. This approach could deepen understanding and retention by engaging multiple cognitive pathways. It might lead to a more holistic view of learning, where success is measured not just by short-term recall but also by long-term comprehension and application.

The shift toward sensory learning and long-term comprehension and application aligns with the potential for AI to foster curiosity-driven plasticity.

The rise of AI also requires a reimagining of educational curricula, moving beyond mere memorization. Many countries still require students to memorize multiplication tables for quick mental math, despite the ubiquity of calculators (Morrow & Alphonso, 2014; Department for Education & The Rt Hon Damian Hinds MP, 2023; Korbey, 2023). While basic numeracy remains important, this approach may not fully prepare students for the complexities of modern mathematics and problem-solving. There are multiple mathematical rationales – such as calculus and geometry – that transcend rote memorization, emphasizing conceptual understanding and application. AI's capacity for rapid calculations and data processing further underscores the need to shift focus from memorization to higher-order thinking skills. Future curricula might prioritize greater experience and application of mathematical reasoning, pattern recognition, and creative problem-solving over merely solving equations or fractions. This could better equip students to leverage AI tools effectively while developing the critical thinking skills necessary for innovation.

3.3.4 Case Studies of Successful Implementation

In Margarida Rodrigues' school, teachers do not fear AI literacy in fifth and sixth grade classrooms. Their students frequently use ChatGPT in projects to digest large chunks of information that they search online, structure presentations, and maintain conversations with a large language model (LLM). They have recently started using the projects function to upload information they choose online and hold thought provoking conversations with LLMs to learn more about a specific topic; they feed it the information they want it to process. Rodrigues explains that these conversations teach students the art of crafting thought-provoking queries and mastering the follow-up, enabling them to engage in profound dialogues they can apply with humans. The immersive and sensory learning environment invites these students to use LLMs to reflect on and think through important questions rather than probing it for quick answers that thwart critical thinking.

In higher education, AI may also promote creative and critical thinking while preparing students for an AI-centric future. At Washington and Lee University, Professor Elizabeth Gilbert continuously refines her classes to integrate AI. In her Organizational Behavior class, she introduces GenAI in the context of a high-stakes written case analysis. First, she outlines the assignment's learning goals and discusses AI's use with students. Then, she gathers their in-class thoughts and asks them to anonymously submit their written thoughts on AI's use in the assignment. She then develops a consensus policy that students must adhere to. Typically, students agree that AI's use is acceptable for brainstorming, clarifying course material, proofreading, and identifying the areas for improvement, but the bulk of thinking and writing should be done independently.

Once the rules have been established and agreed upon, Professor Gilbert provides students with a "quickstart guide," offering a basic introduction to AI tools, sample prompts, and tips for effective use. The course also includes broader discussions and readings about AI's impact on the workplace to prepare students for future workforce demands and to explore the ethical implications of using AI, particularly in work-related contexts. She asks students to list all AI tools used in the assignment, describe their use, explain the aspects of the assignment where they did not use AI, and justify how the final product demonstrates the knowledge and skills gained through the course.

Professor Gilbert emphasizes that while AI can offer time-saving benefits, one of the most significant advantages for students is enhanced self-efficacy. She also anticipates that AI will potentially change the skill set of incoming students. She thus stresses the importance of using AI in education not simply because it's novel but because it either directly supports learning goals or frees up time and energy for other important learning objectives. Professor Gilbert uses this opportunity for students to experience what AI can do for them and get to know its limitations.

3.4 Personalized Learning

While we hold immense hope for AI to drastically change the current educational system, we are confident it can significantly hinder students if the system remains the same. AI has the potential to make students lazy (Ahmad et al., 2023), lacking in cognitive and analytical skills (Pokkakillath & Suleri, 2023) such as problem-solving, and too dependent on technology (Habib et al., 2024). Because of the wonderful benefits AI provides through personalized learning – instant feedback, enhanced explanations, and accessibility to different fields – it can easily be used to cheat and replace critical thinking if we continue to support a fixed mindset educational system.

Personalized learning through AI offers exciting possibilities by adapting to individual needs and providing tailored exercises. For instance, an AI tool could offer targeted practice for a student struggling with thesis statements. However, in the current education system, this convenience raises concerns about stunted critical thinking (Dergaa et al., 2024). While AI can provide quick solutions, it might inadvertently rob students of the opportunity to grapple with complex problems independently (Dergaa et al., 2024).

The instant feedback provided by AI represents a significant leap in educational technology, allowing students to identify and rectify mistakes immediately. Language learning apps like Duolingo exemplify this, offering real-time corrections on pronunciation and grammar. Yet, in traditional models, this immediacy could lead to reduced cognitive effort (Dergaa et al., 2024) as it may diminish students' productive struggle – "expend[ing] effort (. . .) to figure something out that is not immediately apparent" (Hiebert & Grouws, 2007, p. 287). The productive struggle of working through problems independently is crucial for deep learning, enhancing memory consolidation and problem-solving strategies.

AI's ability to provide enhanced explanations across multiple formats caters to diverse learning styles, potentially fostering a deeper, more interconnected understanding of subjects. For example, an AI system could explain photosynthesis through verbal, visual, and interactive models. Still, in the current education system, this ease of access to information might inadvertently diminish creativity (Dergaa et al., 2024). Students might rely heavily on AI-generated content rather than cultivating their own creative processes, potentially leading to a homogenization of thought.

The accessibility to different fields that AI provides democratizes knowledge, allowing students to explore subjects beyond their school's curriculum. This expanded access could broaden horizons and uncover hidden talents. It could also enable students, particularly adolescents, to learn during optimal times according to their circadian rhythms – a crucial factor given that teenagers' biological clocks naturally shift to later sleep and wake times, often conflicting with traditional early morning school schedules (Walker, 2017). Yet, in traditional models, accessibility raises concerns about neural rewiring, especially in developing brains (Dergaa et al., 2024). The constant availability of AI assistance might alter cognitive pathways, potentially affecting motivation and the sense of achievement associated with independent learning (Martín-Núñez et al., 2023).

However, just as AI could potentially melt children's brains by making them superfluous, it could also make them more curious and incite lifelong learning as they become adults. This is not an overly optimistic view from people who study AI, but a reality some students already experience in non-traditional education systems. The possibilities for altering brain plasticity are endless; they *simply* require changes in the current education system.

In immersion and sensory educational programs, AI-driven personalized education can provide students with a plethora of benefits that traditional models cannot match. While it lacks a face-to-face component alone, when used in a school context, it can engage students with content and reach many students at the same time at a limited price. Rather than relying on a sink or swim approach where only a few students can thrive, personalized learning can adapt to different learning needs and styles and unlock neurodivergent students' potential, according to the education specialist Dr. Emily Carter (Stefanic, 2024). For skill development, tools such as AI Career Coach by

CareerVillage.org move beyond traditional "cookie-cutter" approaches where students must follow a single path. Instead, these AI tools can engage students in dynamic dialogues, assessing their readiness, connecting their skills and preferences to various academic paths and potential careers, and offering guidance on identifying and developing important skills for their specific academic path. Table 3.2 highlights the differences between AI-driven personalized education in immersion and sensory education programs and traditional educational programs.

TABLE 3.2 AI-Driven Personalized Education Compared to Traditional Models

	AI-Driven Personalized Education	Traditional Education Models
Customization	Highly tailored to individual needs and learning styles	One-size-fits-all approach with limited personalization
Accessibility	24/7 access to diverse fields of knowledge beyond curriculum	Limited by classroom hours and set curriculum
Feedback and Assessment	Instant, real-time feedback and corrections	Delayed feedback, often limited to periodic assessments
Scalability	Highly scalable, can serve many students simultaneously	Limited by physical classroom size and teacher availability
Engagement	Interactive and multi-format content, potentially more engaging	Varies, but often less interactive and diverse in format
Cost-Effectiveness	Potentially more cost-effective at scale	Can be costly due to human resource requirements
Inclusion	Adapts to diverse learning needs and styles (particularly important for neurodivergent students)	May struggle to accommodate all learning differences
Data Utilization	Extensive use of data for personalization and improvement	Limited data utilization for personalization
Skill Development	Can focus on specific skills, encourage productive struggles, and foster critical thinking when properly implemented	Often stunts creative and critical thinking due to standardized "cookie-cutter" approaches
Challenges	Potential for over-reliance, reduced cognitive effort, and creativity diminishment	Difficulty in meeting individual needs, less engaging for some students
Opportunities	Promotes lifelong learning, curiosity, and exploration of diverse subjects	Develops traditional academic skills and face-to-face interaction abilities

3.5   AI in Education: Recommendations

Given the potential benefits and challenges of AI-driven personalized learning and its use in immersion and sensory learning models, it's crucial to consider how we can best implement these technologies in our educational systems. The following recommendations provide a roadmap for educators, parents, students, and policymakers to effectively integrate AI into educational practices while maintaining focus on immersive and sensory learning experiences.

As we navigate the integration of AI into education, it's crucial to approach this transformation thoughtfully and collaboratively. For educators, the journey begins with immersion and sensory learning. Before introducing AI tools, test them with hands-on, experiential learning techniques in your classroom. Once comfortable with these methods, gradually integrate AI tools to complement immersive learning. Use AI to personalize learning experiences, spark curiosity, and foster critical thinking skills. Throughout this process, document your experiences and share insights with colleagues to build a community of practice around AI in education.

Parents play a vital role in this educational evolution. Advocate for immersive learning by seeking out and supporting educational programs that offer rich, hands-on experiences for your children. Engage with AI alongside your children, participating in their usage rather than just monitoring it. Explore AI tools together, focusing on topics that interest them. Guide your children in questioning and verifying AI-generated information to foster essential digital literacy skills.

Students, as the primary beneficiaries of these changes, should approach AI as a tool for exploration rather than a shortcut. Instead of relying on AI for quick answers, use it to explore complex questions and dive deeper into subjects that fascinate you. Challenge AI outputs by critically evaluating the information provided and cross-referencing with other sources. Leverage AI to pursue passion projects and explore topics beyond your standard curriculum, taking charge of your learning journey.

Policymakers have a crucial role in facilitating this educational transformation. It's time to update outdated educational policies to accommodate the integration of AI and immersive learning experiences into classrooms. Invest in developing and funding AI literacy programs for educators to ensure they can effectively leverage these tools. Make sure to excite them about it; AI should not become another check mark on their long list of curriculum items. Establish comprehensive guidelines for the ethical use of AI in educational settings. For the love of learning, rethink assessment methods, moving away from standardized testing toward more holistic evaluation methods that can measure the skills developed through AI-enhanced learning.

Finally, everyone has a part to play in shaping the future of education. Cultivate curiosity by staying informed about AI developments and their potential impact on education. Engage in lifelong learning by participating in workshops, reading articles, and joining discussions about AI in education. Share your perspectives and experiences with AI in learning, as the future of education is a collective responsibility. We must ensure that AI enhances rather than replaces the human elements essential for effective education.

3.6 Conclusion

The integration of AI into education presents a transformative opportunity to address longstanding issues in our educational systems. As we've explored throughout this chapter, AI has the potential to shift education from rote memorization to practical knowledge application, fostering an environment where learning is dynamic and relevant. Combining AI tools with immersive and sensory learning experiences allows us to create educational environments that engage students on multiple levels, enhancing both comprehension and retention.

AI's role in fostering personalized learning and enhancing critical thinking skills cannot be overstated. It offers the ability to tailor educational experiences to individual needs, pacing, and interests, while simultaneously challenging students to think more deeply and critically about the information they encounter. However, we must strike a balance, leveraging AI while maintaining the essential human elements that are fundamental to education.

As we move forward, it's clear that educators, parents, students, and policymakers all have crucial roles to play in shaping this AI-enhanced educational future. We must work collaboratively to ensure that AI serves as a catalyst for curiosity, critical thinking, and lifelong learning. In this new paradigm, education becomes less about memorizing facts and more about developing the skills to navigate, analyze, and create in an AI-augmented world.

AI, like any tool, is what we make of it. In the hands of curious learners and innovative educators, it has the potential to unlock new realms of understanding and creativity. But it's not a magic Hogwarts wand – it requires thoughtful implementation, and a reimagining of what education can be. Current and future students desperately need environments that encourage immersive, experiential learning, where AI serves as a powerful ally in cultivating curiosity and critical thinking. The goal isn't to create AI-dependent learners, nor is it to shun technology in favor of traditional methods. Instead, it's about leveraging AI to enhance our innate human capacities for learning, creativity, and problem-solving. If we are living in a world where cars drive themselves, why are we still driving our kids' brains like they're Model Ts?

References

Ahmad, S. F., Han, H., Alam, M. M., Rehmat, M. K., Irshad, M., Arraño-Muñoz, M., & Ariza-Montes, A. (2023). Impact of artificial intelligence on human loss in decision making, laziness and safety in education. *Humanities & Social Sciences Communications*, 10(1), 311. https://doi.org/10.1057/s41599-023-01787-8.

Chayer, C., & Freedman, M. (2001). Frontal lobe functions. *Current Neurology and Neuroscience Reports*, 1(6), 547–552.

Department for Education & The Rt Hon Damian Hinds MP. (2023). *More children score full marks in their times tables check*. GOV.UK. https://www.gov.uk/government/news/more-children-score-full-marks-in-their-times-tables-check.

Dergaa, I., Ben Saad, H., Glenn, J. M., Amamou, B., Ben Aissa, M., Guelmami, N., . . . Chamari, K. (2024). From tools to threats: A reflection on the impact of artificial-intelligence chatbots on cognitive health. *Frontiers in Psychology*, 15, 1259845.

Dewey, J. (1938). *Experience and education*. New York: Macmillan.

Dweck, C. S. (2014). *The mindset of a champion*. Psychology at Stanford University.

Dweck, C. S., & Yeager, D. S. (2019). Mindsets: A view from two eras. *Perspectives on Psychological Science*, 14(3), 481–496.

Gelfo, F. (2019). Does experience enhance cognitive flexibility? An overview of the evidence provided by the environmental enrichment studies. *Frontiers in Behavioral Neuroscience*, 13, 150.

Habib, S., Vogel, T., Anli, X., & Thorne, E. (2024). How does generative artificial intelligence impact student creativity? *Journal of Creativity*, 34(1), 100072.

Hiebert, J., & Grouws, D. A. (2007). The effects of classroom mathematics teaching on students' learning. *Second Handbook of Research on Mathematics Teaching and Learning*, 1(1), 371–404.

Kolb, B., Mychasiuk, R., Muhammad, A., & Gibb, R. (2013). Brain plasticity in the developing brain. *Progress in Brain Research*, 207, 35–64.

Kolk, S. M., & Rakic, P. (2022). Development of prefrontal cortex. *Neuropsychopharmacology*, 47(1), 41–57.

Korbey, H. (2023). *Should more time be spent learning math facts?* Edutopia. https://www.edutopia.org/article/how-decreased-practice-time-plays-into-historic-math-declines/.

Martín-Núñez, J. L., Ar, A. Y., Fernández, R. P., Abbas, A., & Radovanović, D. (2023). Does intrinsic motivation mediate perceived artificial intelligence (AI) learning and computational thinking of students during the COVID-19 pandemic? *Computers and Education: Artificial Intelligence*, 4, 100128.

Morrow, A., & Alphonso, C. (2014). Ontario education minister wants the basics: "Learn your multiplication tables." *The Globe and Mail*. https://www.theglobeandmail.com/news/national/education/ontario-education-minister-wants-the-basics-learn-your-multiplication-tables/article17666049/.

Pokkakillath, S., & Suleri, J. (2023). ChatGPT and its impact on education. *Research in Hospitality Management*, 13(1), 31–34. https://doi.org/10.1080/22243534.2023.2239579.

Stefanic, D. (2024). *Neurodiversity and personalized learning*. Hyperspacemv - The Metaverse for Business Platform. https://hyperspace.mv/neurodiversity-learning/.

UN news. (2024). *UN issues global alert over teacher shortage*. United Nations. https://news.un.org/en/story/2024/02/1147067.

Walker, M. (2017). *Why we sleep: Unlocking the power of sleep and dreams*. Scribner.

Yeager, D. S., & Dweck, C. S. (2012). Mindsets that promote resilience: When students believe that personal characteristics can be developed. *Educational Psychologist*, 47(4), 302–314.

4

EXPLORING STUDENTS' PREPAREDNESS FOR USING GENERATIVE ARTIFICIAL INTELLIGENCE TECHNOLOGIES

A Case Study from Nigeria

Yusufu Gambo

4.1 Introduction

The rapid development and integration of Generative Artificial Intelligence (GenAI) technologies, such as ChatGPT, are transforming several sectors, including education. As these tools become more widely used, there is a rising need to determine how well students are prepared to maximize their potential in academic contexts. While GenAI has various advantages, such as improving learning efficiency, personalizing educational experiences, and assisting with complicated problem solving, it also raises serious questions about ethics, data privacy, and the possible impact on critical thinking and creativity. This advancement is now utilized in a variety of disciplines, including educational processes (Nasim et al., 2022; Anders, 2023; Sim et al., 2018). A wider role in society is anticipated for AI as research and technology are already influencing how people live and work (Lockey et al., 2021; Farrokhnia et al., 2023). GenAI like ChatGPT is also applied in the field of education to enhance the teaching and learning process, personalization, easing repetitive administrative work, and creating new research avenues (Zhai et al., 2021; Essel et al., 2022). This technology can provide intelligent tutoring systems, adaptive learning platforms, automated grading systems, virtual reality simulations, data analytics, and visualization, which can support inclusive learning experiences. Today, students can use an AI tool like ChatGPT to create writing assignments, get comments and suggestions for revisions, and get writing guidance. As a result, it can be utilized to support students in discovering their skills and improving the learning process (Fauzi et al., 2023; Dahmash et al., 2020; Anders, 2023).

However, despite the potential advantage of GenAI technology like ChatGPT, there are concerns about its risks to education (Shoufan, 2023;

DOI: 10.1201/9781003422433-4

Wardat et al., 2023; Yan, 2023). The ability of AI to provide precise responses to user inquiries raises concerns over the possibility of academic dishonesty because it might be used to complete homework and exams for students (Chen et al., 2023; Cooper, 2023; Ngo, 2023). Teachers worry that if students rely too much on ChatGPT to produce suitable writing, they may be outsourcing this work to the AI system (Gayed et al., 2022). Additionally, concerns regarding plagiarism, inaccurate information, and unauthorized references have been raised (Abouammoh et al., 2023; Biswas, 2023). To maximize benefits while reducing drawbacks, it is important to determine whether these concerns are generalized and how a student can be supported to inform strategies for integrating this technology into the mainstream of education (Fauzi et al., 2023; Wardat et al., 2023; Ngo, 2023; Chan & Hu, 2023).

To answer the call for more exploratory research studies (Shoufan, 2023; Wardat et al., 2023; Yan, 2023; Fauzi et al., 2023), this study explored students' preparedness to use GenAI in an educational setting. Furthermore, this study aims to ascertain whether students are ready to use ChatGPT in their learning by focusing on their experiences, concerns, and how to support students for strategic and ethical integration of this technology into education. This will bridge the existing research gaps and add to the body of knowledge about exploring GenAI technology. Thus, this study intends to address the following research questions:

1. Do students have experience with GenAI technologies for education?
2. What are the students' concerns about using GenAI technologies?
3. How can students be supported to use GenAI technologies?

The reminder of the chapter proceeds as follows. First, the review of the existing literature on GenAI and student preparedness, followed by the methodology used in our case study, and the results section presents the findings and discusses their implications for educational practice. Finally, the chapter concludes with recommendations for supporting students' preparedness for using GenAI.

4.2 Literature Review

4.2.1 GenAI

GenAI is a sort of AI that generates new information, such as text, photos, audio, or other types of data. GenAI can generate original material based on patterns learned from the data it was trained on (Crompton & Burke, 2023; Cross et al., 2023; Eggmann et al., 2023). This is accomplished with models such as generative adversarial networks (GANs), variational encoders (VAE), and generative pre-trained transformers (GPTs), which are forms of neural networks created expressly for generative tasks (Kohnke et al., 2023; Xiao & Zhi, 2023).

A generative text model, such as GPTs, can, for example, take a prompt or a starting sentence and generate a coherent and contextually suitable continuation or completion of that sentence (Gayed et al., 2022; Xiao & Zhi, 2023). Similarly, with image processing, GenAI can generate new images that mimic real-world objects, settings, or artwork. While GenAI has demonstrated impressive capabilities, it also poses ethical concerns, particularly in areas such as deep fakes, where the technology can be abused to create misleading content (Zhai et al., 2021; Essel et al., 2022). As with any technology, the development and application of GenAI should be driven by ethical standards and a careful examination of its possible societal impact. This technology is now being used in education to support inclusive learning experiences despite the concerns about its usage across many fields of endeavors (Crompton, 2023; Cross et al., 2023; Xiao & Zhi, 2023).

4.2.2 Existing Works

There are several studies that explored students' or faculty's perceptions and concerns about the use of GenAI technologies. This includes Sandu et al.'s (2024) investigation of the impact of ChatGPT on higher education, with an emphasis on its role in improving instructional practices, student engagement, and academic achievement. Researchers conducted a rigorous case study and a survey of 74 students in Australia, revealing that ChatGPT's flexibility and reactivity significantly enhance academic achievements. However, issues such as the tool's limited understanding of complex queries and the lack of human contact highlight considerable opportunities for improvement. Notably, the study highlights the potential for ChatGPT to transform educational methods. Similarly, Essel et al. (2022) explored the impact of using ChatGPT in teaching and learning. The study conducted pre-test-post-test on 68 students. The findings revealed that students who used ChatGPT performed better than those who didn't use it. The study provides critical information on the integration of this technology into teaching and learning. Moreover, Chan & Hu (2023) explored the perception of students on the willingness, benefits, and challenges for the integration of ChatGPT into teaching and learning using a survey among 399 students in Hong Kong public universities. The results revealed students' interest in using ChatGPT in their learning process. However, they expressed concerns about accuracy, ethical issues, and the quality of the outputs. In addition, Elkhodr et al. (2023) investigated the application of ChatGPT, a GenAI tool, in higher education, with a focus on the impact on learning outcomes and student experiences. Through three case studies involving undergraduate and postgraduate ICT students, the study discovered that ChatGPT is regarded as a valuable and enjoyable resource, with the majority of students expressing a desire to employ AI technologies in the future. Furthermore, students who used ChatGPT performed better in terms of functionality, user flow, and material understanding than those who just used standard search engines. However, the study acknowledged the possibility of misuse, underscoring the need for caution in its use.

Furthermore, Shoufan (2023) explored students' perceptions on the use of ChatGPT using mixed-methods approach among 56 students. In the first stage, students evaluated ChatGPT in their own words, and based on the themes generated from their opinions, 27 items of questions were generated and administered using a survey. The results revealed that the students were fascinated with the use of ChatGPT. However, they opined that the outputs from the ChatGPT were not always correct and that it required more background to correct the outputs.

Similarly, Yilmaz & Yilmaz (2023) investigated students' experiences with the use of ChatGPT as a programming tool among 41 cohort undergraduate students. The study used structured open-ended questions and content analysis to understand students' experiences. The findings revealed a significant interest in using ChatGPT for programming and proposed several strategies for integrating ChatGPT into lessons. Moreover, Yan (2023) investigated the students' reflections on their exposure to ChatGPT for writing and reflection activities. The findings revealed the affordance of writing and the automatic workflow that could minimize efficiency. However, students expressed concerns about academic honesty and ethical issues. In addition, Kohnke et al. (2023) explored preparedness for the integration of GenAI among 12 teachers using semi-structured interviews. The study explored digital competency, pedagogical knowledge, and challenges for implementation. The results show the significance of knowledge competency among teachers. Furthermore, teachers reported to require tailored and professional support for effective integration. However, the study recommended that future research should focus on large-scale samples and integrate diverse research methodologies to expand the scope. Moreover, Abouammoh et al. (2023) explored the perceptions and experiences of using ChatGPT among faculties and students using focused group discussion. The study aimed to explore knowledge, benefits, concerns, and limitations among faculties and students. The results of the study show significant knowledge and perception of ChatGPT and an understanding of its roles in teaching and research. Furthermore, the limitations include ambiguity of references, lack of human interactions, trust, and bias. The study recommended further research to expand the scope using a large sample and a variety of research approaches. In addition, Wardat et al. (2023) examined the perspectives of various students and educators on the use of ChatGPT in teaching mathematics. The study adopted a qualitative case study in two stages. The first stage explored the capability of ChatGPT to enhance solutions to mathematical problems and the second stage explored the user experiences. The result of the first stage shows that ChatGPT doesn't have a deep understanding of geometry and cannot correct misconceptions and the second stage shows limited interactions with humans and thus it must be used with caution.

The study by Cross et al. (2023) assessed the integration of ChatGPT into the faculty workflow among 87 faculty using a survey method. The aim is to explore usage, acceptance, and policy to guide the ethical integration of ChatGPT. The results show a significant usage and acceptance among the faculty with mostly used for research and teaching. However, there are concerns among the faculty about the accuracy of information generated from the ChatGPT. Similarly, Ngo (2023) explored the students' experiences with the use of ChatGPT in their learning process using a mixed-methods approach. The results obtained revealed that students were favorable toward ChatGPT, and they recognized its roles in their education process. One of the key concerns of the students is the ability to assess the quality and sources of the information obtained. In addition, Kim & Kim (2022) investigated the perception of teachers on the use of ChatGPT in scientific writing for STEM education. The results revealed significant experiences in using AI tools; however, they raised concerns regarding the outputs generated.

These studies explored the perceptions, knowledge, benefits, and concerns of GenAI technologies, especially ChatGPT. However, there is limited understanding of students' preparedness toward integrating ChatGPT into the mainstream of education. Moreover, most of the studies are surveys without having the voice of the potential users on their experiences and how it can be supported for ethical and strategic integration of this evolving technology into education.

4.3 Methodology

This study used a mixed-methods design to explore students' preparedness for GenAI technologies. The purpose of exploratory analysis is to clarify challenges, define terms, collect interpretations, gain perspectives, eliminate unrealistic conceptions, and establish hypotheses. Research methods such as surveys, seminars, focus groups, and case studies are frequently utilized in exploratory research (Sileyew, 2020; Sim et al., 2018).

A mixed-methods approach is used when one strategy is insufficient for comprehending and solving the problem at hand. It is a methodical and complete approach to addressing the study's objective and conveying respondents' voices and viewpoints to better understand the issues at hand (Creswell & Clark, 2017; Yin, 1994). The study combined qualitative and quantitative data, as well as data triangulation from several sources (Creswell, 2012; Yin, 2004).

The quantitative method explored students' experience with GenAI technologies for education, while the qualitative method investigated students' concerns and supported the need to use GenAI technologies. A random sample of 90 undergraduate students drawn 10 each from the nine departments (Biochemistry, Computer Science, Mathematics, Geology, Chemistry, Physics, Geography, Zoology, and Botany) in the Faculty of Science, Adamawa State University, Mubi, Nigeria, completed the survey using convenience sampling and participated in the focus group discussion. Furthermore, we adhered to the literature (Guest et al., 2017), and the study randomly selected 36 participants to participate in focus group discussions, having 6 focus group discussions with each group consisting of 6 participants. The survey data was analyzed by descriptive analysis using SPSS 25, and the open-ended focus group discussion responses were evaluated by theme analysis using QSR NVivo 12.

4.4   Results and Findings

4.4.1   Demographic Information

Table 4.1 shows the participants' information, which was drawn from nine departments in the Faculty of Science (Botany, Biochemistry, Computer Science, Geography, Geology and Mining, Mathematics, Pure and Applied Chemistry, Pure and Applied Physics, and Zoology). There were 55 males

TABLE 4.1 Participants' Information

Characteristic	n	%
Sex		
Male	55	61.1
Female	35	38.9
Age		
18–23	54	60
24–29	15	16.7
30–34	11	12.2
35- & above	10	11.1
Do you know generative AI technologies like ChatGPT?	62	68.9
Yes	15	16.7
Not sure	13	14.4
No		
Are you willing to use GenAI technologies in the educational process?		
Yes	75	83.3
Not sure	10	11.1
No	5	5.6

(61.1%) and 35 females (88.9%). Furthermore, 54 (61.1%) participants were 18–23 years of age, 15 (16.7%) participants were 24–29 years of age, 11 (12.1%) participants were 30–34 years of age, and 16 (11.1%) participants were aged 35 years and above. More so, 62 (68.9%) knew of GenAI technologies, 15 (16.7%) were not sure of GenAI, and only 13 (14.4%) did not know GenAI technologies. Additionally, 75 (83.3%) were willing to use GenAI technologies in their educational process, 10 (11.1%) were not sure of using GenAI, and only 5 (14.4%) were not willing to use GenAI technologies in their educational process.

4.4.2 Participants' Experiences in Using GenAI Technologies

Table 4.2 shows the level of participants' experiences in using GenAI technologies, with mean scores ranging from 2.04 to 4.12. Specifically, participants with no experiences have a mean score of 4.12 and a standard deviation of 0.92; those with limited experiences have a mean score of 4.02 and a standard deviation of 0.83; those with fair experiences have a mean score of 3.74 and a standard deviation of 1.08; those with average experiences have a mean score of 2.82 and a standard deviation of 1.02; and those with good experiences have a mean score of 2.04 and a standard deviation of 0.72. Moreover, there was a positive correlation ($r = 0.854$; $p < 0.001$) between the participant's knowledge of GenAI technologies and their experiences in using the GenAI technologies. This result means that students who know GenAI technologies were using it for their academic purposes. Furthermore, there is a correlation ($r = 0.292$; $p < 0.001$) between the participant's willingness to use GenAI technologies and experiences in using GenAI technologies, indicating that where there is willingness, there is a possibility of trying to have the experiences.

TABLE 4.2 Participants' Experiences in Using GenAI Technologies

Statement	Mean	SD
I have no experience in using generative AI technologies like ChatGPT in the educational process	4.12	0.92
I have limited experience in using generative AI technologies like ChatGPT in the educational process	4.02	0.83
I have fair experience in using generative AI technologies like ChatGPT in the educational process	3.74	1.08
I have average experience in using generative AI technologies like ChatGPT in the educational process	2.89	1.02
I have good experience in using generative AI technologies like ChatGPT in the educational process	2.04	0.72

4.4.3 Students' Concerns about Using GenAI Technologies

The focus group discussions revealed different concerns students have toward using GenAI technologies. Some participants were optimistic that AI's integration into educational processes can revolutionize the educational paradigm. The themes generated from the focus group discussions are as follows:

Accuracy and transparency: AI-generated content can sometimes produce incorrect or misleading information. In educational settings, this could lead to students learning incorrect information or concepts. One student stated: "We cannot accurately predict or verify the accuracy or validity of AI-generated information. The AI system is sophisticated and opaque to the majority of users, making it difficult to understand how AI makes judgments, and it is always dangerous to use things you cannot understand."

Privacy issues: The use of AI in education requires handling sensitive students' data. Ensuring the privacy and security of this data is crucial to prevent any potential breaches or misuse. As one student put forward, "the power of AI means that they may quickly get our personal information. Since these messages will be utilized to further develop the system, if they are not properly protected, they can pose privacy and security risks."

Ethical issues: There might be ethical concerns related to the generation of content. For example, generating essays or assignments could potentially lead to issues of plagiarism or dishonesty as remarked by one of the students: "I want to know whether I am dealing with an AI bot or AI-generated content. It is currently reasonably easy to detect, but as technology advances, it may become more difficult."

Bias and fairness issues: Like any other AI system, generative models can carry biases in the data they were trained on. This could potentially lead to the reinforcement of existing biases in educational materials. As one of the participants stated, "this may lead to a decrease in critical thinking and making decisions only based on the information that AI provided."

Personalization issues: GenAI might not be able to cater to individual learning needs as effectively as human educators. It might not be able to provide the personalized guidance, feedback, and support that students require. One of the students opined that "AI can provide information to students that couldn't take into consideration the students' characteristics which might not be useful for their learning experiences."

Inhibiting the learning process: If students become too reliant on GenAI tools, they might not engage with the learning material in a meaningful way. This could potentially hinder students' long-term retention and understanding of the subject matter. According to one of the students, "the majority of students may rely on AI to complete their homework and other academic activities, which may make it more difficult for them to participate in the learning process and uphold academic standards."

Critical thinking and creativity: Over-reliance on GenAI could potentially hinder students' development of critical thinking skills and creativity. If students primarily rely on AI for generating content, this might hinder students from developing skills to think critically or express themselves effectively. One of the students stated: "The overuse of generative AI may hinder students' ability to think critically and creatively. Students who entirely rely on AI to generate information may not be able to think critically or communicate themselves."

4.4.4 Supporting Students to Use GenAI Technologies

The focus group discussions revealed that participants reported various approaches which can be used to support students in using GenAI technologies in the educational process.

Guidelines and policies: Ensure that students understand the purpose, limitations, and appropriate contexts for using these technologies. One of the participants stated that "with clear guidelines and policies, Generative AI can be properly integrated into the mainstream of education."

Training and orientation: Provide training sessions or workshops to introduce students to the GenAI tools they will be using. Offer hands-on guidance on how to effectively utilize these tools in their learning process. One of the participants stated: "Good training and awareness is needed for students to properly use Generative AI technologies for research and learning in education."

Emphasize critical thinking: Encourage students to critically evaluate the output of GenAI. Teach them how to verify information and cross-check facts to ensure accuracy and reliability. One of the participants stated: "Teaching students critical thinking processes and providing activities that will improve critical thinking will help students engage with the outputs of Generative AI technologies."

Creativity and originality: Emphasize the importance of using GenAI as a tool to enhance students' creativity and ideas rather than as a replacement for their thinking. Encourage students to use AI-generated content as a starting point for their work. One of the participants put forward: "Emphasizing the need to teach students the ability to produce critical and original content through critical thinking process will help students in developing the AI skills needed to excel in education."

Feedback and iteration: Encourage students to seek feedback from educators and peers on the content they generate using AI. This feedback loop can help improve the quality and relevance of the generated content. One of the participants stated that "teacher should provide timely and critical feedback to help students improve their learning process."

Encourage collaboration and discussion: Foster a collaborative learning environment where students can discuss and share their experiences with GenAI. This can promote peer-to-peer learning and the exchange of best practices. One of the participants stated that "teachers should provide learning activities that encourage collaboration to foster critical thinking and knowledge sharing in a teaching process."

Monitor and provide support: Keep an eye on students' use of GenAI and be available to offer assistance and guidance when needed. Address any questions or concerns they may have promptly. One of the participants stated that "teachers should provide and support students on the use of Generative AI outputs and guide them on using it ethically."

4.4.5   Discussion of Findings

This exploratory study examined how prepared students were to use GenAI tools like ChatGPT in higher education. The results shed light on students' understanding and experiences in using ChatGPT for educational purposes. It is clear that most students are familiar with GenAI technologies and are eager to employ them in their learning processes.

Overall, the participants demonstrated a good awareness of the strengths and weaknesses of GenAI technologies and a favorable attitude toward utilizing these tools in their studies, research, and future professions. The results are consistent with those of Abouammoh et al. (2023), and Essel et al. (2022), who discovered that students had a strong comprehension of GenAI technologies and their limitations in their learning process. Moreover, similar to the findings of Shoufan (2023), Yilmaz & Yilmaz (2023), and Kohnke et al. (2023), there were also concerns about the dependability, privacy, and ethical issues related to GenAI and its potential impact on personal development, career prospects, and societal values. Additionally, students seem to be familiar with the technology and have a good understanding of the advantages and drawbacks of GenAI. Students are typically willing to use GenAI for their coursework and future employment, but they have high expectations and concerns.

Furthermore, the findings revealed that students are concerned about reliance on GenAI technologies, the value of higher education it may affect, and issues with accuracy, transparency, privacy, ethics, and moral issues, particularly plagiarism, because they find it challenging to assess the originality of work produced by GenAI tools, similar to the findings of Dahmash et al. (2020) and Dehouche & Dehouche (2023). Students were also concerned about the effects of GenAI on human values and how it would inspire critical thinking and creativity, similar to the findings of Dahmash et al. (2020), Dehouche & Dehouche (2023), Yan (2023), and Yilmaz & Yilmaz (2023). Similarly, the findings also revealed that students wanted support from their teachers and educational institutions to use the power of GenAI technology in their learning processes through the possibilities of clear guidelines, prompt and timely feedback, and training on the use of the technology and collaborative learning activities.

Although the benefits of using GenAI are clearly remarkable, this enthusiasm was tempered by significant concerns about the ethical implications and potential challenges associated with these technologies. Students typically felt at ease utilizing ChatGPT, particularly for tasks such as research assistance, content creation, and idea exploration. This comfort was frequently associated with past exposure to AI products and perceived ease of use. However, confidence in using AI for more important academic jobs, such as creating original content, some students were concerned about the technology's limitations, such as the possibility of creating false or biased information and the difficulty in determining the originality and authenticity of AI-generated material. Ethical considerations were a major theme among attendees. Students were particularly concerned about plagiarism, data privacy, and the societal implications of using AI. While students recognized the benefits of GenAI in expediting academic activities, they also saw possible downsides, particularly in terms of personal and professional growth. There was concern that relying too heavily on AI might erode critical thinking skills and creativity, all of which are necessary for personal development and future career success. Students were also aware of the potential long-term influence on their future chances, especially in sectors where innovation and ethical considerations are critical.

4.4.6 Recommendations

The study found that university students at Adamawa State University in Mubi, Nigeria, are generally well-prepared to incorporate GenAI technologies such as ChatGPT into their instructional procedures. The participants were well aware of the benefits, strengths, and limitations of these tools, and they reported a positive attitude toward using them in their studies, research, and future professions. However, the study raised concerns about ethical issues, data privacy, and the possible impact on critical thinking and creativity. Students highlighted a need for educational institutions to provide greater support on how to use GenAI successfully and responsibly. Based on the findings, the following recommendations are provided to promote students continued use of GenAI technologies:

I. Professional training and workshops: Institutions should hold workshops and training sessions that focus on the application of GenAI technologies like ChatGPT. These sessions could include hands-on activities, ethical issues, and tools for critically examining AI-generated content. For example, students could be taught how to assess the accuracy and originality of AI-generated work, helping them to avoid potential pitfalls such as plagiarism.

II. Institution should develop guidelines and policy of the use of GenAI: Institutions should create and apply explicit ethical rules for the use of GenAI in academic environments. These standards could cover topics like plagiarism, data privacy, and the proper use of AI. For example, students should be forced to disclose when they utilize AI tools in their work and the percentage of AI accepted in academic submissions, to ensure transparency and academic integrity.

III. Institution should incorporate GenAI in both curriculum and pedagogical framework: Institutions might integrate GenAI into their curriculum across multiple fields, allowing students to interact with the technology in an organized and relevant manner. For example, tasks could be created to incorporate the use of AI technologies, followed by critical evaluation on their impact on the learning process. This method would help students gain a balanced grasp of AI's strengths and limits.

IV. The institution should provide constant assistance for teachers and tutors. Teachers should use GenAI to provide constant help and feedback to their students. This might include individualized advice on how to properly include AI into their research and studies, as well as rapid feedback on AI-generated work. For example, educators may arrange regular office hours or discussions to address students' concerns and queries about AI use.

V. The institution should promote collaborative projects and other academic activities. Encourage collaborative projects in which students can utilize GenAI tools together, promoting peer learning and discussion of the ethical and practical implications of using AI in education. For example, group assignments could include applying AI to solve an issue or developing content, followed by group discussions on the problems.

4.5 Conclusion

The increasing diffusion of GenAI technologies in education calls for a study to understand students' viewpoints and how they can be integrated into the education system. This study explored students' experiences, concerns, and strategies for integrating GenAI into teaching and learning. The findings revealed that students have a good understanding and experience of GenAI tools like ChatGPT and were willing to use it in the educational process. Moreover, the study revealed students' concerns and how this technology can be integrated into teaching and learning.

However, the findings have some limitations; the sample size was small, which would limit the findings' relevance to the greater student population at Adamawa State University, Mubi, Nigeria. Furthermore, because of the cross-sectional structure of the study, it was not possible to look at how students' perceptions evolved as their exposure to and experiences with GenAI technology could change over time.

The study has several implications for teachers, policymakers, and developers. To support students in getting familiar with GenAI technologies and their ethical and societal implications, educational institutions should first consider providing workshops and instructional resources. Furthermore, privacy, accuracy, and transparency should be given top attention in the design, development, and use of GenAI technology to foster confidence and minimize potential risks. For instance, technical professionals could work on AI models that clearly explain their decision-making processes. There should be data protection policies and procedures implemented to protect the privacy of users in educational institutions.

Future research can use larger, more representative samples and longitudinal designs to track changes in students' perceptions of GenAI over time, examine how these technologies can be incorporated into higher education, and examine the relationship between GenAI use and learning outcomes. Future research may investigate a particular group of students from different academic fields, age ranges, or cultural backgrounds in terms of their AI literacy.

4.6 Acknowledgments

The author acknowledged Adamawa State University for supporting their research.

References

Abouammoh, N., Alhasan, K., Raina, R., Malki, K. A., Aljamaan, F., Tamimi, I., & Temsah, M. H. (2023). Exploring perceptions and experiences of ChatGPT in medical education: A qualitative study among medical college faculty and students in Saudi Arabia. *medRxiv*, 2023. DOI: 10.1101/2023.07.13.23292624. https://europepmc.org/article/ppr/ppr692052.

Anders, B. A. (2023). Is using ChatGPT cheating, plagiarism, or both, neither, or forward-thinking? *Patterns*, 4(3).

Biswas, S. (2023). ChatGPT and the future of medical writing. *Radiology*, 307(2), e223312. https://doi.org/10.1148/radiol.223312.

Chan, C. K. Y., & Hu, W. (2023). *Students' voices on generative AI: Perceptions, benefits, and challenges in higher education.* arXiv:2305.00290.

Chen, Y., Jensen, S., Albert, L. J., Gupta, S., & Lee, T. (2023). Artificial intelligence (AI) student assistants in the classroom: Designing chatbots to support student success. *Information Systems Frontiers, 25*(1), 161–182.

Cooper, G. (2023). Examining science education in chatbot: An exploratory study of generative artificial intelligence. *Journal of Science Education and Technology, 32*(3), 444–452.

Creswell, J. W. (2012). *Educational research.* Pearson.

Creswell, J. W., & Clark, V. L. P. (2017). *Designing and conducting mixed methods research.* Sage Publications.

Crompton, H., & Burke, D. (2023). Artificial intelligence in higher education: The state of the field. *International Journal of Educational Technology in Higher Education, 20*(1), 22. https://doi.org/10.1186/s41239-023-00392-8.

Cross, J., Robinson, R., Devaraju, S., Vaughans, A., Hood, R., Kayalackakom, T., & Robinson, R. E. (2023). Transforming medical education: Assessing the integration of ChatGPT into faculty workflows at a Caribbean medical school. *Cureus, 15*(7).

Dahmash, A. B., Alabdulkareem, M., Alfutais, A., Kamel, A. M., Alkholaiwi, F., Alshehri, S., Zahrani, Y. A., & Almoaiqel, M. (2020). Artificial intelligence in radiology: Does it impact medical students' preference for radiology as their future career? *BJR Open, 2*(1), 20200037. https://doi.org/10.1259/bjro.20200037.

Dehouche, N., & Dehouche, K. (2023). *What's in a text-to-image prompt: The potential of stable diffusion in visual arts education.* https://doi.org/10.48550/arXiv.2301.01902.

Eggmann, F., Weiger, R., Zitzmann, N. U., & Blatz, M. B. (2023). Implications of large language models such as ChatGPT for dental medicine. *Journal of Esthetic and Restorative Dentistry.* https://doi.org/10.1111/jerd.13046.

Elkhodr, M., Gide, E., Wu, R., & Darwish, O. (2023). ICT students' perceptions towards ChatGPT: An experimental reflective lab analysis. *STEM Education, 3*(2), 70–88.

Essel, H. B., Vlachopoulos, D., Tachie-Menson, A., Johnson, E. E., & Baah, P. K. (2022). The impact of a virtual teaching assistant (chatbot) on students' learning in Ghanaian higher education. *International Journal of Educational Technology in Higher Education, 19*(1), 1–19, 57. https://doi.org/10.1186/s41239-022-00362-6.

Farrokhnia, M., Banihashem, S. K., Noroozi, O., & Wals, A. (2023). A SWOT analysis of ChatGPT: Implications for educational practice and research. *Innovations in Education and Teaching International,* 1–15. https://doi.org/10.1080/14703297.2023.2195846.

Fauzi, F., Tuhuteru, L., Sampe, F., Ausat, A. M. A., & Hatta, H. R. (2023). Analysing the role of ChatGPT in improving student productivity in higher education. *Journal on Education, 5*(4), 14886–14891.

Gayed, J. M., Carlon, M. K. J., Oriola, A. M., & Cross, J. S. (2022). Exploring an AI-based writing assistant's impact on English language learners. *Computers and Education: Artificial Intelligence, 3*, 100055. https://doi.org/10.1016/j.caeai.2022.100055.

Guest, G., Namey, E., & McKenna, K. (2017). How many focus groups are enough? Building an evidence base for nonprobability sample sizes. *Field Methods, 29*(1), 3–22.

Kim, N. J., & Kim, M. K. (2022, March). Teacher's perceptions of using an artificial intelligence-based educational tool for scientific writing. In *Frontiers in education* (Vol. 7, p. 142). Frontiers.

Kohnke, L., Moorhouse, B. L., & Zou, D. (2023). Exploring generative artificial intelligence preparedness among university language instructors: A case study. *Computers and Education: Artificial Intelligence, 5*, 100156.

Lockey, S., Gillespie, N., Holm, D., & Someh, I. A. (2021). A review of trust in artificial intelligence: challenges, vulnerabilities and future directions. *Hawaii International Conference on System Sciences*, Honolulu, HI, United States, 4–8 January 2021. Honolulu, HI, United States: Hawaii International Conference on System Sciences. https://doi.org/10.24251/hicss.2021.664.

Nasim, S. F., Ali, M. R., & Kulsoom, U. (2022). Artificial intelligence incidents & ethics a narrative review. *International Journal of Technology, Innovation and Management (IJTIM)*, 2(2), 52–64.

Ngo, T. T. A. (2023). The perception by university students of the use of ChatGPT in education. *International Journal of Emerging Technologies in Learning (iJET)*, 18(17), 4–19. https://doi.org/10.3991/ijet.v18i17.39019.

Sandu, R., Gide, E., & Elkhodr, M. (2024). The role and impact of ChatGPT in educational practices: Insights from an Australian higher education case study. *Discover Education*, 3(1), 71.

Shoufan, A. (2023). Exploring students' perceptions of CHATGPT: Thematic analysis and follow-up survey. *IEEE Access*, 11, 38805–38818. https://ieeexplore.ieee.org/document/10105236.

Sileyew, K. J. (2020). Systematic industrial OSH advancement factors identification for manufacturing industries: A case of Ethiopia. *Safety Science*, 132, 104989.

Sim, J., Saunders, B., Waterfield, J., & Kingstone, T. (2018). Can sample size in qualitative research be determined a priori? *International Journal of Social Research Methodology*, 21(5), 619–634.

Wardat, Y., Tashtoush, M. A., AlAli, R., & Jarrah, A. M. (2023). ChatGPT: A revolutionary tool for teaching and learning mathematics. *Eurasia Journal of Mathematics, Science and Technology Education*, 19(7), em2286.

Xiao, Y., & Zhi, Y. (2023). An exploratory study of EFL learners' use of ChatGPT for language learning tasks: Experience and perceptions. *Languages*, 8(3), 212.

Yan, D. (2023). Impact of ChatGPT on learners in an L2 writing practicum: An exploratory investigation. *Education and Information Technologies*, 1–25.

Yilmaz, R., & Yilmaz, F. G. K. (2023). Augmented intelligence in programming learning: Examining student views on the use of ChatGPT for programming learning. *Computers in Human Behavior: Artificial Humans*, 1(2), 100005.

Yin, R. K. (1994). Discovering the future of the case study. Method in evaluation research. *Evaluation Practice*, 15(3), 283–290.

Zhai, X., Chu, X., Chai, C. S., Jong, M. S. Y., Istenic, A., Spector, M., & Li, Y. (2021). A review of artificial intelligence (AI) in education from 2010 to 2020. *Complexity*, 2021, 1–18.

5

STUDENT AND TEACHER PERSPECTIVES REGARDING THE ETHICAL AND RESPONSIBLE USE OF GENERATIVE AI AT KUWAIT UNIVERSITY

A Comparative Case Study

Huda S. Alazmi and Ayeshah A. Alazmi

5.1 Introduction

In recent years, higher education institutions (HEIs) have undergone significant transformations in both teaching and learning (Farrelly & Baker, 2023; Lee et al., 2024; Yusuf et al., 2024). The advent of cutting-edge digital tools and platforms has prompted a critical reevaluation of educational processes, paving the way for more streamlined, personalized, and interactive learning experiences (Wang et al., 2023). Among these innovations, the use of Generative Artificial Intelligence (GenAI) technology has emerged as a significant influence, offering novel ways for both creating and disseminating knowledge.

GenAI can be defined as "a class of artificial intelligence systems designed to generate content or data, such as text, images, video, music, computer code, or even complex combinations of these media, that closely resemble human-created content" (Farrelly & Baker, 2023, P. 2). These systems exploit existing data (via deep learning) and attempt to imitate the patterns, styles, and structures of their training input. For example, OpenAI's GPT-4 (Chat-GPT), a powerful language model, can produce coherent and contextually relevant text based upon a given textual prompt (Mhlanga, 2023). Similarly, DALL-E, another of OpenAI's creations, can generate original images from textual descriptions, showcasing the versatility of GenAI in creative fields (Chan & Hu, 2023).

Today, HEIs around the world have a responsibility for providing their students and teachers with modern, efficient, and relevant learning tools. HEIs must also respond to the rapidly changing technological landscape, of which GenAI is an increasingly prominent feature (Bearman et al., 2023).

DOI: 10.1201/9781003422433-5

However, the integration of such technology with HEIs poses a challenge, as its benefits arrive accompanied by numerous hurdles, encompassing a wide range of areas (Williams, 2024). Some of GenAI's key uses in higher education include automating content creation, personalizing learning experiences, enhancing artistic pursuits and accelerating scientific research. For instance, AI-driven tools can generate adaptive learning materials, offer instant feedback on assignments, and provide writing assistance to students (especially non-native English speakers) thus supporting a more student-centered approach to education (Chan & Hu, 2023; Holmes & Miao, 2023). As HEIs integrate these technologies, they not only enhance the efficiency and effectiveness of educational processes but also prepare students for a future where AI literacy is increasingly essential (Summers et al., 2024).

While GenAI offers numerous benefits to HEIs, it also presents several significant challenges and potential pitfalls. One major concern is the issue of academic integrity, as the ease of generating content could facilitate plagiarism and reduce student incentives for developing original ideas and critical thinking skills (Chaaban et al., 2024). Additionally, privacy and data security are critical issues, since the use of GenAI often involves the collection and processing of vast amounts of personal information, raising concerns about data misuse and breaches (Qadhi et al., 2024). Furthermore, biases embedded in AI algorithms can perpetuate existing inequalities while also introducing new forms of discrimination. These challenges highlight the need for the careful implementation and regulation of GenAI in HEIs to ensure that its adoption does not undermine education's fundamental goals (McDonald et al., 2024: Qadhi et al., 2024).

Research into the educational use of GenAI has grown in recent years. Many studies have emphasized how GenAI can be implemented in classrooms (Chen et al., 2023; Lee & Perret, 2022) while others have explored both its advantages and challenges in educational settings (Baidoo-Anu & Ansah, 2023; Farhi et al., 2023; Firat, 2023; Michel-Villarreal et al., 2023; Mutammimah et al., 2024; Parker et al., 2023). However, few studies have focused on the ethical and responsible use of GenAI so far, and even those efforts have primarily relied upon document and literature analysis. Mhlanga (2023) argues that learning how GenAI can be integrated into HEIs both ethically and responsibly is a complex, multi-dimensional task.

There is presently a lack of empirical research investigating student and teacher understandings regarding the ethical and responsible use of GenAI in an educational setting. This chapter fills this gap in the literature by presenting an empirical study conducted at Kuwait University, the largest government-run university in Kuwait. It explores both student and teacher insights and perspectives regarding the ethical and responsible educational use of GenAI. This study also compares the varying perspectives held by these two groups to identify the similarities and differences using a comparative analysis method.

This study attempts to answer the following research question: "What are the similarities and differences between student and teacher perspectives regarding the ethical and responsible use, concerns, and needs of GenAI tools in Kuwait University?" This chapter offers significant, summarized contributions on several vital points. First, it enables a comprehensive comparative understanding of diverse student and teacher perspectives regarding the ethical and responsible use of GenAI. Secondly, it helps assess the level of understanding for the ethical use of GenAI in the HEI context (Kuwait University) to enable educational leaders to develop training programs and workshops covering the subject more effectively and to ensure that both students and teachers are well equipped to use GenAI ethically, responsibly, and successfully. Finally, the findings from this study can significantly inform the development of future policies and regulations, which will further support the ethical and responsible use of GenAI in higher education.

The chapter begins by examining the context of Kuwait University, detailing its mission and integration of AI technologies, particularly GenAI, into its educational framework. Following this, the conceptual framework for the ethical and responsible use of GenAI is presented, defining the key concepts and principles that guide this research. The methodology section describes the research design, participant selection, data collection methods, and data analysis techniques employed in this study. The results section reports the findings, highlighting the similarities and differences in student and teacher perspectives on the ethical use of GenAI, organized into themes: understanding ethical use, concerns about ethical use, and needs for ethical use. The discussion interprets these findings in relation to the existing literature, explores their theoretical and practical implications, and acknowledges study limitations. Finally, the conclusion summarizes the key findings, offers recommendations for future research and policy, and reflects on the significance of ethical AI use in higher education.

5.1.1 *The Kuwait University Context*

Kuwait is a small Middle East nation which shares borders with Iraq and Saudi Arabia. Established in 1966, Kuwait University is the country's oldest and largest government-run university. With its vision centered upon becoming a hub of innovation and creating an international reputation for excellence, Kuwait University is dedicated toward advancing knowledge, fostering critical thinking, and contributing to the nation's socio-economic development (Kuwait University, 2024). Student enrollment in the fall semester of the 2023/2024 academic year totaled 39,891 students, spread across

16 colleges and supported by 1,695 faculty members. With a diverse student body and a broad array of academic programs, Kuwait University has consistently emphasized the importance of integrating technology into its educational framework to enhance learning outcomes and prepare students for the demands of the modern world. Over the years, Kuwait University has continuously upgraded its information and communication technology (ICT) infrastructure, enhancing facilities such as computer labs with Wi-Fi across its campuses. Additionally, classrooms are equipped with digital projectors and interactive smart boards, further enriching student educational experiences (Alkandari, 2015).

In 2005, Kuwait University introduced its first learning management system (LMS) for electronic learning (e-learning) using Blackboard software as a platform. This initiative to promote integrated learning marked a significant step toward embracing educational technologies, setting the stage for subsequent advancements. Accordantly, Kuwait University's faculty members were encouraged to adopt the Blackboard E-portfolio feature to evaluate students for graduation. E-portfolios compile various student works, such as PowerPoint presentations, lectures, and projects, thus providing a comprehensive assessment tool (Altaher & Atteih, 2012). In response to the COVID-19 pandemic in 2020, Kuwait University transitioned from Blackboard to Moodle, while adopting the Microsoft Teams platform for integrated and distance learning. These platforms come equipped with features which enable faculty members to verify academic integrity and detect plagiarism, helping to ensure the authenticity of student work (Hendal & Alkhezzi, 2022).

Kuwait University takes the issue of academic integrity very seriously, maintaining stringent measures to uphold academic honesty among students, faculty, and staff. Policies are in place to deter academic dishonesty such as plagiarism and cheating. For example, students are expected to adhere to the Kuwait University Policy on Cheating and Plagiarism (Student Guide, Chapter 3, Section 3.2), ensuring the authenticity of their work through proper citation practices and originality (Kuwait University, 2024). Students are required to note all sources and assistance carefully when submitting their work; under no circumstances are they to take credit for the work which is not their own. They should neither receive nor give any unauthorized assistance on any deliverable either.

With the rise of GenAI technologies, Kuwait University now faces increasing challenges to maintaining its academic integrity since students have growing access to AI-driven solutions for writing, research, and problem-solving. To address this situation, Kuwait University's Council of 2024 is preparing for a pivotal assembly to deliberate on the adoption of a GenAI policy (Arab Times, 2024). This policy aims to address key questions regarding GenAI integration into curricula and research programs, ethical guidelines for GenAI usage, collaborative efforts with other institutions, and its impact on the job market and graduate employability. This policy covers key areas such as GenAI concerns and the use of GenAI by students, faculty, and employees. The advantages of embracing a GenAI policy at Kuwait University are manifold: they include keeping abreast of technological developments, enhancing research capabilities, and boosting student competitiveness. However, potential drawbacks, such as the high implementation costs, continual updating, and the ethical dilemmas related to AI algorithms, must be considered carefully.

5.2 Conceptual Framework: Ethical and Responsible Use of GenAI

Integrating GenAI into the educational system requires a robust, ethically based framework to ensure that its implementation enhances learning while providing a safe, ethical, equitable, and meaningful environment. A notable contribution to this subject is UNESCO's (2023) publication, *Guidance for Generative AI in Education and Research* (Holmes & Miao, 2023). In this document, UNESCO offers guidelines for the ethical and responsible use of GenAI in educational settings, focusing on the importance of academic integrity. This guidance is based upon a human-centered approach to AI designed to enhance human rights, cultural diversity, inclusion, equity, and equality. In addition, Mhlanga (2023) published a framework in his study entitled *Open AI in Education, Responsible and Ethical Use of ChatGPT toward Lifelong Learning*. This framework employed a comprehensive document analysis, analyzing digital and physical sources, including blog posts and published journal articles and books. The review concluded that there are six key principles which help to maintain trust and accountability to ensure the ethical use of GenAI tools (see Figure 5.1).

The present study uses the frameworks which UNESCO and Mhlanga published in 2023 as a guide. Mhlanga's study outlined important principles for the ethical use of GenAI which aligned closely with those established by UNESCO; however, each framework provides its own unique perspectives which support the ethical use of the technology in education. By integrating these frameworks, the present study seeks to offer a robust analysis of how GenAI can be ethically and responsibly used in an educational context.

1. **Respect for Privacy** is the first ethical principle in our framework. Many studies argue that protecting privacy must be a primary consideration when students and teachers use GenAI (Alafnan et al., 2023; Mhlanga, 2023; Su &Yang, 2023; Thurzo et al., 2023; Holmes & Miao, 2023). UNESCO (2023) referred to the risk involved in this issue as "use of content without consent." It argues that GenAI models are obtained from vast amounts of data which are frequently gathered from the internet without

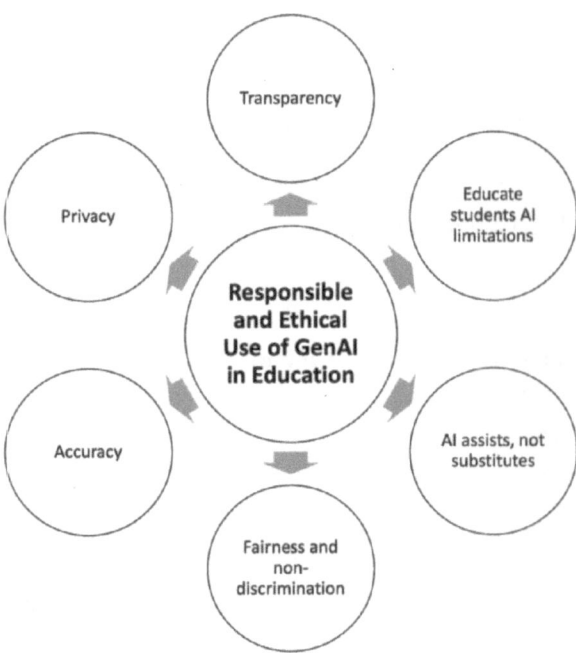

FIGURE 5.1   Responsible and ethical use of GenAI in education (Mhlanga, 2023).

permission from those who actually created the original content. This method of data collection has led to legal concerns about the violation of intellectual property rights (IPR), especially those involving images and coding, because they handle copyrighted content without consent from the original creators. Thus, researchers, teachers, and students must acknowledge the rights of data owners and ensure that any GenAI tools which they use do not violate current laws (Holmes & Miao, 2023). Moreover, academic institutions must maintain the confidentiality of everyone who works in the educational process, such as students, teachers, and other educators. This is an issue because the use of GenAI tools in educational settings often involves the sharing of personal details and sensitive information such as student grades and performance. To protect the confidentiality of those involved, it is essential to prevent illegal or unauthorized access to, the use of, or disclosure of personal data. Myskja (2023) indicates that trust is a vital component in the learning process. If student and teacher rights to privacy are violated, then the trust between them will erode, thus deleteriously affecting learning outcomes and the overall quality of education.

2. **Fairness and Nondiscrimination** is the second ethical principle we considered. UNESCO (2023) explained that GenAI's resources are controlled by

the largest technology companies based in developed countries such as the United States of America, China, and several European nations (Holmes & Miao, 2023). This means that smaller companies and most other nations are generally unable to either direct or access such technology. Marwala (2023) indicated that control of GenAI by certain wealthy countries has lead to a lack of computing power in other nations, thus exacerbating the digital and economic divides between them. Mannuru et al. (2023) argued that there is a need for providing infrastructure and support to ensure that future progress is distributed more equitably rather than broadening pre-existing disparities. In addition, GenAI technology typically collects data from internet-based sources, which frequently contain offensive and discriminatory language (Intahchomphoo & Gundersen, 2020). The absence of stringent regulation and robust monitoring has therefore lead to the metastization of biased, AI-generated content online and the contamination of a significant global source of information for students. Moreover, GenAI systems often generate data which reflect the viewpoints, values, and beliefs buried within the training data. This is because the models which many of these systems employ have a propensity for repeating words that occur frequently in the training set, which typically comprises popular and mainstream ideologies (Evans & Sinha, 2024). This tendency has the potential for restricting the range of available opinions and beliefs, especially when it comes to marginalized communities represented less robustly online. In an attempt to avoid these risks, UNESCO's framework provided three recommendations. For one, teachers, students, and researchers should be made aware of the cultural biases and social norms embedded in GenAI models. Furthermore, it is important for educators, researchers, and students to understand that GenAI technology can produce offensive and unethical content. And finally, teachers, students, and researchers must never accept GenAI-created data at face value; they should always evaluate it critically.

3. **ChatGPT Is Not a Substitute for Human Teachers** is the third principle. Many studies have highlighted concerns that ChatGPT or other GenAI tools could be used as replacements for in-person instruction (Ausat et al., 2023; Alghazali, 2024). This seems unlikely, however, as GenAI uses text-based Generative Pre-trained Transformers (GPTs). These mimic language from training data but do not actually understand it, which is why they are frequently referred to as "Stochastic Parrots" (Holmes & Miao, 2023). These models are unable to produce truly original insights about the world because they are not grounded in human values or real-world observations. Mhlanga (2023) argues that an ethical principle, which both students and teachers should recognize, is that ChatGPT is not intended as a substitute for in-person instruction from certified teachers. To start with, GenAI cannot facilitate human interaction. While ChatGPT does provide

significant ways of facilitating learning, it is unable to offer the same rich social interaction and connection between students and teachers which in-person interaction provides, such as non-verbal cues. Moreover, GenAI tools cannot possess the empathy, emotional intelligence, or interpersonal skills which a human teacher can provide (Mhlanga, 2023). Furthermore, research argues that GenAI tools cannot engage in critical thinking or creativity (Mhlanga, 2023), such as evaluating literature, identifying biases, constructing arguments, or creating new meaning (Holmes & Miao, 2023). However, teachers can encourage students to assess AI-generated content to discover flaws in its logic and work to complete arguments. Indeed, instead of considering whether ChatGPT could be a substitute for actual teachers, we should see it as an effective tool which can supplement in-person instruction and assist student learning.

4. **Responsible AI: Educating Students about AI and Its Limitations** is the fourth principle. Many studies argue the importance of teaching students both how GenAI works and what the limitations and boundaries of such tools are (Jarrah et al., 2023; Kiryakova & Angelova, 2023; Sok & Heng, 2024). As already intimated, while GenAI can produce human-like text and assist students in a variety of assignments, it lacks actual understanding, critical thinking, empathy, and creativity. For example, students need to be aware that ChatGPT and other GenAI tools cannot actually create *new* content but rather they generate content based on existing information in their dataset, which may have been gathered without the consent of the original content creators, and this raises concerns related to plagiarism and intellectual property rights (Holmes & Miao, 2023). Furthermore, ChatGPT was trained via a vast array of textual content gathered from the internet, some of which consists of unreliable, biased, and potentially harmful information. In addition, students must understand the potential ethical and social ramifications which GenAI can involve, as discussed earlier. Therefore, students should be prepared to challenge the veracity of GenAI output, and teachers must also encourage them to think critically about it. In other words, students must be capable of conducting in-depth analyses of GenAI-created content and learn how to distinguish between genuine and unreliable sources of information. UNESCO (2023) recommended that researchers, teachers, and students must also be aware that GenAI systems do not understand the data they create and that the data often includes factually inaccurate statements (Holmes & Miao, 2023). Students and teachers, therefore, need a critical approach to measure the reliability of this data.

5. **Transparency in the Use of ChatGPT** marks the fifth principle regarding the ethical use of GenAI. UNESCO's (2023) guidelines indicate that GenAI systems are frequently characterized as "black boxes," because it

is difficult to both explain and understand their internal workings (Holmes & Miao, 2023). While the basic algorithms these systems employ are readily explainable, the specific model parameters and weights which determine the output remain opaque (Gillani & Haider, 2023). This lack of transparency becomes increasingly problematic as GenAI systems grow more complex, generate unexpected results, and reinforce biases in the data (Varsha, 2023). Consequently, the process creates problems related to public trust; people are less likely to embrace a technology which they neither understand nor comprehend the manner in which its findings arrive. For this reason, it is essential for students and teachers to be open (and clear) about when they use GenAI tools. For example, if students use ChatGPT to create content, even if only in minor ways, then they must disclose this fact to their teachers to ensure academic integrity. Similarly, if teachers use GenAI tools for grading, offering feedback, or class content creation, then they must inform students regarding the role AI played in this process (Mhlanga, 2023). This transparency will help build trust, maintain academic integrity, and enhance the use of ethical and responsible practices, because disclosing when and how GenAI tools are used will promote better understanding of its affordances and limitations. UNESCO (2023) recommends that students, teachers, and researchers who use GenAI tools should follow this practice of transparency to maintain their academic integrity (Holmes & Miao, 2023).

6. **Information Accuracy** is the sixth ethical principle. Numerous studies focus on the informational accuracy of GenAI-created output, because many such tools have a high propensity for producing incorrect, outdated, and/or misleading content (Nguyen et al., 2023). Since GenAI tools were trained to find patterns in the data they access, they can produce content which, while perhaps looking authentic, is factually inaccurate. UNESCO (2023) described this as: "generating deeper deepfakes." It argued that GenAI technologies can also be used to manipulate or produce photographs and/or moving images (videos) which are difficult to distinguish from authentic examples. This has facilitated the advancement of unethical, immoral, and illegal acts by making it simpler to produce the so-called "deepfakes" and "fake news." These practices include the dissemination of false information, encouragement of hate speech, and unauthorized use of human likenesses within fabricated and sometimes deeply disturbing media content. Researchers, teachers, and students need to be aware that image, video, and audio files which they post online may be included in GenAI training data, or even altered and applied unethically (Holmes & Miao, 2023). As already implied, they should also be aware that GenAI-created content may be inaccurate or misleading. Thus, there is an approach to critically assess this content.

5.3 Method

This study used a qualitative comparative case study approach to explore and compare the perspectives of students and teachers about their ethical and responsible use of GenAI at Kuwait University (Corbin & Strauss, 2008). The study seeks to identify the similarities and differences in their perspectives, thus offering a comprehensive insight into their understanding for the ethical and responsible use of GenAI.

5.3.1 Participants

Students and teachers from the humanities and social sciences colleges at Kuwait University participated in this study. A stratified purposive sampling technique was used to ensure that each of them possessed both a relevant background and sufficient knowledge of GenAI (Yin, 2009). Students and teachers were selected based on specific criteria: (1) their engagement with GenAI technologies in their coursework or research, (2) their willingness to participate in the study, and (3) their enrollment/work in humanities and social sciences colleges at Kuwait University during the fall semester of the 2023/2024 academic year. The study sample comprised 42 students and 25 teachers (faculty members) from these collages. A majority of the participants were female (31 students and 16 teachers) and the remaining participants were male (11 students and 9 teachers). Among the teachers, 9 (36%) were assistant professors, 11 (44%) were associate professors, and 5 (20%) were full professors. Most students were in their second academic year ($N = 29$, 69%) and the remaining students were distributed across the first ($N = 29$, 69%), third ($N = 29$, 69%), and fourth year or higher ($N = 29$, 69%). The participants belonged to Kuwait University's College of Education (students, $N = 8$; teachers, $N = 6$), College of Arts (students, $N = 9$; teachers, $N = 5$), College of Social Sciences (students, $N = 6$; teachers, $N = 5$), College of Sharia and Islamic Studies (students, $N = 5$; teachers, $N = 2$), College of Administrative Sciences (students, $N = 6$; teachers, $N = 3$), and College of Law (students, $N = 8$; teachers, $N = 4$).

5.3.2 Data Collection and Analysis

Study data were collected via semi-structured interviews, which allowed participants to freely express their perspectives regarding professional agency. As a qualitative study, it aimed to explore the personal interpretations of participant responses and experiences, structured around several key questions (Cresswell, 2013). The researchers gained ethical approval for the study from Kuwait University prior to recruiting participants. The latter were obtained via an invitational email outlining the study objectives sent to every student and teacher of the university's humanities and social sciences colleges; 42 students and 25 teachers agreed to take part. Table 5.1 shows the participants characteristics.

TABLE 5.1 Participants' Characteristics

Demographic Category	Students (N = 42)	Teachers (N = 25)	Total (N = 67)
Gender			
Female	31	16	47
Male	11	9	20
Academic Position			
Assistant Professor	—	9 (36%)	9
Associate Professor	—	11 (44%)	11
Full Professor	—	5 (20%)	5
Academic Year			
First Year	3 (7%)	—	3
Second Year	29 (69%)	—	29
Third Year	3 (7%)	—	3
Fourth Year or Higher	7 (17%)	—	7
Colleges			
College of Education	8	6	14
College of Arts	9	5	14
College of Social Sciences	6	5	11
College of Sharia and Islamic Studies	5	2	7
College of Administrative Sciences	6	3	9
College of Law	8	4	12

Participant anonymity and etc. Participant anonymity and confidentiality were assured, as was their right to withdraw from the study at any stage. Consent was obtained before scheduling face-to-face interviews, which took place at the university during the fall semester of the 2023/2024 academic year.

Three primary questions guided each interview, supplemented with follow-up questions to delve more deeply into the initial responses: (1) *What are your perspectives regarding the ethical and responsible use of GenAI tools at Kuwait University?* (2) *What are your perspectives regarding the ethical and responsible concerns of GenAI tools at Kuwait University?* (3) *What are your perspectives regarding the ethical and responsible needs of GenAI tools at Kuwait University?* Each 40-to-50-minute audio-recorded interview was conducted in Arabic, with the data being transcribed for analysis. The interview transcriptions were shared with the participants to validate data accuracy and authenticity.

Data analysis was performed in two stages:

Stage 1: The researchers initially employed constant comparative analysis, as described by Corbin and Strauss (2008), with each of them analyzing the interview transcripts independently, following the within-case analysis

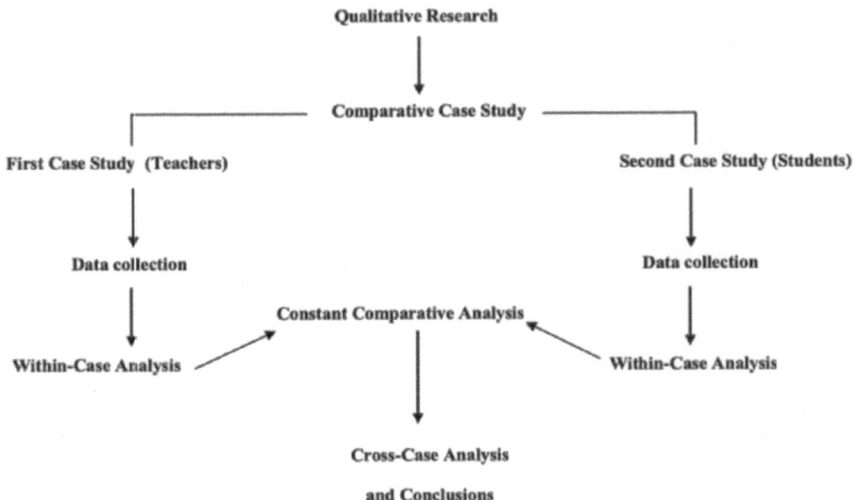

FIGURE 5.2 Research methodology.

approach outlined by Yin (2009). Each primary transcript was read multiple times and underwent open coding, wherein every potentially relevant piece of data was identified and coded (Merriam, 2015). Following this, the researchers exchanged their analyses to cross-verify their findings for each case, ensuring a comprehensive and unbiased interpretation of the data, while enhancing its trustworthiness. The researchers then reviewed and validated the initial codes together. These codes, which emerged from the data via open coding, were then examined for similarities and differences to identify common themes and patterns related to the ethical and responsible use of GenAI. The researchers consolidated similar codes into categories and subcategories. They then compared the categories, which enabled the development of the study's main themes and propositions.

Stage 2: In the second stage, the cases were compared against each other using cross-case analysis to identify both their similarities and differences (Miles et al., 2014). This cross-case comparison helps in a deep investigation of a single phenomenon (i.e., how well do students and teachers at Kuwait university understand the ethical and responsible use of GenAI), while also carefully comparing the similarities and differences within each case. Figure 5.2 shows a summary of the research methodology applied in this study.

5.4 Results

This section reports the findings from the current study. Within each section, the findings are presented with reference to the similarities and differences

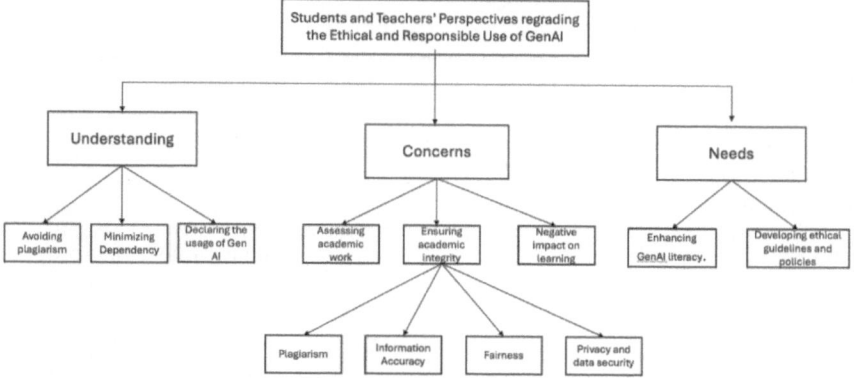

FIGURE 5.3   Results by overall themes, categories, and sub-categories.

between student and teacher perspectives regarding the ethical and responsible educational use of GenAI. The findings are presented based on the specific themes, as shown in Figure 5.3.

5.4.1   Understanding for the Ethical and Responsible Use of GenAI

Teachers and students were asked about their understanding regarding the responsible and ethical use of GenAI. Their answers were then grouped into categories (see Table 5.2).

5.4.1.1   Avoiding Plagiarism

Student Perspectives. Most students (N = 31) indicated that the responsible and ethical use of GenAI means using the technology without plagiarizing. They highlighted two ways of avoiding plagiarism: (1) proper attribution and (2) paraphrasing. Indeed, students clarified that they must always cite the use of GenAI tools in their work, as one student explained: "When students use ChatGPT, they must cite ChatGPT." They also indicated the importance of paraphrasing content to avoid plagiarism. In this case, paraphrasing implies that a student rewrites the AI-generated content in their own words but without changing either its meaning or the ideas involved. Student (S17) explained this point with the following: "I believe that ethical use is using ChatGPT and citing that this content was taken from ChatGPT. . . [and that] I have not copied everything 100% the same, but I must paraphrase this content in my own words."

Teacher Perspectives. Many teachers (N = 12) also emphasized that the responsible and ethical use of GenAI tools requires that students avoid plagiarism. They highlighted how students should be aware of the correct

TABLE 5.2 Student and Teacher Perspectives Regarding Their Understanding for the Ethical and Responsible Use of GenAI

Theme: Understanding for the Ethical and Responsible Use of GenAI	Degree of Similarity			Description
	Not Similar	Somewhat Similar	Similar	
Avoiding Plagiarism	√			Students believe that proper attribution, like citing ChatGPT, and paraphrasing of content are sufficient to avoid plagiarism. However, teachers indicated that understanding source authenticity and respecting IPR are essential to avoid plagiarism.
Minimizing Dependency		√		Both groups agreed that students' use of GenAI should be kept to a minimum. Students focused on the amount of their dependency, while teachers tended to focus on how to minimize its use.
Declaring the usage of GenAI			√	Both groups highlighted the importance of declaring instances of GenAI use to teachers.

processes for avoiding plagiarism, noting it can be achieved via the following: (1) understanding source authenticity and (2) respecting intellectual property rights (IPR). They stressed that students should seek out and properly cite original sources when using information obtained from AI tools rather than solely relying on the AI-generated outputs. As one teacher (T3) stated: "It is not acceptable to cite ChatGPT for the information it provides, because ChatGPT compiles data from other sources and most of the time does not generate original content." Additionally, teachers indicated that students must recognize author copyrights, ensuring that IPR is respected. With respect to the above, teacher (T19) noted: "I believe that students should understand the importance of tracing back to the primary sources and providing accurate citations to maintain academic integrity and respect for authorship."

5.4.1.2   Minimizing Dependency

Student Perspectives. Many students ($N = 15$) believe that the ethical and responsible employment of GenAI tools involves using them as infrequently as possible for academic work. When students were asked to list ways in which they could minimize their dependency upon these tools, their answers focused mainly on the quantity of work rather than content itself. For example, student (S2) stated: "When I use ChatGPT on my research or report, I should take no more than two or three sentences." She emphasized that students should perform the majority of the work but that ChatGPT could be used to assist that task. Another student offered their own understanding for this point with the following: "I think each student must not exceed 10% of the whole work [with ChatGPT]."

Teacher Perspectives. Many teachers ($N = 12$) thought that responsible and ethical use of GenAI entailed students minimizing their use of the tools when working on school assignments. Teacher perspectives regarding student dependency upon GenAI technology are as follows: (1) use AI to brainstorm and (2) use AI as a supportive tool. Regarding the first point, many teachers argue that student use of GenAI tools must be limited to brainstorming to help them generate ideas or provide suggestions with which to build their own work. Teacher (T11) summarized this concept, noting: "To ethically use GenAI tools . . . they must be used to create ideas, such as ideas for presentations, projects, or research." Regarding the second point, some teachers ($N = 6$) reported that AI can be used ethically as a supportive tool. More specifically, they meant that GenAI tools can be used for *content assistance*, where necessary. However, this dependency should only involve supplementary information, or as teacher (T4) reported: "Students can take some [AI generated] content to add examples, or some clarifications to their work." Three teachers also suggested that students should use GenAI tools as a learning aid.

5.4.1.3   Declaring the Usage of GenAI

Student Perspectives. During their interviews, students indicated that in order to employ ChatGPT ethically, they must be open and honest about their usage of the tool, especially with their teachers. This means asking their teachers for permission to use the GenAI on a project *before* actually using it, and then citing the technology properly in their references once they do. They further highlighted that the declaration of GenAI usage is a crucial component of ethical academic behavior, student (S4) stating: "I believe that the ethical use of ChatGPT means I must be honest about the usage with my teacher . . . because by declaring the usage of ChatGPT, I acknowledge the potential risks of these tools."

Teacher Perspectives. Teachers believed that, ethically, students should disclose their use of GenAI programs. From their perspective, this disclosure serves multiple purposes, with the primary emphasis being on academic integrity and ensuring scholastic honesty. As teacher (T18) stated:

In my classes, it is essential to be open and honest about the using of ChatGPT. . . . This empowers students to use GenAI tools knowledgeably, and ensures that these technologies are integrated in a manner consistent with Kuwait University's ethical values.

Furthermore, teachers believe that such transparency influences the assignment assessment process, providing a clearer understanding of student abilities and ensuring alignment with educational objectives.

5.4.2 The Ethical and Responsible Concerns of Using GenAI

Teachers and students were asked about their concerns regarding the responsible and ethical use of GenAI. Their answers were then grouped into categories (see Table 5.3).

5.4.2.1 Assessing Academic Work

Student Perspectives. The primary concern which students expressed regarding their use of GenAI tools to complete assignments is that it may negatively affect the assessment of their work. Indeed, students ($N = 15$) feared that it could lead to pejorative attitudes, which may unfavorably affect their grades. Students highlighted their beliefs that many teachers have a negative perception regarding GenAI use on assignments or research, and one stated: "Sometimes they considered this behavior as cheating, which affects my grades." Another student (S40) reported: "I remembered that I used ChatGPT on my assignment last semester, and I declared this point for my teacher . . . however, students who used GenAI tools got lower grades compared with those who did not use it."

Teacher Perspectives. Teachers are concerned that student use of GenAI tools for academic work will complicate and undermine the accuracy of the assessment process. For example, teachers may struggle to distinguish between a student's own work and the contributions to it from GenAI programs, making its evaluation potentially unfair. Additionally, teachers are interested in using software which detects the use of GenAI, but this technology (just like AI itself) may sometimes be inaccurate and remains under development. Referring to this, teacher (T11) stated: "In some cases, assignments are submitted, and I feel that the student may have used ChatGPT to complete the task, but I have no conclusive evidence, leaving me uncertain about assigning a fair grade." Adding to this, another teacher

TABLE 5.3 Student and Teacher Perspectives Regarding the Ethical and Responsible Concerns of Using GenAI

Theme: Ethical and Responsible Concerns Regarding the Use of GenAI	Degree of Similarity			Description
	Not Similar	Somewhat Similar	Similar	
Assessing academic work	√			While students were concerned that their use of GenAI might negatively affect their grades, teachers were more worried about the best assessment techniques for evaluating AI-assisted student work.
Ensuring academic integrity				
1. Plagiarism		√		Students were concerned about what constitutes plagiarism and whether paraphrasing is sufficient to avoid it, whereas teachers were more concerned about whether students understood source authenticity and respected intellectual property.
2. Information Accuracy			√	Both groups were concerned about the accuracy of information produced via GenAI.
3. Fairness		√		Both groups were worried about the universal accessibility to GenAI tools. However, teachers held broader concerns which considered the GenAI information quality gap between developed and developing countries such as Arab nations.
4. Privacy and Data Security	√			Teachers expressed significant concerns regarding privacy and data security associated with GenAI use, but students did not mention this issue.
Negative Impact on Learning		√		Both groups were concerned about how students' use of GenAI tools may negatively affect their thinking and writing skills. However, while students focused on the immediate impact, teachers centered upon the long-term effects.

(T2) expressed: "What worries me is that some students can make minor changes to AI-generated work which AI detection programs cannot track."

5.4.2.2 Ensuring Academic Integrity

Both groups (teachers and students) were concerned that using GenAI tools may affect academic integrity. This category is divided into three main sub-categories:

5.4.2.2.1 Plagiarism

Student Perspectives. Many student concerns focused on plagiarism. They worried about how they could maintain honesty and avoid academic plagiarism when using GenAI tools. Students also expressed concerns over whether using GenAI tools might be considered plagiarism or cheating, even if they cited its use in their references. Some students were also uncertain whether paraphrased AI-generated content would be considered plagiarism or not, even if cited. Student (S9) emphasized these concerns, stating: "I am not sure if using GenAI tools is considered plagiarism or not . . . I am confused, and I am worried about this point [and whether it] will negatively affect my grades."

Teacher Perspectives. Many teachers (N = 16) showed significant concern regarding student understanding for the concept of academic plagiarism and how it relates to the use of GenAI tools. They felt students believe that merely citing an AI program as a source of information protects them from the consequences of academic plagiarism, which is not necessarily the case, according to teacher participants. They believe that the issue of academic plagiarism extends well beyond any immediate consequences and that it will profoundly impact scientific integrity and the ethical treatment of IPR over the long term. Teachers contend that as students use GenAI tools, there is an increased risk of unintentional plagiarism due to a potentially inadequate understanding of attribution and originality in digital content creation, as teacher (T7) expressed:

As a teacher, I observe that students often have a misguided understanding of avoiding academic plagiarism, such as citing AI programs as sources of information without recognizing that the majority of data within AI models like ChatGPT constitutes generated content rather than original sources.

5.4.2.2.2 Information Accuracy

Student Perspectives. Students are concerned that GenAI tools may generate inaccurate content, leading to misconceptions and poor understanding. Their worries centered around two main issues, the first being that GenAI tools can produce false information. Student (S1) summarized this, stating: "We know that ChatGPT generates information, but sometimes, unfortunately, this information is wrong and inaccurate." The other concern is the low quality of information which AI can sometimes produce and that this may negatively affect their work since the AI-generated content quality is generally inferior to the primary and secondary sources. Furthermore, this issue is even more pronounced for AI-generated Arabic content, since the Arabic language AI training data set is considerably smaller than that available in English. Student (S11) illustrated some of these concerns, stating: "I believe that the quality of work, such as the accuracy of information, is not similar to the content from authentic books and resources, especially in Arabic."

Teacher Perspectives. Teachers are concerned about the information accuracy of content produced by GenAI systems, as this is crucial to educational integrity. Teachers stressed the significance of ensuring that GenAI output is accurate, reliable, and reflective of reality in order to maintain educational standards. Teacher (T3) epitomized this issue, stating: "The accuracy of information is paramount in education to ensure that teaching materials are trustworthy . . . AI's ability to process and disseminate accurate information directly influences learning outcomes." Teacher concerns were rooted in how such information could potentially influence the analysis and comprehension of reality, as well as the decision-making processes on diverse matters. This apprehension arises from the realization that AI-derived information may lack accuracy, verifiability, or objectivity in its presentation. Moreover, teachers argued that students must be able to evaluate the information which GenAI tools produce, as teacher (T17) stated: "I believe that my students should possess the foundational knowledge to judge and evaluate the outputs of these AI tools."

5.4.2.2.3 Fairness

Student Perspectives. Students were also concerned about the fairness of using GenAI tools. More specifically, some students ($N = 8$) worried about the potentially unfair grading disparity between those students who use GenAI tools in their work and those who do not. Students explained that the work of those who use ChatGPT may be more effectively structured and polished than that produced by their peers who write papers independently. They fear this may lead to higher grades for students who used GenAI tools even though they likely put less effort into their work and had a poorer understanding for its content than those who opted not to use AI. One student (S23) stressed this point, stating: "When teachers compare two research papers written by two students, one of them using GenAI tools and the other [not] . . . perhaps the students who used GenAI tools wrote a better paper, which got a higher mark with lower effort."

Teacher Perspectives. Most of the teachers (N = 21) were concerned about the fairness in GenAI application. Their perspectives covered two main points, the first involving student access to the technology itself. Teachers explained that only some students have the means to use these technologies. Kuwait University should, as one teacher suggested, "provide institutional access to ChatGPT, ensuring that all students and teachers have equal and reliable access to GenAI technologies." Teachers also believe that there is a broader dimension of bias related to fairness at the national and regional levels, where the quality of information depends heavily upon the availability and comprehensiveness of the input data and references that AI can mine for information, and these data sources are mostly in English. This leads to a gap in information quality between developed countries and developing countries. In regions like the Arab world, disparities exist in digital resources, affecting the effectiveness and fairness of AI-driven educational initiatives. Teacher (T5) noted: "In the Arab regions, there is a lack of foundational books in digital form, which creates a kind of inequity and bias."

5.4.2.2.4 Privacy and Data Security

Student Perspectives. Student participants did not express any opinions regarding these aspects.

Teacher Perspectives. Teachers expressed significant concerns regarding the privacy and security implications associated with the use of GenAI tools. Nearly every teacher (N = 23) was worried about safeguarding student data confidentiality and ensuring adherence to privacy regulations amidst the integration of GenAI technologies into teaching and research. Highlighting this, teacher (T22) stated: "I think that the protection of users' personal information is an essential concern." Teachers explained that GenAI tools can handle sensitive information, such as grades and personal details, a fact which they felt all stakeholders should be aware of. Teachers stressed the critical need for the secure handling of personal information within educational institutions and to encourage students to only access GenAI tools via institutional portals. They also emphasized how AI platforms must adhere strictly to privacy regulations to safeguard the confidentiality of each individual involved in the educational process.

5.4.2.3 *Negative Impact on Learning*

Student Perspectives. Many students (N = 13) expressed concerns that they may become over-reliant upon GenAI tools and that such dependence may impair their learning. They felt that this could manifest itself in two key-ways, with the first involving the atrophy of writing skills. Student (S1) explained this succinctly stating: "Using ChatGPT in writing will encourage students to just copy-and-paste the content without *writing* their content." Students also worried that AI may diminish their thought processes. For example, an over-reliance on these AI tools could lead students to simply accept the generated answers without questioning it or performing analysis and synthesis to gain deeper understanding of the content. This, they felt, would reduce their ability to think critically and independently. Student (S2) summarized this aspect, stating: "Using these tools to generate ideas and suggest solutions will stifle creativity, as students might rely on these tools instead of developing their own original ideas."

Teacher Perspectives. Many teachers ($N = 11$) worried about how GenAI may negatively affect student abilities to learn skills, undermining the overall quality of education. More specifically, teachers were concerned that students might lose the ability to write effective essays or solve tasks without using these tools. Moreover, teachers cautioned against viewing GenAI as a substitute for human educators, emphasizing that while GenAI can play a supportive role in education, it cannot replicate the unique talents, experiences, and perspectives which human teachers bring to the classroom. In their discussions, teachers noted that GenAI lacked cultural awareness, which would affect its interactions within diverse educational contexts. This deficiency underscores the importance of human educators, who do typically understand cultural nuances and can provide contextually relevant learning experiences. As teacher (T24) reported: "Although ChatGPT has the potential to contribute to education, it should not replace actual teachers."

5.4.3 Ethical and Responsible Needs for Using GenAI

Teachers and students were asked about the ethical needs for using GenAI tools. Their answers were then grouped under the categories shown in Table 5.4.

5.4.3.1 Enhancing GenAI Literacy

Student Perspectives. Many students expressed the need to incorporate GenAI literacy within curricula, reporting that most of their peers lack the knowledge and skills to use GenAI tools ethically. They further clarified the importance of providing students with essential knowledge and skills about the technical, ethical, and societal implications of using GenAI. Educators, as student (S8) stated, must explain "how GenAI tools work, what are their risks and limitations, and how can students use them ethically." They emphasized how clarifying these points will help them use such tools with fewer risks.

TABLE 5.4 Student and Teacher Perspectives Regarding the Ethical and Responsible Needs for Using GenAI

Theme 3: Ethical and Responsible Needs Regarding the Use of GenAI Tools	Degree of Similarity			Description
	Not Similar	Somewhat Similar	Similar	
Enhancing GenAI literacy			√	Both students and teachers expressed the need for developing GenAI literacy.
Developing ethical guidelines and policies for GenAI tool use	√			Students focused upon guidelines, while teachers were primarily concerned about the need to develop and implement policies.

Teacher Perspectives. Teachers believe that GenAI literacy should encompass both students and teachers, highlighting the need for improving the status quo through the instruction of appropriate techniques. First, universities should provide short courses and workshops focusing upon essential GenAI knowledge and skills. Secondly, teachers suggested that Kuwait University could create an ethical GenAI proficiency test, which all students and teachers should fulfill before completing their first academic year at university. This would ensure that all members of the academic community were properly prepared to engage with GenAI technologies, both from ethical and practical perspectives.

5.4.3.2 Developing Ethical Guidelines and Policies for Using GenAI

Student Perspectives. Many students reported on the need for ethical guidelines to control the use of GenAI tools in academic settings. They acknowledged that although GenAI can serve as a valuable academic resource, it is essential for them to be properly aware of the potential pitfalls associated with its use, such as plagiarism, fairness, and information accuracy. Therefore, there is a need to develop a systematic set of guidelines clarifying the ethical use of these tools, as student (S29) noted: "The university should provide clear instructions on how to integrate these tools ethically into our work."

Teacher Perspectives. Most teachers ($N = 18$) agreed on the need for developing and implementing GenAI-related policies which fully uphold academic standards to ensure that the technology supports and enhances the integrity of academic work. They felt that this could be achieved, in part, if universities developed comprehensive frameworks to ensure GenAI is used responsibly. They also highlighted the need for institutions to update academic integrity policies to incorporate AI technologies. Teacher (T4) summarized this, stating: "I think that Kuwait University should develop effective policy frameworks to ensure that GenAI is used ethically and responsibly in education. . . . We need a clear policy that promotes transparency, accountability, and fairness in AI-driven educational practices."

5.5 Discussion

This chapter investigated student and teacher perspectives regarding the ethical and responsible use of GenAI technologies. It affected this, in part, by looking for the common ground which these groups share with respect to GenAI usage in higher education, along with their differences. The study offers an insightful understanding of these varying viewpoints, highlighting the distinct ethical concerns and needs each group associates with the use of GenAI in educational contexts.

5.5.1 The Ethical and Responsible Use of GenAI: Insight and Discussion.

Regarding the first theme, both groups agreed that this involves three major points: (1) avoiding plagiarism, (2) minimizing dependency on technology, and (3) declaring the usage of GenAI whenever it is applied. Even so, the two groups interpreted each of these categories quite differently at times. In comparison to students, teachers generally held a broader view and deeper understanding for the ethical and responsible use of GenAI. For example, both groups understood that this involves avoiding plagiarism, but there were differences when it came to each group's actual understanding of plagiarism and the mechanisms for avoiding it. While students believe that this simply involves providing proper attribution for any ChatGPT-developed content in their references and by paraphrasing the said content, teacher concerns extend beyond these mitigation strategies. Indeed, teachers believed that a student merely citing the use of such tools in their references and content is insufficient to avoid plagiarism. They indicated that GenAI tools generate content derived from pre-existing data via algorithms, rather than anything the author using them has contributed. Wardat et al. (2024) noted that ChatGPT and other AI language models fail to link/attribute the produced content to its original source(s), which is a direct violation of IPR. Indeed, as our study also found, Chen et al. (2023) argue that most students do not understand how GenAI tools work and they think that simply citing the sections of their work derived from GenAI will help them avoid plagiarism. This gap between each group's understanding of plagiarism led to differences in expectations and practices between them, potentially causing misunderstandings regarding the regulation of GenAI tools in academic settings. UNESCO (2023) argues that students and teachers must be aware that ChatGPT cannot generate *new* content, but rather that it produces content based on existing data, which may raise the concern of IPR infringement (Holmes & Miao, 2023).

Both groups understood that the ethical and responsible use of GenAI involves minimizing their reliance upon the application of such technology in academic work. This result concurred with previous studies which viewed excessive student dependence upon GenAI as an impediment to gaining understanding for a subject while also facilitating cheating, both of which impair academic integrity (Mhlanga, 2023). In the present study, while students focused primarily on the volume of work which they could ethically derive from ChatGPT, teachers prioritized "how to minimize student dependency on GenAI technologies." Students noted that ChatGPT should provide no more than 10% or perhaps up to three sentences of their work on a particular project. In contrast, teachers delved deeper, discussing how to reduce student use of ChatGPT even further. They argued that students could use GenAI tools only as a supportive aid. In a written report, for example, they could use ChatGPT to add clarifications and/or examples of existing content. They also noted that students could use ChatGPT for brainstorming. For instance, if students were looking for ideas for their research or other projects, they could ask GenAI to offer suggestions. They further indicated that ChatGPT should not provide the primary content for a student's work, but rather that it could serve as a technology-assisted aide. This perspective aligns with UNESCO's (2023) guidelines, which argue that students and teachers can use GenAI technologies as a tool to supplement and assist learning.

Furthermore, students and teachers concurred regarding the importance of disclosing when they use GenAI programs in their work; both groups considered it a fundamental aspect of respecting ethical principles and responsibilities. This agrees with Mhlanga (2023), whose framework also notes that "transparency in the use of ChatGPT" is a primary principle in the ethical and responsible educational application of GenAI. He argued that both students and teachers *must always* be open and clear about their use of the technology whenever and wherever they apply it. For example, if students use ChatGPT to help generate content for an assignment, then they must disclose this assistance to their teachers. Transparency helps build reciprocal trust between students and teachers which, in turn, helps both maintain academic integrity and enhance ethical and responsible practices. In this regard, Luo (2024) argued that integrating GenAI into higher education can impair the trusting relationships between teachers and students. Thurzo et al. (2023) argued that transparency in GenAI use is essential to fostering trust and mitigating the biases inherent in AI algorithms.

5.5.2   *Discussion of the Concerns*

Regarding the second theme, student and teacher perspectives were grouped into three categories. In the first category, *Assessing Academic Work*, most student concerns involved grading, while teachers were focused primarily on the tools used either to assess content generated by GenAI or to detect its use. For example, students worried that using GenAI tools would lead to negative teacher perceptions of their work which would, in turn, affect their grades. Moreover, teachers were more concerned about how they could assess GenAI-created content or, if students did not declare its use, how they could detect it. This result agrees with Chan and Hu's (2023) concern that Chat-GPT poses a risk to the validity of assessment practices, particularly those involving written assignments, and that it highlights a significant threat to academic integrity. While AI detection programs are intended to address this issue, they are neither foolproof nor fully developed. Alafnan et al. (2023) explained that this AI detection deficiency stems from the fact that ChatGPT can effectively paraphrase generated content in a way which anti-plagiarism software struggles to identify. This will lead, as Sok and Heng (2024) noted, to a situation where students who use ChatGPT to complete their classroom assignments are likely to get higher grades than those who do not. To address that issue, Kiryakova and Angelova (2023) argued that there is the need to replace traditional assessment methods with innovative techniques which can appraise student work more fairly.

Both students and teachers were concerned about "how they could ensure academic integrity" while using GenAI technologies. Students and teacher perspectives encompassed four major topics related to academic integrity, namely plagiarism, fairness, information accuracy, and privacy. Teachers clearly demonstrated a broader understanding than students for all topics in this category. For example, regarding plagiarism, students were primarily concerned with the ambiguity surrounding plagiarism when using AI-generated content, even if proper citations were provided. This uncertainty promotes confusion and anxiety about whether paraphrasing AI-generated text and citing it correctly amounts to cheating or plagiarism. Teachers, however, are concerned that students lack sufficient understanding for what actually constitutes academic plagiarism and that simply citing the use of a GenAI tool does not address the core issue of intellectual honesty. Teachers believe that reliance on AI-generated content without a proper understanding for originality and attribution could erode scientific integrity and ethical standards in academia over time. Regarding information accuracy, both students and teachers recognized that the information which GenAI tools provide may be imprecise or even wholly incorrect. While students stressed how inaccurate information may affect the quality of academic work, teachers were concerned that the real danger of poor/misleading information lies in its potential to improperly shape student decision-making, their understanding of complex issues, and/or academic rigor (Holmes & Miao, 2023).

With respect to fairness and privacy concerns, it is clear that teachers have broader and deeper views in comparison to students. For example, while students focused on how GenAI may unfairly benefit the grades of those students who have personal access to the technology, teachers looked beyond that, emphasizing the importance of providing institutional GenAI access equally for all students and teachers. Moreover, teachers discussed how fairness concerns also include the fact that GenAI tools are largely controlled by powerful high-tech companies and wealthy countries, resulting in generated content which primarily serves the interests of these nations, thus creating a significant imbalance with respect to the needs of developing countries, such as Kuwait (Holmes & Miao, 2023; Marwala, 2023). This access inequity raises significant ethical concerns about fairness and inclusivity in educational settings. Unequal access to AI technologies exacerbates educational disparities, potentially widening the gap between privileged and marginalized student groups (Paulus & Langford, 2022; Carvalho et al., 2022).

Regarding privacy and security, while every teacher worried about how GenAI programs could compromise information confidentiality, not one student mentioned this concern. Indeed, there is a lack of student understanding regarding data privacy and security related to GenAI use. Teachers emphasized the importance of raising student awareness for these issues (Holmes & Miao, 2023; Mhlanga, 2023). They stressed that students should not use GenAI programs until after the development of privacy protection techniques, so that the technology does not pose a threat to the inadvertent release of their personal information.

Students and teachers expressed concerns that GenAI tools may "negatively impact learning." Both groups indicated that using GenAI tools may undermine student skills for writing and critical thinking. They cautioned against an over-reliance upon AI technologies. It must be noted that student concerns in this area focused primarily upon the immediate effects which such technologies may have on their ability to write and think. Teachers, however, were more concerned about the long-term negative effects these technologies may hold for student knowledge and skills. Furthermore, teachers expressed their fears regarding how GenAI technology may affect the future quality of education. They also discussed their perceptions about the potential which GenAI technologies may have for replacing in-person instruction, explaining that despite GenAI's affordances, the technology currently lacked the ability to actually replace a human instructor. This perspective confirmed previous studies which argued that GenAI models were unable to generate original insights about the world because they are not grounded in human values or empathy (Ausat et al., 2023; Al Ghazali et al., 2024). Mhlanga (2023) found that the challenge lies in striking an equitable balance between leveraging

GenAI for enhanced educational experiences while preserving the value of human-centered learning environments.

5.5.3   *Discussions of the Needs*

Regarding the third theme, student and teacher discussions centered on two main areas. First, both groups argued that there is a need for enhancing GenAI literacy. They felt that students and teachers must be provided with the essential knowledge and skills to use GenAI technologies ethically. Mhlanga (2023) indicated the importance of educating students and teachers so that they understand how GenAI works, what its limitations are, and how they can handle them. Secondly, both groups also highlighted the need for developing ethical guidelines and policies for GenAI tools in an educational context. For this aspect, students focused mainly on the need for guidelines to help them understand how to use the technology ethically within the existing framework, whereas teachers prioritized the development (and enforcement) of policies to maintain academic standards. Indeed, several studies have indicated that the lack of clear policies and structured frameworks for the application of GenAI in teaching and learning processes remains a significant barrier (Felten et al., 2021). Moreover, the implementation of GenAI declaration policies, as observed in some institutions, serves as a step toward enhancing transparency and accountability in AI-mediated educational assessments (Luo, 2024).

5.6   Conclusion

5.6.1   *Contributions of the Study*

While numerous studies have investigated either student perspectives or teacher perspectives regarding the ethical use of GenAI (Chan & Hu, 2023; Farhi et al., 2023; Firat, 2023; Mutammimah et al., 2024; Parker et al., 2023), few studies, so far, have explored the *differences* between them. This study attempts to address this gap in the literature by comparing student and teacher perspectives regarding the ethical and responsible use of GenAI in higher education. This effort has provided valuable insights into how these groups understand the ethical and responsible use of GenAI, the concerns they have, and their needs. As such, it offers a unique contribution to the field.

Furthermore, this study breaks new ground for higher education in Kuwait. Kuwait University is now working on developing guidelines to ensure that GenAI can be used ethically and responsibly within the institution. The findings presented in this chapter could help develop the ethical guidance for doing so.

This study also contributes to the body of knowledge regarding the methodology of comparative research, serving as a model for using the comparative analysis approach to identify the gap between student and teacher understandings. Instead of simply using qualitative analysis to investigate either student or teacher perspectives independently, this study went further by comparing the perspectives of these two groups with each other. This study, therefore, serves as an example for future educational research in how to use the comparative approach for investigating the gap between student and teacher understandings regarding other issues.

5.6.2   Practical Implications

The study's practical implications center on two major points, the first being the need to develop a framework for clarifying the policies and guidelines for the ethical and responsible use of GenAI at Kuwait University. This technology is newly emerging and changing rapidly, which has placed considerable stress on academic institutions to adapt to it worldwide, not just Kuwait University. The university has put a lot of effort into addressing such challenges this year and is working to develop GenAI guidelines which encourage the use of these tools while firmly ensuring that academic integrity is preserved. This framework for guiding the ethical use of GenAI could build upon what UNESCO developed and published in 2023, while tailoring it for the cultural context of Kuwait. The second point is the need to improve the AI literacy of both students and teachers at Kuwait University. This could be achieved if the university offered workshops, short training courses, and lectures to provide both groups with the essential knowledge and skills for the ethical use of GenAI. In these courses, students should learn both how GenAI works and what the expected practices are for ensuring the ethical and responsible use of such technologies. Moreover, teachers must learn about the best practices for assessing students who use GenAI in their classwork along with how they can teach students to use these technologies ethically. Kuwait University must also consider the rapidly changing nature of GenAI; AI literacy standards will need regular revisions to ensure that students and teachers are well prepared to use such technologies appropriately.

5.6.3   Limitations of the Study and Future Directions

We recognize that a possible limitation to the current study is that it focuses mainly on student and teacher *perspectives* regarding the ethical and responsible use of GenAI; it does not explore their actual experiences and practices in that realm. The latter aspect may merit further investigation to offer a more comprehensive understanding of the ethical practices in the use of GenAI. Another limitation to this study is that its participants came only from colleges in the humanities and social sciences, which may not adequately represent the variety of perspectives across the university as a whole. This disciplinary focus may therefore limit the generalizability of the results in colleges where GenAI might be used differently. Future research may consider including a more diverse sample of teachers and students to create a broader understanding for how students and teachers understand the ethical and responsible use of GenAI university-wide. Furthermore, GenAI technologies have experienced rapid and significant improvements over the last few years, a growth cycle which continues at an ever more rapid rate. As a result, student and teacher understandings regarding the ethical and responsible use of GenAI are expected to change year after year. Future research may implement long-term, follow-up investigations, such as a longitudinal study, to observe and investigate the evolution of how students and teachers use and understand GenAI over time.

5.7   Conflict of Interest Declaration

None.

5.8   Funding

The authors received no financial support for the research, authorship, or publication of this article.

References

Al Ghazali, S., Zaki, N., Ali, L., & Harous, S. (2024). Exploring the potential of ChatGPT as a substitute teacher: A case study. *International Journal of Information and Education Technology*, 14(2), 271–278.

AlAfnan, M. A., Dishari, S., Jovic, M., & Lomidze, K. (2023). Chatgpt as an educational tool: Opportunities, challenges, and recommendations for communication, business writing, and composition courses. *Journal of Artificial Intelligence and Technology*, 3(2), 60–68.

Alkandari, B. (2015). *An investigation of the factors affecting students' acceptance and intention to use e-learning systems at Kuwait university: Developing a technology acceptance model in e-learning environments* (Doctoral dissertation, Cardiff Metropolitan University).

Altaher, R., & Atteih, R. (2012). *Quality of e-learning contemporary vision*. Dar Algamaa Al Gadida: Alexandria.

Arab Times. (2024). https://www.arabtimesonline.com/news/kuwait-university-council-to-discuss-adoption-of-ai-policy/.

Ausat, A. M. A., Massang, B., Efendi, M., Nofirman, N., & Riady, Y. (2023). Can chat GPT replace the role of the teacher in the classroom: A fundamental analysis. *Journal on Education*, 5(4), 16100–16106.

Baidoo-Anu, D., & Ansah, L. O. (2023). Education in the era of generative artificial intelligence (AI): Understanding the potential benefits of ChatGPT in promoting teaching and learning. *Journal of AI*, 7(1), 52–62.

Bearman, M., Ryan, J., & Ajjawi, R. (2023). Discourses of artificial intelligence in higher education: A critical literature review. *Higher Education*, 86, 369–385. https://doi.org/10.1007/s10734-022-00937-2.

Carvalho, L., Martinez-Maldonado, R., Tsai, Y. S., Markauskaite, L., & De Laat, M. (2022). How can we design for learning in an AI world? *Computers and Education: Artificial Intelligence*, 3, 100053.

Chaaban, Y., Qadhi, S., Chen, J., & Du, X. (2024). Understanding researchers' AI readiness in a higher education context: Q methodology research. *Education Sciences*, 14(7), 709.

Chan, C. K. Y., & Hu, W. (2023). Students' voices on generative AI: Perceptions, benefits, and challenges in higher education. *International Journal of Educational Technology in Higher Education*, 20(1), 43.

Chen, Y., Jensen, S., Albert, L. J., Gupta, S., & Lee, T. (2023). Artificial intelligence (AI) student assistants in the classroom: Designing chatbots to support student success. *Information Systems Frontiers*, 25(1), 161–182.

Corbin, J., & Strauss, A. (2008). *The basics of qualitative research* (3rd ed.). Los Angeles, CA: Sage.

Cresswell, J. (2013). *Qualitative inquiry & research design: Choosing among five approaches*. SAGE Publications, 2007.

Evans, R., & Sinha, N. (2024, May). Bridging the gap: Diversity initiatives in AI education. *Proceedings of the AAAI Symposium Series*, 3(1), 474–477.

Farhi, F., Jeljeli, R., Aburezeq, I., Dweikat, F. F., Al-shami, S. A., & Slamene, R. (2023). Analyzing the students' views, concerns, and perceived ethics about chat GPT usage. *Computers and Education: Artificial Intelligence*, 100180.

Farrelly, T., & Baker, N. (2023). Generative artificial intelligence: Implications and considerations for higher education practice. *Education Sciences*, 13(11), 1109.

Felten, E., Raj, M., & Seamans, R. (2021). Occupational, industry, and geographic exposure to artificial intelligence: A novel dataset and its potential uses. *Strategic Management Journal*, 42(12), 2195–2217.

Firat, M. (2023). What ChatGPT means for universities: Perceptions of scholars and students. *Journal of Applied Learning and Teaching*, 6(1), 57–63.

Gillani, S. I. A., & Haider, A. (2023). Impact of digitalization and artificial intelligence on local tourism industry. *Journal of World Research*, 3(2), 43–48.

Hendal, B. A., & Alkhezzi, F. A. (2022). Kuwait university students' evaluation of the e-learning experience during the coronavirus pandemic. *Journal of the Gulf & Arabian Peninsula Studies*, 48(185).

Holmes, W., & Miao, F. (2023). *Guidance for generative AI in education and research*. UNESCO Publishing.

Intahchomphoo, C., & Gundersen, O. E. (2020). *Artificial intelligence and race: A systematic review*. Legal Informa.

Jarrah, A. M., Wardat, Y., & Fidalgo, P. (2023). Using ChatGPT in academic writing is (not) a form of plagiarism: What does the literature say. *Online Journal of Communication and Media Technologies*, 13(4), e202346.

Kiryakova, G., & Angelova, N. (2023). ChatGPT – a challenging tool for the university professors in their teaching practice. *Education Sciences*, 13(10), 1056.

Kuwait University. (2024). http://kuweb.ku.edu.kw/ku/index.htm.

Lee, D., Arnold, M., Srivastava, A., Plastow, K., Strelan, P., Ploeckl, F., . . . Palmer, E. (2024). The impact of generative AI on higher education learning and teaching: A study of educators' perspectives. *Computers and Education: Artificial Intelligence*, 6, 100221.

Lee, I., & Perret, B. (2022, June). Preparing high school teachers to integrate AI methods into STEM classrooms. *Proceedings of the AAAI Conference on Artificial Intelligence*, 36(11), 12783–12791.

Luo, J. (2024). How does GenAI affect trust in teacher-student relationships? Insights from students' assessment experiences. *Teaching in Higher Education*, 1–16.

Mannuru, N. R., Shahriar, S., Teel, Z. A., Wang, T., Lund, B. D., Tijani, S., . . . Vaidya, P. (2023). Artificial intelligence in developing countries: The impact of generative artificial intelligence (AI) technologies for development. *Information Development*. https://doi.org/10.1177/02666669231200628.

Marwala, T. (2023). *Artificial intelligence, game theory and mechanism design in politics*. Springer Nature.

McDonald, N., Johri, A., Ali, A., & Hingle, A. (2024). *Generative artificial intelligence in higher education: Evidence from an analysis of institutional policies and guidelines*. arXiv:2402.01659.

Merriam, S. B. (2015). Qualitative research: Designing, implementing, and publishing a study. In *Handbook of research on scholarly publishing and research methods* (pp. 125–140). IGI Global.

Mhlanga, D. (2023). Open AI in education, the responsible and ethical use of Chat-GPT towards lifelong learning. In *FinTech and artificial intelligence for sustainable development: The role of smart technologies in achieving development goals* (pp. 387–409). Cham: Springer Nature Switzerland.

Michel-Villarreal, R., Vilalta-Perdomo, E., Salinas-Navarro, D. E., Thierry-Aguilera, R., & Gerardou, F. S. (2023). Challenges and opportunities of generative AI for higher education as explained by ChatGPT. *Education Sciences*, 13(9), 856.

Miles, M. B., Huberman, A. M., & Saldaña, J. (2014). *Qualitative data analysis: A methods sourcebook* (3rd ed.). London, UK: SAGE.

Mutammimah, H., Rejeki, S., Kustini, S., & Amelia, R. (2024). Understanding teachers' perspective toward ChatGPT acceptance in English language teaching. *International Journal of Technology in Education*, 7(2), 290–307.

Myskja, B. K. (2023). Technology and trust–a Kantian approach. In *Technology ethics* (pp. 122–129). Routledge.

Nguyen, A., Ngo, H. N., Hong, Y., Dang, B., & Nguyen, B. P. T. (2023). Ethical principles for artificial intelligence in education. *Education and Information Technologies*, 28(4), 4221–4241.

Parker, L., Carter, C., Karakas, A., Loper, A., & Sokkar, A. (2023). Ethics and improvement: Undergraduate students' use of artificial intelligence in academic endeavors. *International Journal of Intelligent Computing Research (IJICR)*, 13(2).

Paulus, M. J., & Langford, M. D. (Eds.). (2022). *AI, faith, and the future: An interdisciplinary approach*. Wipf and Stock Publishers.

Qadhi, S. M., Alduais, A., Chaaban, Y., & Khraisheh, M. (2024). Generative AI, research ethics, and higher education research: Insights from a scientometric analysis. *Information*, 15(6), 325.

Sok, S., & Heng, K. (2024). *Opportunities, chassllenges, and strategies for using ChatGPT in higher education: A literature review*. Journal of Digital Educational Technology, 4(1), ep2401. https://doi.org/10.30935/jdet/14027.

Su, J., & Yang, W. (2023). Unlocking the power of ChatGPT: A framework for applying generative AI in education. *ECNU Review of Education*. https://doi.org/10.1177/20965311231168423.

Summers, A., El Haddad, M., Prichard, R., Clark, K. A., Lee, J., & Oprescu, F. (2024). Navigating challenges and opportunities: Nursing student's views on generative AI in higher education. *Nurse Education in Practice*, 104062.

Thurzo, A., Strunga, M., Urban, R., Surovková, J., & Afrashtehfar, K. I. (2023). Impact of artificial intelligence on dental education: A review and guide for curriculum update. *Education Sciences*, 13(2), 150.

Varsha, P. S. (2023). How can we manage biases in artificial intelligence systems–a systematic literature review. *International Journal of Information Management Data Insights*, 3(1), 100165.

Wang, S., Sun, Z., & Chen, Y. (2023). Effects of higher education institutes' artificial intelligence capability on students' self-efficacy, creativity and learning performance. *Education and Information Technologies*, 28(5), 4919–4939. https://doi.org/10.1007/s10639-022-11338-4.

Wardat, Y., Tashtoush, M., AlAli, R., & Saleh, S. (2024). Artificial intelligence in education: Mathematics teachers' perspectives, practices and challenges. *Iraqi Journal for Computer Science and Mathematics*, 5(1), 60–77.

Williams, R. T. (2024, January). The ethical implications of using generative chatbots in higher education. In *Frontiers in education* (Vol. 8, p. 1331607). Frontiers Media SA.

Yin, R. K. (2009). *Case study research: Design and methods* (4th ed.). Thousand Oaks, CA: SAGE Publications.

Yusuf, A., Pervin, N., & Román-González, M. (2024). Generative AI and the future of higher education: A threat to academic integrity or reformation? Evidence from multicultural perspectives. *International Journal of Educational Technology in Higher Education*, 21(1), 21.

6

REVOLUTIONIZING PERSONALIZED LEARNING

Exploring the Role of Artificial Intelligence in Enhancing Education

T. K. Jijeesh and Smita Sail

6.1   Introduction to Personalized Education and AI

Today's colleges and universities face a wide range of challenges, including disengaged students, high dropout rates, and the ineffectiveness of a traditional "one-size-fits-all" approach to education. But when big data analytics and artificial intelligence (AI) are used correctly, personalized learning experiences can be created, which may in turn help resolve some of these challenges (Rouhiainen, 2019).

Personalized learning guarantees that every learner gets a tailored educational experience that is precisely crafted following their talents and requirements. Implementing this method has the potential to enhance student motivation and decrease the likelihood of students dropping out. Moreover, it furnishes educators with a greater understanding of individual learning processes, hence augmenting their ability to instruct effectively.

AI-driven educational systems have the potential to furnish teachers with crucial insights into pupils' learning preferences, aptitudes, and accomplishments. This information equips educators possess the capacity to customize teaching methodologies to meet the specific needs of students. For example, students who struggle with learning may get extra support or tutoring, while those who are advancing quickly could benefit from an introduction to new study materials or projects. Solutions based on AI address diverse requirements, empowering students to optimize their capabilities and reducing dropout rates by identifying and fixing issues in their early phases. Nevertheless, the efficacy of these systems relies on the availability of ample data for training. The ethical concerns regarding the use of this data, as discussed

DOI: 10.1201/9781003422433-6

in later sections of this article, are quite significant, and it is crucial to educate students about how their data may be utilized by AI algorithms.

AI has revolutionized personalized learning by personalizing educational experiences to fulfil the unique needs, preferences, and learning styles of individual learners. AI systems can use complex algorithms and data analysis to track students' progress, determine their strengths and weaknesses, and adjust educational materials appropriately. This personalized strategy improves student engagement, motivation, and academic performance. In addition, AI empowers educators to improve their understanding of students' learning processes, hence easing the implementation of more impactful teaching strategies. AI can significantly revolutionize education by offering tailored learning experiences that maximize achievement for learners.

A study result of the effectiveness of AI in personalized education from Ronilo Berondo's article (Berondo, 2023) is briefly described below:

> The study sought to uncover crucial determinants that determine the efficacy of artificial intelligence in personalised learning, analyse its effects on student learning outcomes and engagement, and evaluate its viability in diverse educational environments. The study comprised a group of 100 students with varied educational backgrounds and levels. The participants were chosen using a random selection method. Data was collected through surveys, interviews, and observations. Additionally, a pre-test and post-test were administered to evaluate the influence of individualised learning via Artificial Intelligence on student academic achievement. The findings indicated that AI has multiple applications in personalised learning and was observed to be more efficacious in enhancing student learning outcomes compared to conventional teaching approaches.

Table 6.1 shows the mean scores for the pre-test and post-test. The mean score for the pre-test was 65.2%, indicating that students had a moderate level of understanding of the concepts being tested before the intervention. After the intervention, the mean score for the post-test increased to 87.5%, indicating a significant improvement in student learning outcomes. It also shows the standard deviation for the pre-test and post-test scores. The standard deviation for the pre-test was 8.2%, indicating that the scores were moderately dispersed around the mean. The standard deviation for the post-test was 5.4%, indicating that the scores were more tightly clustered around the mean. This suggests that the intervention was effective in improving student performance, as there was less variation in the post-test scores.

The results suggest that personalized learning using AI can have a significant positive impact on student learning outcomes. The findings also

TABLE 6.1 Mean Scores for the Pre-Test and Post-Test

Test	Pre-Test Mean	Post-Test SD	Post-Test Mean	Post-Test SD
Maths	60.5	8.2	75.3	7.1
Science	68.2	6.9	80.7	5.8
Language Arts	75.6	4.5	86.9	3.6

TABLE 6.2 Impact of AI on Student Outcomes

	Control Group	AI Group	p-Value
Mean score Test 1	80	85	0.3
Mean score Test 2	75	87	0.001
Mean score Test 3	82	89	0.02
Engagement rate	70%	80%	0.05

highlight the potential of AI to enhance personalized learning and improve student engagement and motivation in the learning process.

Proponents of AI-based systems argue that these technologies can provide personalized learning experiences that adapt to the unique needs and preferences of individual students, leading to improved academic performance and engagement (Koedinger and Corbett, 2006). For instance, AI-based systems can analyze students' learning patterns and provide customized feedback, enabling them to progress at their own pace and address the areas of weakness (Zawacki-Richter et al., 2019).

Anuyahong and co-writers in their article (Anuyahong et al., 2023) show the student outcomes in various fields when using AI in their education process. The survey results are shown in Table 6.2.

Notes: Control Group: A group that did not use AI-based systems.
AI Group: A group that used AI-based systems.

Table 6.2 presents the results of a study that aimed to determine the impact of AI on student outcomes. Two groups were formed for this study: a control group and an AI group. The table shows the mean scores on three different tests and the engagement rate for each group and the p-value of the statistical analysis. The p-value measures the level of significance of the differences between the groups. A lower p-value suggests that the differences between the groups are less likely due to chance. These findings from this chart clearly suggest that the use of AI-based systems has a positive impact on student outcomes, as indicated by the higher test scores and engagement rates in the AI group compared to the control group.

6.2 Theoretical Framework of the Study

The present study integrates several theoretical frameworks, including cognitive psychology, machine learning algorithms, adaptive learning systems, and constructivist theory. These theories are applied to investigate how AI can transform personalized education by enhancing student learning experiences and outcomes.

The following is a discussion of the applications of the theories applied in this study, including cognitive psychology, machine learning algorithms, and adaptive learning systems. The basic tenets of these theories and how they can make a theoretical framework of this theory are given below. They discuss what would be the outcomes when applying those tenets to personalized learning of students.

- **Cognitive Psychology**

Cognitive psychology, which focuses on the research and analysis of mental processes such as perception, memory, and problem-solving, is applied in this study to examine how individuals acquire, process, and retain knowledge. Integrating cognitive psychology in education as a theoretical framework for this study can provide valuable insights into how AI can be used to enhance the learning process by understanding how students think, learn, and remember information. Understanding these cognitive processes is crucial for designing effective individualized learning experiences that align with students' cognitive abilities and preferred learning styles.

The information processing in cognitive psychology views the mind as a complex system that processes information through various stages, including encoding, storage, and retrieval. AI can aid in the creation of adaptive learning systems that display information in a way that is aligned with the cognitive processes and memory storage of the human brain. This can involve utilizing AI to detect instances where a learner is encountering difficulties in the process of encoding new information and consequently offering specific interventions to aid in the consolidation of memory.

Cognitive psychology focuses a great deal on the crucial role of motivation and engagement in the process of learning. The use of AI helps improve student motivation by generating customized learning experiences that are captivating and applicable to individual interests and aspirations. AI can enhance student engagement and motivation to study through gaming, adaptive learning directions, and instant feedback.

Metacognition, in the context of cognitive psychology, refers to the conscious recognition and comprehension of one's own mental processes. Within the realm of education, metacognition refers to the capacity of students to introspect, manage, and govern their own learning strategies and processes. Metacognitive methods encompass the ability to recognize and control one's own learning processes. AI can contribute to the development of metacognitive skills by offering immediate feedback and data analysis on a student's educational advancement. By engaging in this practice, students can enhance their self-monitoring and self-regulation skills, so strengthening their ability to be more efficient and self-sufficient learners.

The cognitive school views (1) learning as an active process "involving the acquisition or reorganization of the cognitive structures through which humans process and store information" and (2) the learner as an active participant in the process of knowledge acquisition and integration (Good and Brophy, 1990, 187). This theory describes knowledge acquisition as a mental activity involving internal coding and structuring by the learner (Derry, 1996; Spiro et al., 1992) and suggests that learning happens best under conditions that are aligned with human cognitive architecture (Sobel, 2001). Cognitive psychologists place more emphasis on what learners know and how they come to acquire it than on what they do. For this reason, the cognitive approach focuses on making knowledge meaningful and helping learners organize and relate new information to prior knowledge in memory. Instruction should be based on a student's existing mental structures or schema to be effective (Ertmer and Newby, 1993).

Overall, integrating cognitive psychology theories into this study can provide a good theoretical framework to understand how AI can enhance personalized learning and improve educational outcomes.

- **Machine Learning Algorithms**

Machine learning, a field of AI, focuses on creating algorithms that learn from data and make predictions. In this study, cognitive psychology principles are applied alongside machine learning algorithms to examine extensive quantities of educational data, including students' performance metrics, learning preferences, and behavioral tendencies. By incorporating cognitive psychology, the study aims to understand how students process and retain information, informing the development of these algorithms. Algorithms such as decision trees, neural networks, and clustering algorithms are employed to detect significant patterns and connections in the data. The integration of cognitive psychology and machine learning techniques seeks to develop adaptive learning systems that customize educational content and interventions in real time, addressing the specific needs of individual students.

Machine learning focuses on creating algorithms that learn from data and make predictions. Anjali Jagwani (Jagwani and Aloysius, 2019):

> Machine Learning is a core sub-area of AI which promotes the reality just to be able to give machines access to data for more ease in human work

and just to learn them for themselves. Learning is a key hallmark of AI. The machines can take real-time data and feedback and improve performance over time and involved the development of self-learning algorithms to gain knowledge from that data to make predictions.

- **Adaptive Systems for Learning**

Adaptive learning systems use advanced algorithms and data-driven technology to tailor the learning experience for individual students. By continuously analyzing a learner's performance and interaction patterns, these systems adjust instructional content, pacing, and feedback in real time to align with each student's unique strengths, weaknesses, and learning preferences. This personalized approach ensures that students receive the most relevant and effective educational interventions, allowing them to progress at their own pace and engage with materials that are optimally challenging and supportive.

The study applies cognitive psychology to understand how these adaptations affect learning processes and outcomes. It explores the philosophical foundations of adaptive learning, utilizing theories from educational psychology and instructional design. Cognitive psychology offers valuable insights into how adaptive systems might customize instructional content to suit individual cognitive demands by studying how learners perceive, process, and retain information. These systems utilize cognitive principles, such as memory recall, problem-solving, and metacognition, to adapt educational materials, pacing, and feedback in response to real-time data on the learner's progress. Adaptive learning systems can promote learner engagement, boost knowledge retention, and enhance academic achievement by tailoring educational experiences to match the individual cognitive processes of each student. This technique guarantees that educational activities are not just customized but also in harmony with the brain's innate learning processes, leading to more efficient and significant learning outcomes. Influential models such as Bloom's taxonomy, which classifies learning objectives into cognitive domains, and Keller's ARCS model of motivation, which enhances learner engagement, guide the design and implementation of adaptive learning systems. Bloom's Taxonomy is a logically sequenced structure depicting the cognitive skills required for students to grasp knowledge comprehensively and meaningfully. The integration of Bloom's Taxonomy into education promotes mastering the cognitive skills and analytical ability of learners (Nurmatova and Altun, 2023).

Adaptive learning systems leverage AI algorithms to assess students' strengths and weaknesses continually. By analyzing data from student interactions, such as quiz results, time spent on tasks, and learning progress, these systems adapt the learning content and pace to suit each student's needs. Adaptive learning platforms like Knewton and DreamBox Learning provide personalized learning paths, ensuring that students receive targeted instruction aligned with their abilities.

All adaptive learning systems include a fundamental architecture known as a "closed loop" that collects data from the learner and utilizes them to evaluate progress, suggest learning activities, and deliver customized feedback (Wang et al., 2020).

- **Constructivist Learning Theory**

The constructivist learning theory states that learners are involved in the active construction of their own comprehension and knowledge of the world by means of experiences and later reflection on those experiences. Lev Vygotsky, a Russian psychologist, made a substantial contribution to constructivist theory by highlighting the social environment in which learning takes place and introducing the concept of the zone of proximal development (ZPD). The ZPD refers to the difference between what a learner can accomplish on their own and what they can achieve with guidance and support.

By applying constructivist theory in this study, active learning and engagement of the students can be improved. AI can be used to create interactive simulations and virtual labs where students can experiment, make decisions, and observe outcomes in a risk-free environment. This can help them actively construct knowledge through hands-on experiences. Additionally, by developing AI-driven platforms that present interactive content, such as multimedia presentations, interactive videos, and gamified learning modules, students can actively involve in the learning process.

In the constructivist learning theory, scaffolding refers to the assistance and advice offered by a teacher, a peer, or an educational tool to aid a learner in accomplishing a task that they may not be able to accomplish on their own. AI systems that offer personalized support and guidance to meet the unique requirements of every student need to be developed. These systems can provide suggestions, cues, and supplementary materials to assist students in advancing through learning assignments at their individualized speed. These tools are beneficial due to their customized approach to schooling.

One of the basic tenets of constructivist theory is problem solving through which students "construct knowledge." AI can be used to create learning activities that are based on real-world problems and scenarios. This can help students see the relevance of what they are learning and apply their knowledge in practical contexts. Here, students themselves create knowledge with the help of AI.

6.3 AI Tools and Technologies for Personalized Education

The rapidly evolving landscape of education is increasingly intertwining with advanced technological innovations. Among these, AI has emerged as a driving force for personalizing the learning experience, bringing about a paradigm shift in conventional instructional methods (Jian, 2023). At its core, personalized learning refers to tailoring educational experiences to accommodate individual learners' unique needs, learning styles, and pace (Pane et al., 2017).

The descriptions of some of such tools are as follows:

- **Intelligent Tutoring Systems (ITS)**

Intelligent tutoring systems replicate individualized tutoring sessions by employing AI methods such as natural language processing (NLP) and machine learning. An ITS system customizes educational activities and strategies based on students' characteristics and needs (Mousavinasab et al., 2018). These systems offer individualized assistance, feedback, and explanations that are customized to match the skill level and learning rate of each student. Platforms such as Carnegie Learning's Mika and Duolingo utilize Intelligent Tutoring Systems (ITS) to provide personalized language learning experiences. These systems alter the lessons according to the learners' level of proficiency and performance.

- **Recommender Systems**

In the realm of personalized education, a recommender system is an AI-powered tool that offers individualized suggestions for learning resources, activities, and pathways depending on the unique requirements, preferences, and learning styles of students. These systems utilize data analytics and machine learning algorithms to offer personalized educational experiences.

In reality, it is observed that some students in fact find a guided, structured way of teaching helpful while others benefit from the opportunity for self-motivated exploration and discovery (Tang et al., 2020). Because of this, it is becoming increasingly important to evaluate the requirements of a specific student or a group of students and to construct a collaborative structure in which the primary focus will be on the educational needs of a student.

Recommender systems utilize user data, including previous actions and preferences, to suggest suitable learning resources, courses, or activities. Personalized education systems assist students in identifying content that is in line with their individual interests and learning objectives. Platforms such as Coursera and Khan Academy employ recommender algorithms to propose courses, videos, and activities based on participants' past interactions and preferences.

- **Natural Language Processing**

The natural language process is an effective process to assist students in the process of scientific learning. Implementing NLP in the educational setting not only helps in developing effective language processes but is also significant in enhancing academic performance. The NLP techniques follow the approach of the natural process of language acquisition integrated with the scientific approach of using computer programs (Khaled, 2014).

NLP enables AI systems to understand and generate human language, facilitating personalized interactions in education. Chatbots and virtual assistants powered by NLP can engage with students in natural language conversations, answering questions, providing feedback, and offering assistance in real time. Examples include IBM's Watson Assistant for Education and Squirrel AI, which employ NLP to deliver personalized learning experiences through dialogue-based interactions.

- **Gamification and Adaptive Game-Based Learning**

Gamification is the application of game design elements and principles in non-game contexts to engage and motivate learners. The integration of gamification characteristics with AI-powered adaptivity results in engaging learning experiences that are customized to suit the needs of each learner. Adaptive game-based learning (AGBL) combines the motivational aspects of gamification with personalized learning experiences. AGBL utilizes AI to adapt the content and difficulty of educational games based on the individual learner's progress, preferences, and needs. Adaptive game-based learning platforms utilize AI algorithms to modify game mechanics, obstacles, and content difficulty according to learners' performance and preferences. Smart Sparrow and Legends of Learning utilize gamification to offer personalized learning experiences that inspire and captivate students.

- **Data Analytics and Learning Analytics**

Data analytics approaches are used to evaluate large quantities of educational data to extract insights about students' learning behaviors, preferences, and outcomes. Learning analytics solutions utilize AI to monitor student progress, identify areas of learning deficiencies, and forecast future academic achievement. By using data-driven insights, educators can tailor curriculum, interventions, and support measures to better address the individual needs of children.

- **Emotional AI and Student Well-being**

Emotional AI refers to AI systems designed to comprehend and react to human emotions. Emotional AI has the potential to significantly improve student well-being and learning experiences within the realm of individualized education. Emotional AI utilizes complex algorithms and data analysis to monitor the emotional state of students and provide them with emotional assistance. Emotional AI utilizes facial recognition, audio analysis, and physiological sensors to accurately identify and monitor the emotional states of students in real time. Emotional AI enhances a pleasant and inclusive learning environment by creating a supportive and responsive educational setting, where students feel valued and understood.

> AI's ability to analyse complex emotional behaviour patterns through data collected during the learning process enables a deeper understanding of each student's needs. By employing advanced algorithms, AI can detect signs of frustration, boredom, or enthusiasm, allowing educators to tailor their teaching methods more effectively. Additionally, AI can provide instant, personalized feedback based on emotional analysis, thereby creating a learning environment that is more attuned to students' emotional well-being.
>
> *(Vistorte et al., 2024)*

6.4   Implementation Challenges and Ethical Considerations

Despite the numerous potential advantages of implementing AI in education, its utilization remains limited mostly due to a lack of comprehension among educators and policymakers. Some people may lack enough expertise with this technology to confidently incorporate it into their lessons. In addition, the use of dependable training algorithms necessitates the availability of top-notch data, which frequently suffers from incompleteness or inconsistency across various systems. This is a major obstacle to the general use of AI solutions in educational environments. The potential applications of AI in education are vast, but certain obstacles must be overcome before it can be widely used.

One of the most complex issues faced by AI in education is safeguarding student privacy and data security. With the increased use of AI technologies in classrooms, a large quantity of sensitive information such as grades, attendance records, and behavioral patterns is being generated, making it essential to put into place suitable policies and protocols for protecting these data (Zeide, 2019; Pardo and Siemens, 2014).

There is also potential for bias within AI algorithms. These systems will only be unbiased if they are trained on impartial datasets; so, when biased training data is used instead, any resulting outcomes from these systems can be prejudiced (Citron and Pasquale, 2014). Moreover, further complexities arise with regard to digital inequalities that may occur due to the implementation of AI in educational sectors. If certain schools or students lack access to the appropriate technology or infrastructure required for utilizing AI solutions, then they may suffer disadvantageous effects compared to those who have such resources available (Grau-Valldosera and Minguillon, 2014).

Implementing AI technologies in education faces the formidable challenge of cost, encompassing significant initial investments in software, hardware, infrastructure development, and specialized training for educators. Cost remains an important factor when considering how best to integrate AI into educational settings. Although technology investments can be costly up-front, they can also yield long-term benefits by providing more efficient instruction methods (Bates, 2019). Ongoing expenses include maintenance, data management, and scaling up implementation across multiple departments or campuses. Despite the financial barriers, addressing these costs is essential for realizing the potential benefits of AI in education, including improved learning outcomes and operational efficiency. Collaborative efforts between governments, educational institutions, and technology providers are necessary to overcome these challenges and make AI-driven education accessible and sustainable for all stakeholders.

Here are some implementation strategies to overcome challenges:

- **Teacher Training and Support**

The integration of digital technologies and AI into education stands as a pivotal trend within the contemporary educational landscape. Consequently, there arises a compelling need to investigate the effectiveness and potential applications of these technologies in the preparation of pedagogical professionals (Wu et al., 2023). Integrating AI into classrooms requires educators to develop new skills and adapt their teaching methods. Providing comprehensive training and ongoing support for teachers is essential to maximize the potential of AI technology and ensure its successful implementation.

- **Access and Equity**

One of the most significant issues is making sure that all students, regardless of their socioeconomic status or geographic location, have access to the various tools and technology that are associated with AI. There is a possibility that the digital divide may deepen and that educational disparities will become even more apparent if sufficient access is not provided. Afzal et al. (2023) in their article observed that the digital divide poses a significant challenge in education, creating disparities in access to and use of technology among students. The implications of this divide are far-reaching, as it affects students' ability to engage with digital resources and participate in online learning platforms.

The authors present the study results on the digital divide based on internet technology across various demographic groups. This study was conducted using data collected from 400 participants some years back. The digital divide is still presenting the modern period. The data are provided in various tables, two of which (Tables 6.3 and 6.4) are shown below.

TABLE 6.3 Barriers to Technology Access

Barriers	Percentage of Students Affected
Lack of Internet at Home	40
Limited Computer Skills	25
High Cost of Devices	20
Limited Internet Speed	15

TABLE 6.4 Internet Access by Income Level

Income Level	Percentage of Individuals with Internet Access
Low Income	65
Middle Income	80
High Income	95

It is obvious that the income level of a person, the location where a person resides, and various other technical issues affect the accessibility of technology for students.

- **Customization and Personalization**

AI can personalize learning experiences for students based on their specific needs and preferences; but to achieve significant customization, complex algorithms and accurate assessment of student progress are needed. There is a substantial problem associated with striking a balance between the advantages of customization and concerns regarding the accuracy of data and algorithmic bias.

- **Infrastructure and Resource Constraints**

Putting AI technology into practice frequently necessitates making substantial investments in infrastructure, which may include hardware, software, and network capabilities. There is a possibility that educational institutions with few resources will have difficulty affording the initial expenditures of implementing AI and the continuous maintenance costs, which will impede wider adoption.

- **Data Privacy and Security**

AI systems typically require substantial amounts of data to operate efficiently. Nevertheless, the collection, storage, and analysis of student data give rise to significant concerns regarding privacy and security. Educational institutions must prioritize the execution of strong data protection measures to ensure the security of sensitive information. The incident of Gnostic Players stealing 932 million user records from 44 companies in China (Wang et al., 2020) does prove the presence of a potential threat while operating an AI-powered system.

- **Ethical Considerations**

In an era where AI pervades our daily lives, the ethical oversight of AI technology becomes paramount. AI systems, capable of amplifying biases and privacy concerns, introduce complex ethical challenges (Li, 2023). AI systems can inadvertently perpetuate biases present in the data they're trained on, leading to unfair outcomes or reinforcing existing stereotypes. Addressing ethical concerns and ensuring transparency and accountability in AI algorithms is crucial to building trust in educational applications.

First and foremost, AI systems integrated into extensive datasets have the potential to strengthen societal biases, resulting in unjust outcomes in critical domains such as employment, lending, and the criminal justice system. In addition, AI systems frequently function in an opaque manner, especially in crucial industries like healthcare and autonomous vehicles, which offer challenges in terms of transparency and interpretability. In addition, the issue of ownership becomes a concern when it comes to creating digital art using AI, particularly if it is generated using AI systems developed by others. Persistent issues such as the spread of false information and manipulation on social media continue to be a concern, as AI algorithms have the ability to worsen social divisions and interfere with elections. The rapid advancement of AI technology has sparked growing concerns regarding personal privacy, security, and surveillance. It is crucial to establish strong safeguards to address these problems. In addition, the rise of AI automation poses a significant risk of job displacement, while the development of AI-powered autonomous weapons has sparked ethical concerns. This has led to a growing demand for international regulations and agreements to address these issues.

6.5   Future Directions and Recommendations

The future of education is significantly impacted by the present acceleration of technological advancements, particularly in the area of AI and its widespread application in education. Most people think AI can drastically change. The future prospects of AI in the education sector are promising. In the future, AI will become a huge part of our daily life. The impact of AI in the field of education will be more massive (Sharma et al., 2021). In the future, another game-changing aspect of AI in education is the implementation of intelligent tutoring systems. These systems use AI to provide personalized instruction and feedback to students, identifying knowledge gaps and offering targeted support to help them achieve their learning goals. For example, platforms like MATHia by Carnegie Learning use AI to analyze student performance and provide customized hints, feedback, and explanations for each need (Boser, 2021).

When considering the future of education, it is important to take into account the impact of AI and personalized learning. From this perspective, several significant directions and recommendations come to light. Firstly, it is important to emphasize the significance of ongoing research and development to improve AI algorithms. This will help ensure that they can effectively adapt to a wide range of learning styles and preferences. In addition, promoting collaboration among educators, technologists, and policymakers can result in the development of ethical guidelines and standards to guide the use of AI in education. Ensuring equitable access to AI-powered educational tools requires prioritizing investment in infrastructure, such as high-speed internet access and device availability. In addition, it is important to focus on seamlessly integrating AI into current educational frameworks, enhancing traditional teaching methods rather than replacing them. Ultimately, encouraging continuous learning and developing digital literacy skills will enable people to effectively navigate and leverage the potential of AI technologies, creating a workforce that is prepared for an AI-driven future.

6.6 Conclusion

Ultimately, this chapter highlights the immense impact that artificial intelligence (AI) can have on revolutionizing personalized learning in the field of education. Through an examination of personalized education and AI, the study highlights the numerous advantages and capacities of AI technologies in altering educational experiences for each learner. Nevertheless, the path to harnessing AI for educational improvement is not without its obstacles. From overcoming implementation challenges to addressing ethical concerns, educational stakeholders face a complex journey to fully utilize the power of AI in education. However, by addressing these challenges and prioritizing ethical and fair practices, there is great potential for AI to positively transform the field of education in the future. With the ever-changing landscape of the field, this chapter offers valuable insights on how to improve the integration of AI into educational settings. By doing so, it aims to create a more personalized and effective learning environment for everyone. George Siemens, a renowned education technologist from the University of South Australia (UniSA) has contributed many studies in this area. His research in learning analytics, digital learning, personalized learning, and human–machine augmentation reveals the transformative potential of AI in education. Siemen's words are quoted in Sam Dewes's articleas follows: "The interaction of AI will allow us to move beyond traditional models and embrace a more adaptive and learner-centric approach" (Dawes, 2023).

References

Afzal, Arfa, Khan, Saima, Daud, Sana, Ahmed, Zahoor & Butt, Ayesha. (2023). Addressing the Digital Divide: Access and Use of Technology in Education. *Journal of Social Sciences Review* 3, 883–895. 10.54183/jssr.v3i2.326.

Anuyahong, Bundit, Rattanapong, Chalong & Patcha, InteeraInteera. (2023). Analyzing the Impact of Artificial Intelligence in Personalized Learning and Adaptive Assessment in Higher Education. *International Journal of Research and Scientific Innovation (IJRSI)* 10(4), 91.

Bates, R. (2019). The Potential of Artificial Intelligence in Education. *TechTrends* 63(6), 651–653.

Berondo, Ronilo. (2023). Harnessing the Power of Artificial Intelligence for Personalised Learning in Education. 12, 1243–1251. 10.48047/ecb/2023.12.10.089202 3.30/06/2023.

Bhutoria, Aditi. (2022). Personalized Education and Artificial Intelligence in the United States, China, and India: A Systematic Review Using a Human-in-the-Loop Model. *Computers and Education: Artificial Intelligence* 3, 100068. ISSN 2666–920X.

Boser, Ulrich & Baker, Ryan S. (2021). *High-Leverage Opportunities for Learning Engineering.* https://learninganalytics.upenn.edu/Learning_Engineering_recommendations.pdf

Citron, Danielle Keats & Pasquale, Frank. (2014). The Scored Society: Due Process for Automated Predictions. *Washington Law Review* 89, 1–33.

Dawes, Sam. (2023). *How AI Can Deliver Personalised Learning and Transform Academic Assessment.* University of South Australia. https://www.unisa.edu.au/connect/enterprise-magazine/articles/2023/how-ai-can-deliver-personalised-learning-and-transform-academic-assessment/

Derry, Sharon. (1996). Cognitive Schema Theory in the Constructivist Debate. *Educational Psychologist* 31, 163â174. 10.1207/s15326985ep3103&4_2.

Ertmer, P. A. & Newby, T. J. (1993). Behaviourism, Cognitivism and Constructivism; Comparing Critical Features from an Instructional Design Perspective. *Performance Improvement Quarterly* 6, 50–66.

Good, T. L. & Brophy, J. E. (1990). *Educational Psychology: A Realistic Approach*, 4th ed. Longman.

Grau-Valldosera, J. & Minguillon, J. (2014). Rethinking Dropout in Online Higher Education: The Case of the Universitat Oberta de Catalunya. *The International Review of Research in Open and Distributed Learning* 15(1), 290–308.

Jagwani, Anjali & Aloysius, StSt. (2019). A Review of Machine Learning in Education. *International Journal of Emerging Technologies and Innovative Research*, 6(5), 384-386, (www.jetir.org). ISSN:2349-5162, May-2019, Available: http://www.jetir.org/papers/JETIR1905658.pdf. https://www.jetir.org/view?paper=JETIR1905658

Jian, Maher. (2023). Personalized Learning Through AI. *Advances in Engineering Innovation* 5. 10.54254/2977–3903/5/2023039.

Khaled, Dr. (2014). Natural Language Processing and Its Use in Education. *International Journal of Advanced Computer Science and Applications* 5. 10.14569/IJACSA.2014.051210.

Koedinger, K. R. & Corbett, A. T. (2006). Cognitive tutors: Technology bringing learning science to the classroom. In *Handbook of Educational Psychology* (pp. 645–654). Routledge.

Li, Ni. (2023). Ethical Considerations in Artificial Intelligence: A Comprehensive Discussion from the Perspective of Computer Vision. *SHS Web of Conferences* 179. 10.1051/shsconf/202317904024.

Mousavinasab, E. et al. (2018). Intelligent Tutoring Systems: A Systematic Review of Characteristics, Applications, and Evaluation Methods. *Interactive Learning Environments* 29(1), 142–163. 10.1080/10494820.2018.1558257.

Nurmatova, Shohidahon & Altun, MustafaMustafa. (2023). A Comprehensive Review of Bloom's Taxonomy Integration to Enhancing Novice EFL Educators' Pedagogical Impact. *Arab World English Journal* 14, 380–388. 10.24093/awej/vol14no3.24.

Pane, J. F., Steiner, E. D., Baird, M. D. & Hamilton, L. S. (2017). *Informing Progress: Insights on Personalized Learning Implementation and Effects*. RAND Corporation.

Pardo, Abelardo & Siemens, GeorgeGeorge. (2014). Ethical and Privacy Principles for Learning Analytics. *British Journal of Educational Technology* 45, 438–450.

Rouhiainen, Lasse. (2019). How AI and Data Could Personalize Higher Education. *Harvard Business Review*. hbr.org/2019/10/how-ai-and-data-could-personalize-higher-education

Sharma, U., Tomar, P., Bhardwaj, H. & Sakalle, A. (2021). Artificial intelligence and its implications in education. In *Impact of AI Technologies on Teaching, Learning, and Research in Higher Education* (pp. 222–235). IGI Global.

Sobel, C. P. (2001). *The Cognitive Sciences: An Interdisciplinary Approach*. Mayfield.

Spiro, R. J., Feltovich, P. J., Jacobson, M. J. & Coulson, R. L. (1992). Cognitive flexibility, constructivism, and hypertext: Random access instruction for advanced knowledge acquisition in ill-structured domains. In *Constructivism in Education*, edited by Steffe, L. P. & Gale, J. Lawrence Erlbaum Associates.

Tang, Y., Liang, J., Hare, R. & Wang, F. Y. (2020). A Personalized Learning System for Parallel Intelligent Education. *IEEE Transactions on Computational Social Systems* 7(2), 352–361.

Vistorte, A. O. R., Deroncele-Acosta, A., Ayala, J. L. M., Barrasa, A., López-Granero, C. & Martí-González, M. (2024). Integrating Artificial Intelligence to Assess Emotions in Learning Environments: A Systematic Literature Review. *Frontiers in Psychology* 15, 1387089.

Wang, S., Christensen, C., Cui, W., Tong, R., Yarnall, L., Shear, L. & Feng, M. (2020). When Adaptive Learning is Effective Learning: Comparison of an Adaptive Learning System to Teacher-Led Instruction. *Interactive Learning Environments* 31, 793–803.

Wu, Wei, Burdina, Gulnara & Gura, AlenaAlena. (2023). Use of Artificial Intelligence in Teacher Training. *International Journal of Web-Based Learning and Teaching Technologies* 18, 1–15. 10.4018/IJWLTT.331692.

Zawacki-Richter, O., Marín, V. I., Bond, M. & Gouverneur, F. (2019). Systematic Review of Research on Artificial Intelligence Applications in Higher Education–Where Are the Educators?. *International Journal of Educational Technology in Higher Education* 16(1), 39.

Zeide, Elana (2019, Summer). Artificial Intelligence in Higher Education: Applications Promise and Perils and Ethical Questions. *Educause Review* 54(3).

7

IMPACT OF GenAI ON STUDENT OUTCOMES

G. S. Divya

7.1 Outline of the Chapter

Chapter 7, "Impact of GenAI on Student Outcomes," explores how Generative Artificial Intelligence (GenAI) is reshaping education by enhancing various aspects of learning. It starts by introducing GenAI and its pivotal role in modern education. The chapter details how GenAI improves personalized learning through individualized content recommendations and customized learning experiences that cater to students' specific needs. It also covers the advancements in adaptive assessment and feedback, where GenAI dynamically adjusts content and provides tailored responses, supporting effective formative assessments. The discussion extends to how GenAI fosters creativity and critical thinking by utilizing AI-powered creative tools, simulation-based environments, and problem-solving scenarios, while also considering how students perceive and interact with these AI tools. The chapter also addresses how GenAI contributes to developing social and emotional intelligence, featuring social interaction platforms, virtual mentors, and exercises aimed at building empathy. Long-term skill development is highlighted, focusing on lifelong learning strategies, continuous skill assessment, and preparation for future careers. The chapter concludes with practical recommendations for leveraging GenAI effectively, emphasizing its transformative potential to enhance learning outcomes and the importance of careful integration. This summary captures GenAI's impact on personalized learning, adaptive assessment, creativity, social-emotional skills, and skill development, along with the challenges and considerations for its successful implementation in educational settings.

DOI: 10.1201/9781003422433-7

7.2 Introduction

In recent years, the merging of artificial intelligence (AI) and education has sparked a surge of innovation, fundamentally altering traditional teaching and learning approaches. Within the wide array of AI applications in education, GenAI-empowered learning emerges as a particularly promising advancement. GenAI signifies a significant shift in educational technology, harnessing the capabilities of GenAI algorithms to construct immersive, tailored, and adaptable learning experiences for students [1–3]. Figure 7.1 provides a chronological summary of notable advancements in AI and GenAI across different decades. It begins in the 1950s with the introduction of the term "artificial intelligence" and the proposal of the Turing test, followed by the development of early AI programs in the 1960s and the emergence of expert systems and rule-based AI in the 1970s. The 1980s witnessed a transition toward connectionism and neural network research, along with the widespread adoption of expert systems. In the 1990s, the AI Winter commenced, characterized by diminished funding and interest in AI. However, the 2000s saw a resurgence in AI driven by machine learning, deep learning, and the impactful role of big data. The 2010s saw notable advancements in deep learning, the emergence of GANs and variational autoencoders (VAEs), as well as progress in natural language processing and reinforcement learning. In the 2020s, AI continued to progress with a particular emphasis on refining GenAI models such as GANs and VAEs, while also addressing ethical and societal concerns and exploring applications in creative domains and data augmentation [4–8].

Since ChatGPT launch on November 30, 2022, it quickly gained over a million subscribers within a week, showcasing its advanced capabilities. This AI tool has stirred mixed reactions among educators, particularly in its

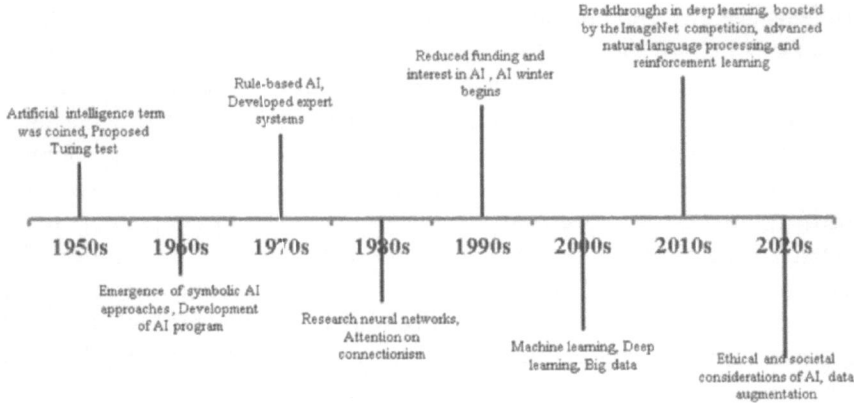

FIGURE 7.1 Advancement in AI.

potential to revolutionize education. An exploratory study highlights Chat-GPT's benefits, such as personalized learning and formative assessment support, alongside limitations like generating inaccurate information and privacy concerns. Recommendations stress the importance of collaboration among stakeholders to maximize the safe and constructive use of Chat-GPT and similar AI tools in education [9]. Individuals have the opportunity to swiftly retrieve information and knowledge via a streamlined natural language-based search method facilitated by ChatGPT. GenAI, a subset of AI methodologies, creates novel data, such as images, text, or entire virtual environments, by leveraging learned patterns from existing datasets, showcasing remarkable proficiency across various domains like natural language processing, computer vision, and creative arts. In the education sector, GenAI holds vast potential to revolutionize learning, instruction, and content generation. Fundamentally, GenAI-empowered learning seeks to enrich the educational process by utilizing AI to customize learning experiences, develop immersive educational settings, support adaptive learning trajectories, foster creativity and collaboration, and instill lifelong learning competencies [10, 11]. Through comprehensive analysis of student data, GenAI algorithms tailor instruction to match individual learning preferences, strengths, and areas for improvement, ensuring each student receives targeted assistance. These platforms also generate interactive simulations and multimedia content, enabling students to engage in experiential learning and address real-world challenges dynamically. Furthermore, GenAI continuously adjusts learning materials in response to real-time feedback, optimizing difficulty levels and pacing to enhance learning outcomes. It empowers students to nurture their creativity and collaborate with peers, aiding in the cultivation of vital 21st-century skills such as critical thinking, problem-solving, and digital literacy [12–14]. GenAI -empowered learning represents a transformative frontier in education, offering personalized, immersive, adaptive, creative, and lifelong learning opportunities. Nonetheless, it's imperative for educators, researchers, and technologists to contemplate ethical, privacy, and equity considerations to ensure fair access to high-quality education for all students [15–17]. AI systems support online learning by personalizing experiences, automating tasks, and facilitating assessments. However, their impact on student–instructor interactions and associated norms remains unclear. Understanding perceptions of AI's impact is crucial for identifying barriers and ensuring interaction safety [18, 19]. Through speed dating sessions with storyboards, with a cohort of 12 students and 11 instructors, a range of AI applications were investigated. While AI can enhance interactions, concerns exist about social boundaries, responsibility, and surveillance. To address these, AI systems should prioritize explainability, human involvement, and data handling. This study contributes by designing AI system storyboards, capturing concerns, and proposing practical implications for maximizing benefits while minimizing negatives [20].

GenAI offers significant benefits in enhancing personalized learning, assessment, creativity, social-emotional intelligence, and long-term skill development, as listed in Figure 7.2.

The impact of GenAI on student outcomes encompasses personalized learning experiences tailored to individual needs, adaptive assessments offering timely feedback and challenge, enhanced engagement through interactive tools, accessibility features aiding students with disabilities, data-driven insights for educators, opportunities for lifelong learning, and ethical considerations regarding privacy, bias, and equity. GenAI promises to revolutionize education by optimizing learning experiences, improving assessment practices, fostering inclusivity and engagement, and supporting continuous skill development. However, it necessitates careful implementation and monitoring to ensure equitable access, mitigate potential risks, and uphold ethical standards in education [21, 22]. In spite of many advantages of ChatGPT, many people stated that ChatGPT and similar GenAI systems have the capability to offer general support and information, yet they might lack the ability to tailor instruction to address the specific requirements of each student [23]. The use of ChatGPT presents several significant challenges that must be addressed. One concern revolves around its impact on assessments and examinations, as GenAI tools like ChatGPT could potentially influence these

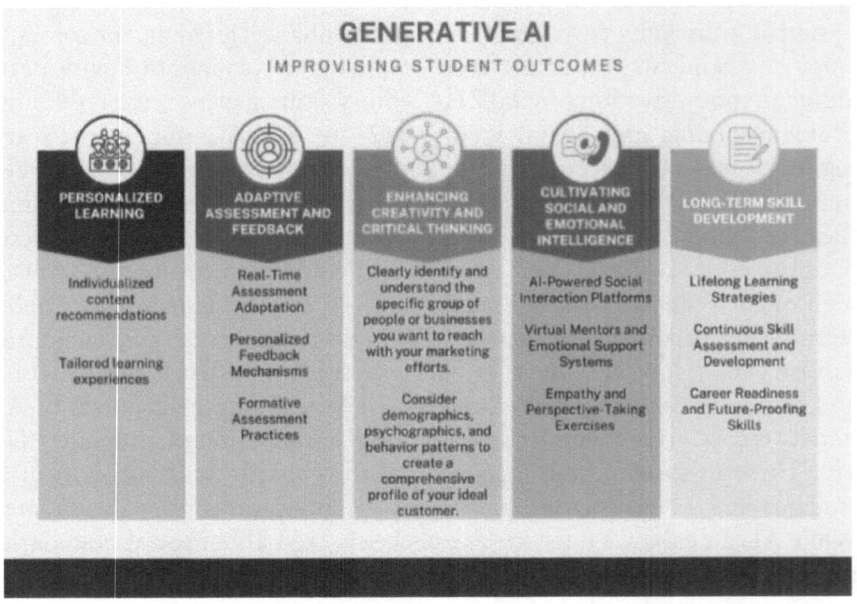

FIGURE 7.2 Empowering Students through GenAI.

processes. Another challenge involves controlling plagiarism and cheating among students, as ChatGPT offers more powerful capabilities compared to existing tools, making it difficult for teachers to detect generated assignments. This could undermine the integrity of academic work. ChatGPT may negatively affect students' motivation to learn writing and their ability to think independently and express themselves linguistically. These challenges highlight the need for strategies to mitigate the potential drawbacks of integrating ChatGPT into educational settings [24, 25].

7.3 Personalized Learning

Personalized learning is an innovative educational approach that places students at the forefront of their learning journey by tailoring instruction to suit their specific needs, preferences, and learning pace. Several variables, as depicted in Figure 7.3, affect individualized learning of students. Understanding their diverse approaches to learning, prior knowledge, and interests allows educators to tailor instruction effectively. Recognizing cultural diversity promotes inclusivity and addressing social and emotional needs ensures a supportive learning environment. Allowing students to progress at their own pace and providing continuous feedback are crucial for individualized learning paths. Educators play a key role in personalizing instruction through expertise in curriculum design and assessment practices. By considering these

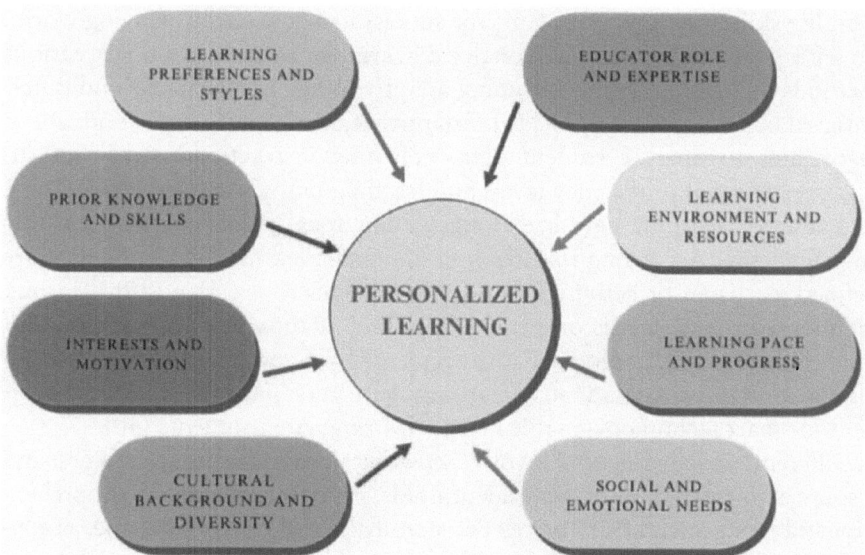

FIGURE 7.3 Factors impacting personalized learning.

factors, educators can create personalized learning experiences that enhance outcomes and engagement.

Unlike traditional uniform teaching methods, personalized learning recognizes the diverse backgrounds, learning styles, and abilities of students. This shift involves comprehensively understanding each learner, considering factors such as their academic strengths and weaknesses, cultural background, socio-economic status, and personal motivations. Zhen et al. examined how GenAI tools can improve personalized learning in a flipped classroom, using a music course as an example. Results show differing views between teachers and students, prompting analysis and suggestions. GenAI aids personalized guidance and feedback for learners, supporting educators in course design. Despite ethical concerns, the study underscores AI's potential in higher education for adapting to changing information landscapes [26, 27]. GenAI presents unparalleled chances to improve personalized learning through accurate adaptation, scalability, dynamic content creation, adaptive feedback, and innovative teaching strategies that exceed the capabilities of conventional methods. Utilizing AI's capabilities, educators can develop personalized learning experiences that are more efficient and captivating, tailored to meet the diverse requirements of modern students.

Personalized learning represents a comprehensive and student-cantered approach to education that aims to maximize each student's potential. By tailoring instruction, leveraging technology, and prioritizing data-driven decision-making, personalized learning creates a learning environment where every student feels valued, supported, and empowered to succeed. This method not only boosts academic performance but also fosters the growth of vital life skills, equipping students for success in a constantly evolving world. To effectively implement personalized learning, educators utilize various methods and technologies, including adaptive learning platforms and differentiated instruction strategies [28]. Adaptive learning platforms use advanced algorithms to analyze student data, adjusting instruction in real-time to match individual proficiency levels and learning paths. Personalized learning and adaptive learning have been longstanding focal points of smart learning environments. According to Huang et al., smart learning environments are defined as spaces or activities that facilitate efficient learning [29]. Kinshuk highlighted the emphasis on personalized and adaptive learning within SLE in an interview. Technological advancements have made personalized learning more adaptive and adaptive learning more personalized, particularly evident in smart technology-enabled smart learning environments [30].

Differentiated instruction involves creating varied learning activities and resources to cater to different student needs, encouraging deeper comprehension and engagement. Data-driven decision-making plays a crucial role, as educators gather and analyze diverse data points to guide instructional planning and intervention efforts. Personalized adaptive learning has emerged as a result of advancements in big data technology, leading to its integration into digital learning environments. This evolution, influenced by the paradigm shift toward data-intensive science, marks a significant milestone in educational technology research. Rooted in historical educational philosophies such as Confucian and Socratic teachings, personalized learning has regained prominence with the shift toward student-cantered approaches in education [31–33]. In a research investigation conducted by a university employing an adaptive learning system fueled by AI, students witnessed notable enhancements in their educational achievements. This system incorporated GenAI algorithms to assess students' learning behaviors, pinpoint weak areas, and customize educational content to suit individual needs. Consequently, students noted heightened levels of involvement, deeper comprehension of intricate topics, and enhanced grades across their courses. They commemorated their accomplishments by exchanging success stories with peers and educators, fostering a sense of assurance and enthusiasm in their academic endeavors [34].

Personalized learning emphasizes the holistic development of students, nurturing socio-emotional skills essential for achievement in academic and practical contexts, leading to enhanced academic achievement and overall well-being. Students have noted that enhancing the personalization of learning materials and interactions with instructors is highly effective in boosting student engagement, whether in well-resourced settings or underserved communities. Although the correlation between personalization and student performance is widely acknowledged, its full integration into classrooms has yet to fully capitalize on this potential. Technology, particularly GenAI, could significantly contribute to the development of materials tailored for more personalized, almost individualized, use [35–37].

7.3.1   Individualized Content Recommendations

Individualized content recommendations powered by GenAI offer a groundbreaking approach to improving student outcomes in education. GenAI refers to machine learning systems generating new content like text and images. In higher education, it can transform learning through personalized experiences, task automation, and interactive content creation. AI offers adaptive learning tailored to students' abilities, enhancing education quality. Applications include personalized feedback via AI-powered chatbots and interactive textbooks. These technologies optimize learning resources and engagement. GenAI streamlines administrative tasks, allowing educators to focus on student support. It revolutionizes traditional teaching methods, making learning more effective and engaging. Through adaptive learning, AI fosters individualized education, catering to diverse student needs. Overall, GenAI promises to revolutionize education, offering personalized, interactive, and efficient learning experiences [38–40].

By analyzing extensive student data, including academic performance and learning preferences, GenAI algorithms generate personalized content suggestions tailored to each student's unique needs and abilities. These recommendations enable educational platforms to provide targeted learning materials and activities aligned with individual learning objectives. One notable advantage is the capability to address a wide range of needs and learning approaches, with algorithms identifying effective content types for each student, whether it is visual explanations, hands-on activities, or interactive simulations [41]. This personalization not only enhances engagement but also helps students overcome learning barriers by recommending resources to address weaknesses or knowledge gaps. Personalized recommendations encourage student independence and self-guided learning, empowering them to delve into subjects of interest at their preferred speed. By promoting ownership of the learning journey, GenAI-powered platforms cultivate lifelong learning habits beyond the classroom. With ongoing refinement, these technologies hold tremendous potential to revolutionize student learning experiences and academic achievement.

Individualized content recommendations powered by GenAI have the potential to significantly improve student outcomes in education. By analyzing student data and generating personalized recommendations, these algorithms can address diverse learning needs, overcome barriers to learning, and promote student autonomy and self-directed learning. As educators and developers continue to refine and optimize GenAI-powered platforms, they hold great promise for revolutionizing the way students learn and achieve academic success [42].

7.3.2 Tailored Learning Experiences

Tailored learning experiences powered by GenAI are revolutionizing education by offering customized and adaptive pathways that optimize student outcomes. Leveraging vast datasets encompassing academic performance, preferences, interests, and progress, GenAI algorithms create customized learning experiences designed for individual needs and capabilities. They are adept at adapting to various learning methods and preferences. By identifying effective instructional methods for each student, whether through visual aids, interactive simulations, or hands-on activities, educators deliver engaging and effective learning experiences. Moreover, GenAI-driven platforms pinpoint areas of weakness or knowledge gaps, providing targeted interventions such as additional practice problems, instructional videos, or personalized feedback to support students in methicastering challenging concepts and fostering confidence. Furthermore, by affording students autonomy to explore topics at their own pace and access resources aligned with their interests and goals, these tailored experiences not only enhance engagement and motivation but also cultivate lifelong learning habits beyond the traditional classroom setting. As educators and developers continue to refine and optimize GenAI-driven platforms, they have the potential to reshape the educational landscape, revolutionizing how students learn and achieve academic success [43].

Tailored learning experiences enabled by GenAI hold tremendous potential to improve student outcomes in education. By analyzing student data and generating personalized learning pathways, these algorithms can address diverse learning needs, overcome barriers to learning, and promote student autonomy and self-directed learning. As educators and developers continue to refine and optimize GenAI-powered platforms, they have the opportunity to revolutionize the way students learn and achieve academic success [44].

7.4 Adaptive Assessment and Feedback

Adaptive assessment and feedback systems significantly enhance student performance by providing personalized learning journeys that address the strengths and weaknesses of each student, offering targeted intervention to address areas of struggle, and delivering immediate feedback to accelerate learning. Figure 7.4 illustrates how adaptive assessment and feedback help in success of students. The personalized nature of these systems, along with features like gamification, motivates students to engage actively in their learning journey. Adaptive systems allow educators to obtain valuable insights into student performance through analysis driven by data, promote inclusivity by accommodating diverse learning needs, and facilitate the retention and transfer of knowledge through scaffolder learning experiences. These systems enable students to assume responsibility for their learning, promoting a

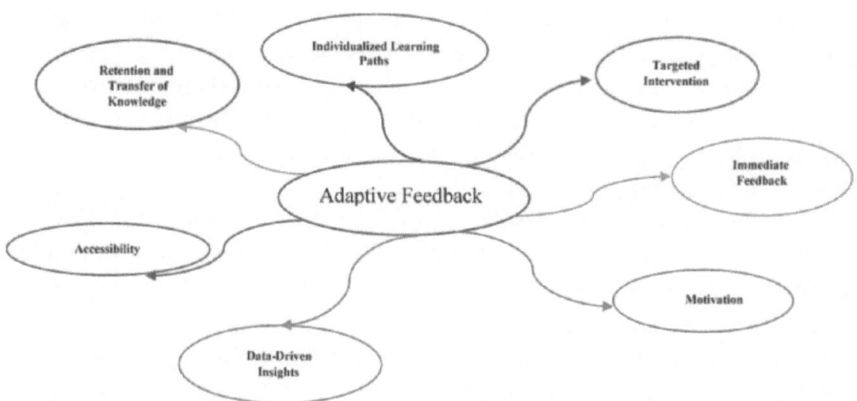

FIGURE 7.4   The impact of adaptive feedback on student success.

positive and productive learning atmosphere, and contribute to continuous improvement and academic growth.

Adaptive assessment and feedback, with the integration of GenAI, reshape education by delivering personalized evaluation and guidance to students. AI presents numerous opportunities to enhance teaching in higher education. These include personalized learning, automated assessment, virtual assistants, content creation, and more. These developments provide advantages such as tailored learning experiences and language skill enhancement, simplified learning processes, academic assistance, and tailored feedback [45–48]. By utilizing AI algorithms to analyze comprehensive student data, including performance on assessments and learning patterns, these systems adjust assessment processes in real time and offer targeted feedback to address individual needs. This approach ensures accurate assessment of student knowledge, promotes deeper learning through tailored feedback, and supports differentiated instruction by identifying and addressing specific learning gaps. Ultimately, adaptive evaluation and feedback mechanisms powered by GenAI have the potential to revolutionize education by improving student outcomes through personalized evaluation and instruction.

Real-time assessment adaptation, personalized feedback mechanisms, and formative assessment practices are integral to modern education, particularly when combined with GenAI. These components play a vital role in shaping student outcomes by offering customized evaluation, guidance, and support throughout the learning journey. Leveraging GenAI, educators can adapt assessments in real time, deliver personalized feedback, and facilitate formative assessment practices. This integration enhances teaching and learning, fostering more engaging and effective educational experiences that ultimately lead to enhanced student outcomes. During a writing workshop tailored for high school students, an AI writing assistant driven by GenAI was seamlessly incorporated into the program. This AI tool offered instantaneous feedback on students' writing endeavors, furnishing recommendations to enhance grammar, style, and coherence. The students marked their accomplishments by crafting top-notch essays, garnering accolades from their instructors, and triumphing in writing competitions. They expressed gratitude toward the AI tool for aiding in their progression as writers and for facilitating acknowledgment of their efforts [49–51].

GenAI has both advantages and challenges, which are listed in Table 7.1. On the positive side, GenAI is highly effective at personalization, quickly adjusting content and feedback to fit individual needs and learning preferences. It boosts efficiency by delivering prompt responses and handling numerous queries at once. Another benefit is its scalability, as it can accommodate many users without needing additional resources. Its 24/7 availability removes barriers related to time and location. Responses remain consistent due to set algorithms, and the system can enhance its performance by learning

TABLE 7.1 Benefits and Challenges of GenAI

Aspect	Benefits	Challenges
Personalization	Tailors to individual needs and styles	Needs accurate data; may miss nuances
Efficiency	Provides rapid responses; handles high volume	Risk of generating irrelevant info
Scalability	Scales easily for many users	Requires significant computational resources
Accessibility	Available 24/7 from any location	Depends on technology and internet access
Consistency	Delivers uniform responses based on training	Lacks contextual understanding
Learning	Improves from data inputs over time	Risk of perpetuating biases; needs monitoring
Cost	Can lower costs for repetitive tasks	High initial development costs

from the ongoing interactions. However, GenAI also has challenges such as the need for precise data to ensure accurate personalization, the potential for producing irrelevant information, and substantial initial setup costs. Additionally, it demands considerable computational power and might struggle with understanding context and providing empathetic feedback, possibly reinforcing biases present in its training data.

7.4.1 Real-Time Assessment Adaptation

Real-time assessment adaptation involves dynamically adjusting assessment content, difficulty levels, and pacing based on students' responses and performance. With the integration of GenAI, these adaptations can occur instantaneously, ensuring that assessments accurately reflect each student's knowledge and understanding. For example, if a student demonstrates proficiency in a particular concept, the assessment can automatically progress to more advanced material, challenging the student appropriately. Conversely, if a student struggles with a concept, the assessment can provide additional support or resources to help them master the material before moving forward. This adaptive approach ensures that assessments are both challenging and achievable for each student, leading to more accurate evaluations of their learning progress and ultimately improving student outcomes.

AI can aid educators in generating educational content, improving student engagement through tasks like generating test questions, summarizing texts, and recommending pertinent resources. AI chatbots offer real-time content for conversations, including images, saving time for educators and providing additional resources for students [52]. Students can enhance their language abilities using AI-driven chatbots for inquiries. AI-enabled language learning apps and translation tools aid students and educators in surmounting language barriers, making education more inclusive by offering real-time translation into various languages, benefiting diverse student populations like international students [53]. Training sessions and workshops could target enhancing the AI literacy of students and educators, enabling them to utilize AI tools confidently. AI literacy entails critical thinking, which involves recognizing constraints and biases, problem-solving by applying AI techniques to real-world challenges, and effective communication skills [54].

7.4.2 Personalized Feedback Mechanisms

Personalized feedback mechanisms leverage GenAI for tailored and personalized feedback provided to students according to their performance and learning needs. Instead of generic feedback, personalized feedback mechanisms analyze students' responses and learning patterns to deliver feedback that addresses specific misconceptions, errors, or areas needing enhancement. Tailored feedback not only assists students in comprehending where they went wrong but also provides guidance on how to improve in the future. For instance, if a student encounters difficulty with a specific mathematical concept, the feedback might incorporate supplementary explanations, examples, or practice problems related to that concept. By providing personalized feedback in real time, these systems enable students to assume responsibility for their learning and make meaningful progress toward mastery, ultimately leading to improved student outcomes.

AI-driven systems simplify the grading of quizzes, tests, and assignments saving time and maintaining consistency. ChatGPT, for instance, automates test grading, offering swift feedback and enabling tutors to focus on personalized assessments. Adaptive assessments modify the difficulty levels according to student responses, providing instant feedback and insights for course improvement. AI is commonly used for automated assessment, facilitating self-regulated learning and enhancing educator engagement. Future research should explore metrics like student performance, engagement, and satisfaction to assess the influence of AI on teaching effectiveness and learning results [55–57]. Ivica et al. introduced an accessible GenAI tool for personalized learning, proposing an affordable approach for creating tailored learning materials within a learning management system. The tool generates materials in three styles, including traditional and pop-culture influenced formats, with accompanying multiple-choice questions. A preliminary experiment involving 20 software engineering college students found that while traditional materials were primarily used, students found multiple variants that were engaging and helpful for assessment. Though the small sample size limits generalization, the study offers valuable insights for forthcoming studies on educational strategies supported by AI [58].

7.4.3 Formative Assessment Practices

Conventional assessment techniques find it challenging to fully grasp students' knowledge and skills, as they lack tools to assess non-cognitive abilities. Also, these traditional approaches do not account for the lack of chances for international collaboration in higher education. To tackle these obstacles, incorporating AI is suggested, providing customized coursework tailored to individual learning patterns and predictive analytics to pinpoint and assist students at risk [59]. Formative assessment practices involve ongoing assessment and feedback throughout the learning process to monitor student progress and inform instructional decisions. When integrated with GenAI, formative assessment practices can be enhanced through real-time adaptation and personalized feedback mechanisms. Teachers can use GenAI-powered tools to administer formative assessments that adapt to students' responses and provide immediate feedback on their understanding of key concepts.

In assessment and feedback, AI supports the grading of student assignments and the evaluation of their work. including identifying similarities using Turnitin, tracking participation in library resource usage, and delivering prompt and accurate feedback. This technology also allows instructors to dedicate more time to teaching by automating these tasks. Additionally, AI-driven chatbots provide learners with instant and tailored support for academic and administrative inquiries, such as course material clarification or registration information. These systems effectively analyze student data to predict potential academic challenges or dropout risks [60, 61]. AI holds promise for transforming how educators interact with learners and meet their obligations in higher education. Many institutions have employed AI tools to enhance productivity in learning activities [62]. Research highlights users' attitudes regarding the adoption of AI for personalized professional development, course design, grading, assessment, and student support [63].

When comparing GenAI techniques with traditional assessment and feedback methods, several differences become apparent, as tabulated in Table 7.2. GenAI offers immediate feedback, greatly accelerating response times compared to the slower, manual processes of traditional methods. It also stands out in its ability to provide dynamic, personalized feedback, whereas traditional methods are typically more standardized and less customized. A notable advantage of GenAI is its scalability, efficiently managing many users at once, unlike traditional approaches which can be more resource-intensive to scale. GenAI excels in analyzing large datasets quickly and thoroughly, while traditional methods depend on manual analysis, which may be less detailed.

TABLE 7.2 Comparison of GenAI Techniques with Traditional Assessments and Feedback Methods

Aspect	Generative AI Techniques	Traditional Methods
Feedback Speed	Instant feedback in real time	Slower feedback due to manual processes
Customization	Dynamic, personalized feedback	Often standardized; less tailored
Scalability	Handles many users simultaneously	More resource-intensive to scale
Data Analysis	Analyzes large data sets efficiently	Manual, less thorough analysis
Bias and Fairness	May inherit or amplify existing biases	Bias can be addressed manually
Human Interaction	Limited empathetic understanding	Provides personal interaction and support
Cost	Reduces long-term costs and high setup costs	Costly in terms of time and resources
Adaptability	Quickly adapts to new needs	Slower to update and adapt

Although GenAI may reinforce existing biases in its training data, traditional methods can address biases through manual review. Traditional methods also excel in providing personal interaction and support, an area where GenAI may fall short. Although GenAI has the potential to reduce long-term costs, it requires a significant initial investment, whereas traditional methods often involve ongoing expenses related to time and resources. GenAI adapts swiftly to new information and changing needs, whereas traditional methods may be slower to adapt.

7.5 Enhancing Creativity and Critical Thinking

Critical thinking and creativity are crucial for student success and innovation. Critical thinking begins with observation and comprehension, allowing students to dissect problems accurately. Creativity complements this by enabling the generation of innovative solutions and connections between different ideas. Together, these skills help students tackle complex issues, devise creative solutions, and adapt to new challenges. Critical thinking assesses and refines ideas, while creativity fosters imaginative problem solving. By developing skills in observation, analysis, idea generation, and adaptation, students are well-prepared for academic and societal contributions. Figure 7.5 illustrates the phases of critical thinking and creativity. The cyclical process involves observing and understanding, evaluating problems, brainstorming solutions, analyzing options, implementing chosen solutions, and continuously refining

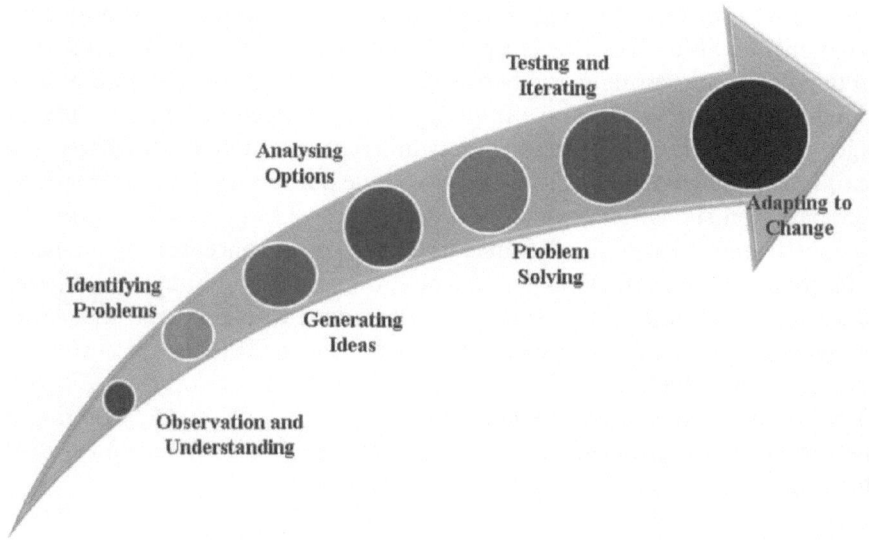

FIGURE 7.5   Phases of implementing critical thinking and creativity.

them based on feedback. This process ensures that critical thinking and creativity drive effective problem-solving and goal achievement.

7.5.1 AI-Powered Creative Tools

AI-powered creative tools are instrumental in improving student outcomes as they cultivate creativity, innovation, and self-expression. These tools offer innovative platforms for students to explore and experiment. Through the utilization of AI algorithms, these tools can provide personalized guidance, suggestions, and feedback tailored to each student's unique preferences, skills, and learning objectives [64]. This personalized approach encourages students to deeply engage with the creative process, resulting in heightened motivation, confidence, and satisfaction in their endeavors. AI-powered creative tools aid students in overcoming creative barriers and exploring fresh ideas by offering inspiration, generating diverse perspectives, and facilitating collaborative opportunities with peers. The exploration of AI in education involves investigating the use of AI technologies in conventional academic disciplines, such as aiding in the mastery of reading and writing and exploring their potential applications in acquiring skills beyond traditional academic realms [65, 66].

The study investigated how humans utilize AI, using storytelling as a test case. Participants were asked to craft sea adventure narratives, with those using ChatGPT-4 generating more innovative and practical stories than those without AI assistance. Seeking multiple ideas from AI further improved story originality and usefulness. Reliance on AI led to increased narrative similarity among users. Interestingly, the benefits of AI were more pronounced among individuals with lower creative thinking abilities, suggesting that its advantages may be limited to those with less inherent creativity [67]. Cherry and Latulipe introduced the creativity support index, a tool evaluating creativity aids based on six aspects, which is widely employed in research. Studies by Gero et al. and Koch et al. confirmed its effectiveness, concentrating on users' subjective experiences. Assessing learning outcomes and subjective significance is vital in impacting creativity in education, with potential indicators for everyday creativity like frequency of engagement. AI tools can customize prompts, bolstering human creativity by refining idea development [68–70]. These tools enhance student outcomes by nurturing creativity, fostering a supportive learning atmosphere, and improving problem-solving and critical thinking skills, ultimately leading to academic success.

7.5.2 Simulation-Based Learning Environments

AI's integration into education, especially through simulation-based learning, represents a major shift in how students, teachers, and technology interact. A review of 59 studies highlights trends in AI applications, such as virtual agents, affective computing, and AI-powered assessments, offering insights for future AI education research [71]. Traditional teaching methods often fail to cater to diverse learning styles, leading to the adoption of simulation-based learning to connect theory with practice. Research on World Health Organization's World Health Assembly Simulation (WHA Sim) shows significant improvements in critical thinking, communication, and collaboration, supporting its use in global health education [72]. Simulation-Based Learning Environments provide hands-on experiences, enhancing theoretical understanding and problem-solving skills. They improve academic performance and real-world readiness by engaging students in immersive tasks and collaborative efforts [73, 74].

Duchatelet et al. proposed a framework for evaluating learning in simulations, emphasizing the need for a detailed approach considering contextual factors and simulation dynamics. Their longitudinal case study of a political simulation discusses the integration of theory and research [75]. Heidy et al. found that simulation-based learning (SBL) in Model United Nations (MUN) frameworks significantly improved critical thinking and academic performance among undergraduates [76].

In middle school STEM programs, AI-enhanced simulations facilitated interactive experiments and deepened understanding of STEM concepts. AI applications in STEM education utilize a range of techniques to improve instructional quality and student success. These include intelligent tutoring systems (ITS) that offer customized tutoring and feedback, learning prediction algorithms that anticipate student performance, and data mining to track learning behaviors. Automation plays a crucial role, with tools like AutoLEP providing automatic assessment and question creation and educational robots like LEGO MINDSTORMS EV3 enabling interactive learning in programming and technology courses. These AI technologies foster active learning and higher-order thinking skills, such as computational thinking and problem solving. In non-STEM fields, AI enhances adaptive learning through interactive AI textbooks that tailor content to student progress and group formation algorithms that optimize collaborative projects based on student profiles and performance data. Overall, AI's transformative potential in both STEM and non-STEM education lies in personalizing learning experiences, increasing engagement, and improving educational outcomes. Table 7.3 shows specific examples of how AI can assist students in various domains such as STEM and non-STEM [77]. A meta-analysis of 145 studies shows that simulations significantly boost learning outcomes, with tailored scaffolding methods benefiting learners differently based on prior knowledge [78]. Universities use AI to create interactive simulations and VR experiences, enhancing engagement and understanding, particularly in fields like science and engineering [79]. Simulations and games, popular in various higher education subjects, provide immersive learning experiences and insights into real-world scenarios, making complex concepts more accessible [80].

7.5.3 Problem-Solving Challenges and Scenarios

GenAI-powered problem-solving challenges enhance student outcomes by promoting critical thinking, creativity, and adaptability. These challenges are dynamically tailored to students' skills and progress, presenting authentic problems that require analytical and innovative solutions [81]. Engaging with these challenges helps students build resilience, perseverance, and confidence. Research on online collaborative problem solving (CSCL and CPS) has increased, focusing on aspects like feature extraction and task analysis, with further study needed on identity awareness and interdisciplinary collaboration [82]. GenAI adjusts difficulty based on student performance, ensuring personalized learning and fostering collaboration and communication skills [83]. Collaborative problem-solving, where students work together to brainstorm and devise solutions, enhances teamwork and peer learning [84]. Wismath et al.'s study on university students involved in puzzle-solving tasks highlights the importance of collaborative skills and individual initiative [85]. By replicating real-world problems, these AI-powered challenges prepare students for academic and professional success, developing crucial skills for both environments [86–88].

TABLE 7.3 Examples of AI Applications in STEM and Non-STEM Domains

Domain	AI Application	Description	Examples
STEM	Learning Prediction	Anticipating students' academic performance and outcomes	Using ensemble machine learning methods to forecast student success
STEM	Intelligent Tutoring Systems (ITS)	Offering customized tutoring and feedback	AI-driven systems providing tailored instructions in subjects such as mathematics
STEM	Student Behavior Detection	Monitoring and analyzing students' learning behaviors	Employing data mining techniques to understand the behavior of programming students
STEM	Automation	Automatic assessment and question creation	Tools like AutoLEP for evaluating programming skills; systems for generating tests
STEM	Educational Robots	Enhancing interactive learning with robots	AI-powered robots like LEGO MINDSTORMS EV3 used in technology courses
Non-STEM	AI Textbooks	Delivering interactive and adaptive learning materials	AI-enhanced textbooks that adjust content according to student progress
Non-STEM	Group Formation	Optimizing group work by forming balanced teams	Algorithms that create groups based on student profiles and performance data
Non-STEM	Language Learning	Providing customized language learning experiences	AI-based language learning apps that adapt to individual learning styles and progress

7.5.4 AI Integration into Education

The integration of AI, exemplified by tools like ChatGPT, has notably transformed education, particularly in higher education, where academic libraries are increasingly utilizing AI chatbots. The influence of AI-generated content on students' critical thinking is a significant concern. While AI tools offer efficiency, there are concerns that they could hinder critical thinking skills and creativity. Despite concerns, students generally have positive attitudes toward AI tools, citing benefits like efficiency [89–92]. A commonly agreed-upon description of creativity entails blending ideas that are deemed to possess unique value, utility, or significance to different individuals involved. The creative process involves both divergent thinking, which generates numerous ideas, and convergent thinking, which selects the most suitable ideas, to arrive at innovative solutions or decisions [93–95]. GenAI involves leveraging AI-powered creative tools, simulation-based learning environments, and problem-solving challenges and scenarios to foster the development of these essential skills. The integration of AI-powered creative tools, simulation-based learning environments, merging theory with practice to bolster critical thinking and problem-solving skills and problem-solving challenges and scenarios into educational settings enhances creativity and critical thinking among students. By providing opportunities for hands-on experimentation, exploration, and problem solving, GenAI empowers students to become more innovative, adaptable, and analytical thinkers, ultimately leading to improved academic outcomes and readiness for future challenges [96, 97].

7.5.5 Student Attitudes and AI Content Tools

Research on AI content tools highlights their impact on students' critical thinking and attitudes. Xiaozhu et al. explored the impact of AI content tools on the critical thinking skills and attitudes of students. The study involving 851 students from a Chinese university examined students' usage patterns, motivations, perceived advantages, and risks, and the significance of critical thinking abilities. It identifies a gap in research regarding the differential usage of AI tools among male and non-binary students. Motivations for usage include time and effort saving, while students also recognize the possible risks and constraints, highlighting the importance of critical thinking when navigating content generated by AI. The findings suggest implications for academic libraries, emphasizing the need for education and training in AI literacy and critical thinking to empower students. Libraries can contribute by offering resources, workshops, and guidance in fostering informed and critical thinking practices [98].

Hoyos et al. explored AI's functions in classrooms, emphasizing its advantages such as promoting equality in academics, assisting with organization, and providing tailored recommendations. However, they also recognize limitations in fostering critical thinking and creativity. Understanding AI's opportunities and limitations is vital for its effective integration into education. Effective training in the use of AI tools is essential to fully capitalize on these benefits, although addressing challenges such as cheating fears necessitates thoughtful approaches. Despite obstacles, the emphasis remains on harnessing AI's potential to enrich educational experiences [99, 100]. Empowering students with GenAI, as shown in Figure 7.6, enhances their problem-solving, innovation, and creativity skills, leading to improved academic performance. It promotes collaboration, personalizes learning, and

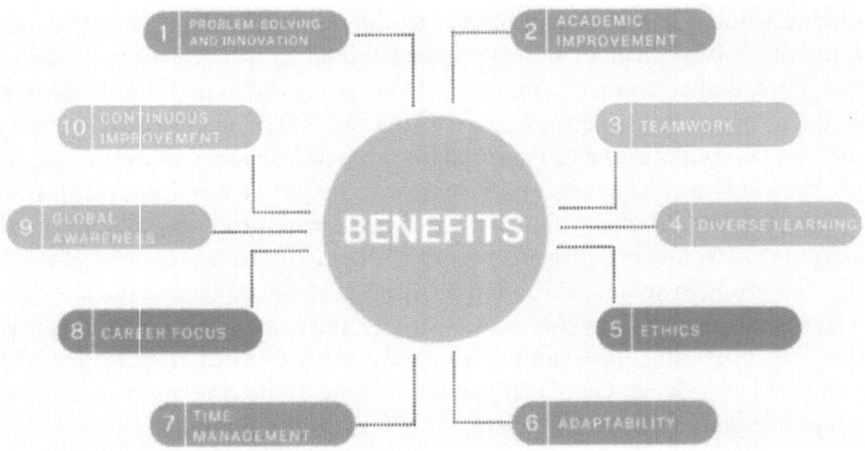

FIGURE 7.6 Effects of GenAI-empowered critical thinking and creativity on student performance.

speeds up prototyping and experimentation. GenAI encourages interdisciplinary exploration, critical thinking, and ethical decision-making, preparing students for future careers and boosting their confidence. It also improves comprehension, communication, adaptability, curiosity, resilience, and time management. Additionally, it fosters a growth mindset, global awareness, and a culture of continuous learning, shaping students into well-rounded contributors to society.

7.6 Cultivating Social and Emotional Intelligence

Leveraging GenAI to cultivate social and emotional intelligence possesses significant potential. It can substantially augment student performance [101]. This is achieved by furnishing personalized interventions, feedback, and interactive experiences tailored to individual needs and aptitudes. Through the sophisticated analysis of extensive student data, GenAI has the capacity to discern both the strengths and areas necessitating development in social and emotional skills, thereby offering bespoke feedback and guidance conducive to holistic growth. Figure 7.7 illustrates how GenAI revolutionizes student learning by empowering factors that cultivate social and emotional intelligence, ultimately enhancing student outcomes. It encompasses personalized guidance, social interaction facilitation, and emotional support systems, all contributing to resilience and well-being. GenAI fosters empathy, self-awareness, and cultural sensitivity through exercises and feedback mechanisms while promoting essential life skills development through simulated conflict resolution, collaborative learning, and mindfulness practices. This holistic approach facilitates comprehensive student growth.

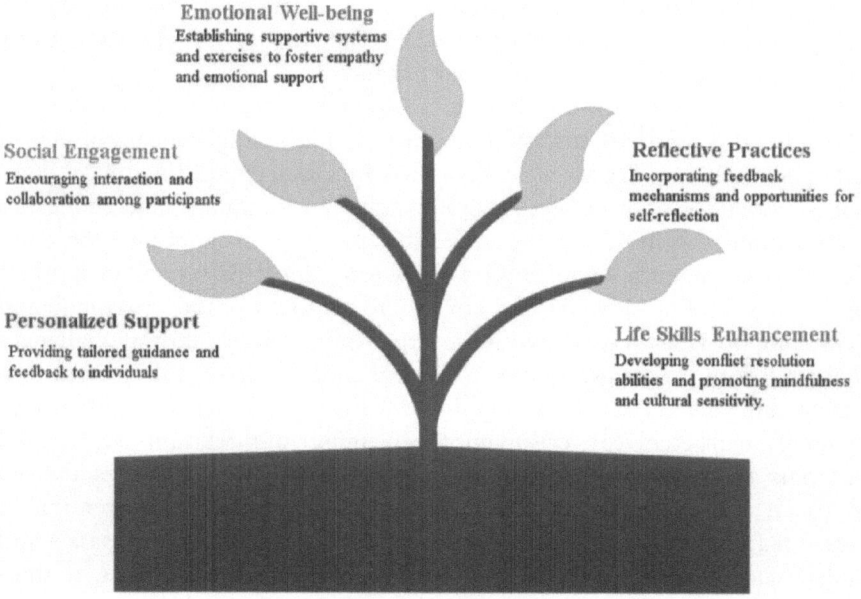

Emotional Well-being
Establishing supportive systems
and exercises to foster empathy
and emotional support

Social Engagement
Encouraging interaction and
collaboration among participants

Reflective Practices
Incorporating feedback
mechanisms and opportunities for
self-reflection

Personalized Support
Providing tailored guidance and
feedback to individuals

Life Skills Enhancement
Developing conflict resolution
abilities and promoting mindfulness
and cultural sensitivity.

FIGURE 7.7   Factors contributing for cultivating social and emotional intelligence.

Integration of AI-driven simulations and scenarios into educational contexts provides students with invaluable opportunities to actively engage in navigating diverse social situations, adeptly resolving conflicts, and adeptly fostering relationships within controlled yet authentic environments, thereby facilitating experiential learning and skill refinement. Concurrently, collaborative tasks orchestrated by AI platforms serve as fertile grounds for fostering peer learning and honing communication competencies, thereby fostering a synergistic learning environment wherein students can thrive collectively. By embedding GenAI into educational frameworks to cultivate social and emotional intelligence, educators stand to craft environments that not only prioritize academic achievement but also foster emotional resilience and social acumen, thereby empowering students to excel holistically in both academic endeavors and interpersonal relationships.

7.6.1   Social Interaction Platforms

AI-powered social interaction platforms driven by GenAI play a crucial role in enhancing student performance by nurturing improved communication, collaboration, and interpersonal skills. These platforms harness GenAI algorithms to scrutinize extensive student data encompassing communication patterns, social interactions, and individual preferences, thus tailoring experiences to meet each student's specific needs and educational objectives.

By facilitating virtual engagements like group discussions, debates, or collaborative projects, these platforms enable students to interact meaningfully with peers, irrespective of the physical distance.

The integration of AI into marketing not only transforms business strategies but also impacts student outcomes in marketing education. As AI reshapes marketing practices, students need to understand the ethical challenges associated with its use. By systematically examining these challenges from a multi-stakeholder perspective, students gain insights into the complex interdependencies and tensions between ethical principles in marketing. Understanding how AI can contribute to societal and environmental well-being provides students with the expertise to address ethical challenges in their future marketing careers. This enhances their overall growth and societal influence [102]. By leveraging AI-driven personalized content and channels, marketers can create more engaging and relevant educational materials tailored to individual learners' requirement. This personalized approach enhances student engagement, comprehension, and retention of course material, ultimately leading to improved academic performance and student success [103]. George et al. work delved into the influence of emotional intelligence (EI) on consumer decision-making styles during purchases, especially concerning brand trust (BT) and brand loyalty (BL). Carried out at Accra and West Hills Malls with a sample of 750 participants, the research investigates how EI impacts decision-making styles, which are influenced by BT and BL. Through confirmatory factor analysis and structural equation modeling, it reveals that EI acts as a mediator between BT and BL, particularly exhibiting stronger mediation at higher EI levels. In essence, this chapter aims to underscore the importance of EI in comprehending customer behavior and decision-making tendencies [104]. Liza et al. explored the importance of emotional intelligence (EI) in marketing in the Algerian telecommunications industry, an area that hasn't received much scholarly attention. EI is considered vital for nurturing relationships and facilitating effective communication, especially in light of technological advancements. Through statistical analysis, the study establishes a positive connection between EI and marketing effectiveness, suggesting that enhancing EI skills through targeted training could improve team performance. Emergence of AI-powered social interaction platforms, a product of learning with GenAI, presents an opportunity to incorporate EI principles into these platforms to enhance customer engagement. In summary, the study emphasizes the significance of EI in marketing and calls for further investigation, given the ongoing evolution of technology [105]. Mohammed Nadeem explored the relationship among GenAI, emotional intelligence (EI), and social skills in the context of marketing strategy. Its goal is to transform future marketing approaches by crafting personalized, emotionally engaging, and ethically sound strategies. Using an interdisciplinary approach, it tackles key questions including enhanced personalization, emotionally intelligent content creation, and ethical dilemmas. The research examines the integration of GAI and EI, ethical concerns, cross-cultural adaptability, and the lasting impact of emotionally intelligent marketing strategies. It offers practical insights and innovative strategies to fully utilize GAI, EI, and social skills [106].

Through AI-generated cues, recommendations, and feedback, students can hone crucial skills such as effective communication, active listening, and empathy, vital for academic success and future professional readiness. AI-powered social interaction platforms foster inclusive participation, ensuring all students have the opportunity to contribute and fostering a supportive and equitable learning atmosphere. These platforms may provide real-time monitoring and assessment tools, empowering educators to track students' social and emotional development and offer tailored support as required. By fostering dynamic social interactions and cultivating proficiency in communication, collaboration, and empathy, AI-powered social interaction platforms significantly bolster student engagement, academic attainment, and overall performance.

7.6.2 Virtual Mentors and Emotional Support Systems

Virtual instructors or mentors, also known as animated pedagogical agents, are computer-generated lifelike characters displayed onscreen. They assist learning by offering guidance or instruction within online learning environments. Prior studies have shown that incorporating such animated agents can enhance learning outcomes in online contexts. It plays a significant role in enhancing student outcomes through the provision of personalized guidance, assistance, and resources tailored to individual needs, and emotional wellness [107–109]. Utilizing GenAI algorithms, these systems analyze diverse student data, encompassing academic performance, behavioral patterns, and socio-emotional cues, to develop tailored support mechanisms. Virtual mentors offer individualized academic guidance, career counseling, and assistance with goal setting, aiding students in navigating academic hurdles and planning for their future endeavors [110, 111]. Recent advances in AI tools like Dalle-2 and ChatGPT have showcased new capabilities including synthetic video creation. This study explores the use of AI-generated synthetic video for online education, addressing a gap in research. Through a mixed-methods approach with 83 adult learners, the study compares traditional instructor videos with AI-generated ones. Findings reveal significant learning improvements with both, suggesting AI-generated videos as viable alternatives for high-quality online educational content [112]. The reason why AI-generated synthetic videos didn't show much difference from pedagogical agents and avatars might be because they're made to look like traditional talking head videos, while research on pedagogical agents and avatars focuses on making learning experiences better by using gestures and showing emotions instead of just talking [113].

Emotional support systems equip students with resources and strategies to cope with stress, anxiety, and other emotional challenges, fostering resilience and well-being. By delivering AI-generated responses, prompts, and interventions, students receive timely support and encouragement, fostering a positive mind set and motivation. Additionally, the availability of these systems round the clock ensures that students have access to support whenever needed. Through the creation of a supportive and inclusive learning environment, Virtual Mentors and Emotional Support Systems employing GenAI empower students to surmount obstacles, excel academically, and realize their full potential [114].

7.6.3 Empathy and Perspective-Taking Exercises

In response to the growing prominence of AI systems and concerns over their potential biases, Ruben et al. explored the impact of biased AI on empathy levels. Utilizing virtual reality (VR) to immerse participants in various personas, researchers sought to address this issue and potentially improve student outcomes. Their laboratory study revealed that students who engaged with VR and embodied different personas showed increased levels of empathy toward those characters. This implies that integrating VR technology into educational settings may promote greater empathy and understanding among students. Furthermore, the analysis of the personas embodied offered valuable insights into students' mental model development, potentially enhancing their overall learning experience and outcomes. Empathy and perspective-taking exercises facilitated by GenAI are crucial for enriching students' learning experiences and holistic development [115]. The exercises offer students opportunities to immerse themselves in others' perspectives, comprehend diverse viewpoints, and cultivate empathy. This skill is indispensable for navigating varied social landscapes. Leveraging GenAI algorithms, these exercises customize scenarios and interactions according to each student's distinct needs and capabilities, ensuring tailored learning experiences.

By engaging with AI-generated scenarios, students are prompted to explore alternative viewpoints, empathize with individuals from diverse backgrounds, and grasp complex emotions and situations. This not only deepens their understanding of human experiences but also hones their interpersonal skills, communication abilities, and conflict resolution techniques. Additionally, these exercises foster values such as tolerance, respect, and inclusivity, fostering a nurturing and harmonious learning environment. By incorporating these exercises into educational contexts, educators can effectively nurture students' social and emotional intelligence, equipping them to thrive in interconnected and diverse settings.

Empathy and perspective-taking exercises facilitated by GenAI significantly contributes to enhancing educational excellence by fostering empathy, comprehension, and interpersonal skills essential for success in academic pursuits and real-world scenarios. Empathy is crucial in addressing biases, and VR can aid in this by immersing stakeholders in the experiences of others. Through VR, stakeholders gain a better understanding of biases, fostering openness to diverse perspectives and potentially leading to more equitable AI systems. Research by Peck et al., Chen et al., and Banakou et al. illustrated VR's ability to diminish implicit biases based on race, gender, and age, with these effects enduring over time. This highlights VR's potential to shape societal attitudes and behaviors positively [116–118].

7.7 Long-Term Skill Development

Skill development has become a significant focus in the corporate sector, as skills rank among the top three external factors influencing business, alongside technology and market dynamics. Companies are increasingly recognizing the importance of skills and the negative consequences of skill gaps, as these directly impact the company's return on investment (ROI). Implementing an effective skill development system can cultivate human resources, leading to heightened productivity and contributing to national development. The emergence of AI has revolutionized the workplace, offering solutions to various challenges in skill development training, such as introducing innovative learning methods. AI enables technological advancements, facilitates data-driven analysis for quicker decision-making, and promotes efficiency, resulting in improved outcomes. Traditional job roles are now efficiently and cost-effectively performed by AI-powered systems, robotic process automation, and humanoids. Consequently, industries require new skill sets to operate such AI-powered machinery and systems, necessitating skill development initiatives for repositioning, upgrading, or upskilling workers [119].

In the modern era, our learning journey extends beyond our formal education at school or university; it requires continuous updating and reskilling to align with the rapidly evolving and innovating workforce. A significant paradox arises from a noticeable disparity between the demand for skills and their supply. The skills acquired through traditional education and training programs often fall short of meeting industry demands, a gap that has been exacerbated by the rise of Industry 4.0 and AI [120]. Implementing GenAI for long-term skill development involves a comprehensive strategy incorporating personalized learning, adaptive feedback, and ongoing enhancement. GenAI algorithms scrutinize extensive data to discern individual learning preferences, styles, and areas needing improvement, facilitating customized instruction and content delivery. AI promotes lifelong learning by encouraging self-directed exploration and curiosity, empowering students to pursue continuous growth beyond formal educational environments. By harnessing GenAI to customize learning experiences, deliver adaptive feedback, and foster lifelong learning, educators can foster enduring skill development, equipping students for success in an ever-evolving landscape. By adopting a holistic approach that integrates lifelong learning strategies, continuous skill assessment and development, and career readiness and future-proofing skills, individuals can effectively prepare themselves for long-term success and fulfilment in their personal and professional lives [121].

7.7.1 Lifelong Learning Strategies

The effective implementation of lifelong learning strategies can be achieved by integrating GenAI, which provides personalized and adaptable learning methods tailored to individual needs and preferences. Through GenAI algorithms, extensive data on a learner's interests, learning styles, and areas requiring improvement are analyzed to create customized learning paths and suggest appropriate content. Educational platforms can leverage GenAI to deliver tailored resources, interactive modules, and learning materials aligned with each learner's specific objectives. Furthermore, GenAI facilitates ongoing feedback and evaluation, enabling learners to monitor their progress and receive personalized guidance on areas needing further development. Additionally, GenAI can simulate real-world scenarios and offer virtual mentorship, providing immersive experiences that enhance practical skills and knowledge. By incorporating GenAI into lifelong learning strategies, individuals can embark on self-directed exploration and continuous development, adapting to evolving challenges and seizing new opportunities throughout their lifetimes.

7.7.2 Continuous Skill Assessment and Development

Continuous skill assessment and development can be effectively achieved through the application of GenAI, which enables personalized and dynamic evaluation of an individual's abilities and proficiencies over time. GenAI processes examine different information origins like achievement measurements, educational trends, and individual feedback to offer continuous evaluations for one's competencies and areas needing enhancement. By continually monitoring progress and pinpointing skill gaps, GenAI can suggest tailored learning resources, exercises, and tasks to address specific developmental needs. Furthermore, GenAI can simulate real-life scenarios and offer interactive simulations or virtual laboratories for practical skill enhancement. Moreover, platforms powered by GenAI can provide adaptive feedback, adjusting the complexity and pace of learning materials based on the learner's demonstrated competency. This cyclical process of evaluation and improvement, facilitated by GenAI, ensures that individuals receive targeted assistance and opportunities for advancement, leading to continual refinement of their skills and capabilities over time. Leveraging GenAI for ongoing skill assessment and development enables individuals to remain adaptable and responsive in an ever-changing environment, ensuring preparedness for future challenges and opportunities in both personal and professional spheres.

Within a college exam readiness program, students employed an AI-driven study platform incorporating GenAI to craft tailored study schedules and quiz exercises. By assessing students' proficiencies and shortcomings, the platform adjusted study resources to target areas necessitating improvement. Students rejoiced in their achievements as evidenced by improved exam scores, heightened preparedness and self-assurance during assessments, and ultimately, enhanced grades across their academic pursuits [122].

7.7.3   Career Readiness and Future-Proofing Skills

Integration of GenAI can significantly enhance the development of career readiness and future-proofing skills among students by providing customized guidance, adaptable learning experiences, and practical simulations. Through the analysis of extensive data pertaining to industry trends, job market demands, and emerging technologies, GenAI algorithms offer valuable insights into future skill requirements. Educational platforms powered by GenAI utilize this data to offer personalized career advice, recommending relevant career paths and skill development opportunities tailored to individual interests and strengths. GenAI generates immersive simulations and virtual environments that replicate real-world work scenarios, enabling students to acquire hands-on experience and refine essential skills such as problem solving and collaboration. Moreover, these platforms offer personalized learning pathways that emphasize future-proof skills like critical thinking and digital literacy, ensuring students are equipped to navigate evolving job markets and technological advancements. By integrating GenAI into educational initiatives, students can cultivate the necessary proficiencies to thrive in the workforce of tomorrow, enhancing their readiness for careers and strengthening their skillsets for long-term success.

AI in the workplace offers benefits like improved efficiency, faster decision-making, and innovation. Research on integrating workers and AI is still developing, necessitating understanding emerging themes. This study investigates effective coexistence between workers and AI, revealing key themes such as workers' distrust in AI and the importance of a blend of technical and human skills [123]. More recent theory that amalgamates various perspectives is "AI Job Replacement Theory," formulated by Huang and Rust. This theory posits that the influence of AI on employment restructures jobs and presents both opportunities for innovation and threats. It delineates four types of intelligence essential for tasks, especially in service-related positions and suggests a systematic sequence for AI deployment. As per the theory, AI primarily substitutes human labor at the task level, particularly for simple mechanical tasks. It predicts that, as AI gradually substitutes for lower-level tasks, there will be noticeable shifts in the importance of certain skills over time. As AI takes over analytical tasks requiring logical and rule-based thinking, the significance of analytical skills may diminish. Eventually, AI might also handle intuitive and empathic tasks, revolutionizing the integration of humans and machines in service provision but posing a risk to human employment [124, 125].

Table 7.4 shows the theoretical models for leveraging GenAI in educational contexts, covering personalized learning, adaptive assessment, creativity

TABLE 7.4 Generative AI-Enabled Frameworks for Student Growth

Framework/Model	Description
Personalized Learning [126–128]	Model name: Learner-centric approach Description: This framework leverages generative AI algorithms to analyze individual student data and preferences, allowing for the development of customized learning experiences adapted to individual learners' requirements, speed, and preferences.
Adaptive Assessment [129–131]	Model name: Dynamic assessment framework Description: This model integrates generative AI to continuously adapt assessment content and difficulty levels based on real-time student performance data, enabling personalized feedback and targeted intervention strategies for skill improvement.
Creativity Enhancement [132]	Model name: AI-driven creative toolkit Description: This framework harnesses generative AI tools to stimulate and support creative thinking by generating novel ideas, providing creative prompts, and facilitating exploration and experimentation in diverse creative domains.
Social-Emotional Intelligence Cultivation [133, 134]	Model name: Empathetic AI Framework Description: This model employs generative AI to foster social-emotional intelligence by generating empathy-building scenarios, facilitating perspective-taking exercises, and providing personalized feedback on emotional expression and interpersonal interactions.
Long-Term Skill Development [135, 136]	Model name: Lifelong learning pathway Description: This framework utilizes generative AI to create personalized skill development pathways that adapt and evolve over time based on learner progress, interests, and emerging trends, ensuring continuous growth and readiness for future challenges.

enhancement, social-emotional intelligence cultivation, and long-term skill development. The table shows how GenAI is transforming educational technology by offering models designed to enhance student outcomes. Each framework employs AI to analyze student data, personalize learning experiences, and adapt assessments in real time. The learner- centered approach tailors educational materials to individual needs, while the dynamic assessment framework adjusts assessment content based on performance data. The AI-driven creative toolkit fosters creativity by generating innovative prompts, and the Empathetic AI Framework develops social-emotional skills through empathy-building scenarios and personalized feedback. Lastly, the Lifelong Learning Pathway creates adaptive skill development pathways to support ongoing growth and readiness for future challenges, reflecting both established research and emerging trends in AI and education.

7.8   Recommendations and Outcomes

The chapter on "Impact of GenAI on Student Outcomes" offers valuable insights and recommendations for leveraging GenAI in education. It emphasizes enhancing personalization and engagement by integrating AI tools such as ChatGPT to develop adaptive, individualized learning experiences that meet diverse student needs. This approach fosters critical 21st-century skills, including creativity, collaboration, and problem solving. Addressing ethical, privacy, and equity issues is essential, with clear guidelines and policies needed to protect student data and ensure academic integrity while providing fair access to all learners. Effective AI integration requires cooperation among educators, technologists, policymakers, and other stakeholders to align AI implementations with educational goals and overcome challenges. GenAI should also be used to support lifelong learning through personalized paths, adaptive feedback, and real-world simulations, helping individuals stay competitive in a dynamic job market. Emphasizing the acquisition of new skills for operating AI systems and providing adequate training will help overcome resistance and maximize AI's benefits. This chapter is recommended for readers interested in understanding how GenAI can transform educational practices, improve student outcomes, and prepare individuals for future career and societal demands.

7.9   Conclusion

The integration of AI, particularly GenAI, into education offers transformative potential by creating personalized, immersive, and adaptive learning experiences, driven by advancements in machine learning, deep learning, generative adversarial networks (GANs), and natural language processing (NLP). Tools like ChatGPT demonstrate AI's rapid adoption in educational settings, providing personalized learning pathways and formative assessments. However, these benefits come with challenges, including ethical considerations, privacy concerns, and the need for equitable access to quality education. Addressing these issues requires careful planning and collaboration among educators, technologists, policymakers, and stakeholders. Beyond academics, AI fosters essential 21st-century skills such as critical thinking, creativity, collaboration, and social-emotional intelligence. AI-powered tools and simulation-based learning environments support experiential learning and problem solving, while virtual mentors and emotional support systems offer personalized guidance, enhancing student well-being and success. In the corporate sector, AI profoundly impacts skill development, necessitating continuous reskilling and upskilling to keep pace with technological advancements. GenAI supports lifelong learning by providing personalized learning paths, adaptive feedback, and real-world scenario simulations, ensuring individuals remain competitive in the evolving job market. AI promises to enhance efficiency, decision-making, and innovation in the workplace, while also requiring new skill sets to operate AI-powered systems effectively. The integration of AI into education and the workplace reflects emerging trends in educational technology and underscores the importance of continuous skill development to meet future demands, preparing students and professionals for meaningful societal contributions.

References

1. T. Adiguzel, M. H. Kaya, and F. K. Cansu, "Revolutionizing education with AI: Exploring the transformative potential of ChatGPT," *Contemp. Educ. Technol.*, vol. 15, no. 3, p. ep429, 2023.
2. M. Mariani and Y. K. Dwivedi, "Generative artificial intelligence in innovation management: A preview of future research developments," *J. Bus. Res.*, vol. 175, p. 114542, 2024.
3. A. Yusuf, N. Pervin, and M. Román-González, "Generative AI and the future of higher education: A threat to academic integrity or reformation? Evidence from multicultural perspectives," *Int. J. Educ. Technol. High. Educ.*, vol. 21, no. 1, 2024.
4. F. J. Cantú-Ortiz, N. Galeano Sánchez, L. Garrido, H. Terashima-Marin, and R. F. Brena, "An artificial intelligence educational strategy for the digital transformation," *Int. J. Interact. Des. Manuf.*, vol. 14, no. 4, pp. 1195–1209, 2020.
5. Y. K. Dwivedi, A. Sharma, N. P. Rana, M. Giannakis, P. Goel, and V. Dutot, "Evolution of artificial intelligence research in technological forecasting and social change: Research topics, trends, and future directions," *Technol. Forecast. Soc. Change*, vol. 192, p. 122579, 2023.
6. L. Banh and G. Strobel, "Generative artificial intelligence," *Electron. Mark.*, vol. 33, no. 1, 2023.
7. L. Wang, "From intelligence science to intelligent manufacturing," *Engineering*, vol. 5, no. 4, pp. 615–618, 2019.
8. R. C. Eberhart and R. W. Dobbins, "Early neural network development history: The age of Camelot," *IEEE Eng. Med. Biol. Mag.*, vol. 9, no. 3, pp. 15–18, 1990.
9. D. Baïdoo-Anu and L. Owusu Ansah, "Education in the era of generative artificial intelligence (AI): Understanding the potential benefits of ChatGPT in promoting teaching and learning," *J. AI*, vol. 7, no. 1, pp. 52–62, 2023.

10. Y. Xue and Y. Wang, "Artificial intelligence for education and teaching," *Wirel. Commun. Mob. Comput.*, vol. 2022, pp. 1–10, 2022.
11. H. Yu and Y. Guo, "Generative artificial intelligence empowers educational reform: Current status, issues, and prospects," *Front. Educ.*, vol. 8, 2023.
12. K. Zhang and A. B. Aslan, "AI technologies for education: Recent research & future directions," *Comput. Educ. Artif. Intell.*, vol. 2, p. 100025, 2021.
13. F. Kamalov, D. Santandreu Calonge, and I. Gurrib, "New Era of artificial intelligence in education: Towards a sustainable multifaceted revolution," *Sustainability*, vol. 15, no. 16, p. 12451, 2023.
14. P. C. Verhoef et al., "Digital transformation: A multidisciplinary reflection and research agenda," *J. Bus. Res.*, vol. 122, pp. 889–901, 2021.
15. Z. Bahroun, C. Anane, V. Ahmed, and A. Zacca, "Transforming education: A comprehensive review of generative artificial intelligence in educational settings through bibliometric and content analysis," *Sustainability*, vol. 15, no. 17, p. 12983, 2023.
16. K. Siau and W. Wang, "Artificial intelligence (AI) ethics: Ethics of AI and ethical AI," *J. Database Manag.*, vol. 31, no. 2, pp. 74–87, 2020.
17. L. Lobschat et al., "Corporate digital responsibility," *J. Bus. Res.*, vol. 122, pp. 875–888, 2021.
18. R. Luckin, "Towards artificial intelligence-based assessment systems," *Nat. Hum. Behav.*, vol. 1, no. 3, p. 0028, 2017.
19. B. Ross, A.-M. Chase, D. Robbie, G. Oates, and Y. Absalom, "Adaptive quizzes to increase motivation, engagement and learning outcomes in a first year accounting unit," *Int. J. Educ. Technol. High. Educ.*, vol. 15, no. 1, 2018.
20. K. Seo, J. Tang, I. Roll, S. Fels, and D. Yoon, "The impact of artificial intelligence on learner–instructor interaction in online learning," *Int. J. Educ. Technol. High. Educ.*, vol. 18, no. 1, 2021.
21. A. Haleem, M. Javaid, M. A. Qadri, and R. Suman, "Understanding the role of digital technologies in education: A review," *Sustain. Oper. Comput.*, vol. 3, pp. 275–285, 2022.
22. M. L. Owoc, A. Sawicka, and P. Weichbroth, "Artificial intelligence technologies in education: Benefits, challenges and strategies of implementation," in *IFIP Advances in Information and Communication Technology*. Cham: Springer International Publishing, 2021, pp. 37–58.
23. Y. K. Dwivedi et al., "Opinion paper: 'So what if ChatGPT wrote it?' Multidisciplinary perspectives on opportunities, challenges and implications of generative conversational AI for research, practice and policy," *Int. J. Inf. Manage.*, vol. 71, p. 102642, 2023.
24. S. Schuetz and V. Venkatesh, "Research perspectives: The rise of human machines: How cognitive computing systems challenge assumptions of user-system interaction," *J. Assoc. Inf. Syst.*, pp. 460–482, 2020.
25. F. Brachten, T. Kissmer, and S. Stieglitz, "The acceptance of chatbots in an enterprise context – a survey study," *Int. J. Inf. Manage.*, vol. 60, p. 102375, 2021.
26. H. Zhen and W. A. J. W. Yahaya, "Use of generative AI tools to facilitate personalized learning in the flipped classroom," in *Transforming Education with Generative AI*. IGI Global, 2024, pp. 327–349.
27. N. Bostrom and E. Yudkowsky, "The ethics of artificial intelligence," in *The Cambridge Handbook of Artificial Intelligence*. Cambridge University Press, 2014, pp. 316–334.
28. H. Peng, S. Ma, and J. M. Spector, "Personalized adaptive learning: An emerging pedagogical approach enabled by a smart learning environment," *Smart Learn. Environ.*, vol. 6, no. 1, 2019.
29. R. Huang, G. Chen, J. Yang, and J. Loewen, "The new shape of learning: Adapting to social changes in the information society," in *Reshaping Learning*. Berlin, Heidelberg: Springer Berlin Heidelberg, 2013, pp. 3–42.

30. J. Yang, C. Hong, and H. Yu, "Research focuses and trend on smart learning environments – dialogue with ET&S editor Kinshuk," *E-Educ. Res.*, vol. 36, no. 5, pp. 85–88, 2015.
31. K. M. Tolle, D. S. W. Tansley, and A. J. G. Hey, "The fourth paradigm: Data-intensive scientific discovery (point of view)," *Proc. IEEE Inst. Electr. Electron. Eng.*, vol. 99, no. 8, pp. 1334–1337, 2011.
32. Z. T. Zhu and D. M. Shen, "New paradigm of educational technology research based on big data," *E-Educ. Res.*, pp. 5–13, 2013.
33. Z. T. Zhu and J. Q. Guan, "The construction framework of 'network learning space for everyone,'" *China Educ. Technol*, no. 10, pp. 1–7, 2013.
34. M. Rizvi, "Investigating AI-powered tutoring systems that adapt to individual student needs, providing personalized guidance and assessments," *Eurasia Proc. Educ. Soc. Sci.*, vol. 31, pp. 67–73, 2023.
35. F. Martin and D. U. Bolliger, "Engagement matters: Student perceptions on the importance of engagement strategies in the online learning environment," *Online Learn.*, vol. 22, no. 1, 2018.
36. V. Abou-Khalil, S. Helou, E. Khalifé, M. A. Chen, R. Majumdar, and H. Ogata, "Emergency online learning in low-resource settings: Effective student engagement strategies," *Educ. Sci.*, vol. 11, no. 1, p. 24, 2021.
37. B. S. Bloom, "The 2 sigma problem: The search for methods of group instruction as effective as one-to-one tutoring," *Educ. Res.*, vol. 13, no. 6, p. 4, 1984.
38. O. Zawacki-Richter, V. I. Marín, M. Bond, and F. Gouverneur, "Systematic review of research on artificial intelligence applications in higher education – where are the educators?," *Int. J. Educ. Technol. High. Educ.*, vol. 16, no. 1, 2019.
39. E. Chen and M. Asta, "Using jupyter tools to design an interactive textbook to guide undergraduate research in materials informatics," *J. Chem. Educ.*, vol. 99, no. 10, pp. 3601–3606, 2022.
40. N. Arslan Namli and B. Aybek, "An investigation of the effect of block-based programming and unplugged coding activities on fifth graders' computational thinking skills, self-efficacy and academic performance," *Contemp. Educ. Technol.*, vol. 14, no. 1, p. ep341, 2022.
41. M. Jaboob, M. Hazaimeh, and A. M. Al-Ansi, "Integration of generative AI techniques and applications in student behavior and cognitive achievement in Arab higher education," *Int. J. Hum. Comput. Interact.*, pp. 1–14, 2024.
42. R. C. Sharma and A. Bozkurt, Eds ., "Transforming education with generative AI: Prompt engineering and synthetic content creation," in *Advances in Educational Technologies and Instructional Design*. IGI Global, 7 February 2024.
43. J. S. Jauhiainen and A. Garagorry Guerra, "Generative AI and ChatGPT in school children's education: Evidence from a school lesson," *Sustainability*, vol. 15, no. 18, p. 14025, 2023.
44. S. MacNeil, A. Tran, D. Mogil, S. Bernstein, E. Ross, and Z. Huang, "Generating diverse code explanations using the GPT-3 large language model," in *Proceedings of the 2022 ACM Conference on International Computing Education Research - Volume 2*, 2022.
45. K. Nikolopoulou, "Generative artificial intelligence in higher education: Exploring ways of harnessing pedagogical practices with the assistance of ChatGPT," *Int. J. Changes Educ.*, vol. 1, no. 2, pp. 103–111, 2024.
46. H. Crompton and D. Burke, "Artificial intelligence in higher education: The state of the field," *Int. J. Educ. Technol. High. Educ.*, vol. 20, no. 1, 2023.
47. J. Crawford, M. Cowling, K.-A. Allen, "Leadership is needed for ethical ChatGPT: Character, assessment, and learning using artificial intelligence (AI)," *J. Univ. Teach. Learn. Pract.*, vol. 20, no. 3, 2023.

48. M. Á . Escotet, "The optimistic future of artificial intelligence in higher education," *Prospects*, pp. 1–10, 2023.

49. K. Kaharuddin, "Assessing the effect of using artificial intelligence on the writing skill of Indonesian learners of English," *Linguist. Cult. Rev.*, vol. 5, no. 1, pp. 288–304, 2022.

50. M. Benvenuti et al., "Artificial intelligence and human behavioral development: A perspective on new skills and competencies acquisition for the educational context," *Comput. Hum. Behav.*, vol. 148, 2023.

51. I. Ruthotto, Q. Kreth, J. Stevens, C. Trively, and J. Melkers, "Lurking and participation in the virtual classroom: The effects of gender, race, and age among graduate students in computer science," *Comput. Educ.*, vol. 151, p. 103854, 2020.

52. K. Walczak and W. Cellary, "Challenges for higher education in the era of widespread access to generative AI," *Econ. Bus. Rev.*, vol. 9, no. 2, 2023.

53. T. Wang et al., "Exploring the potential impact of artificial intelligence (AI) on international students in higher education: Generative AI, chatbots, analytics, and international student success," *Appl. Sci.*, vol. 13, no. 11, p. 6716, 2023.

54. S. M. Bender, "Awareness of artificial intelligence as an essential digital literacy: ChatGPT and gen-AI in the classroom," *Chang. Engl.*, vol. 31, no. 2, pp. 161–174, 2024.

55. B. L. Moorhouse, M. A. Yeo, and Y. Wan, "Generative AI tools and assessment: Guidelines of the world's top-ranking universities," *Comput. Educ. Open*, vol. 5, p. 100151, 2023.

56. K. Nikolopoulou, "Self-regulated and mobile-mediated learning in blended tertiary education environments: Student insights from a pilot study," *Sustainability*, vol. 15, no. 16, p. 12284, 2023.

57. H. U. Rahiman and R. Kodikal, "Revolutionizing education: Artificial intelligence empowered learning in higher education," *Cogent Educ.*, vol. 11, no. 1, 2024.

58. I. Pesovski, R. Santos, R. Henriques, and V. Trajkovik, "Generative AI for customizable learning experiences," *Sustainability*, vol. 16, no. 7, p. 3034, 2024.

59. J. Udolph, S. Tan, and S. Tan, "ChatGPT: Bullshit spewer or the end of traditional assessments in higher education?," *J. Appl. Learn. Teach.*, vol. 6, no. 1, 2023.

60. A. Essien, G. Chukwukelu, and V. Essien, "Opportunities and challenges of adopting artificial intelligence for learning and teaching in higher education," in *Fostering Communication and Learning with Underutilized Technologies in Higher Education*. IGI Global, 2021, pp. 67–78.

61. M. Wenge, "Artificial intelligence-based real-time communication and ai-multimedia services in higher education," *J. Mult. Valued Logic Soft Comput.*, vol. 36, no. 1, pp. 231–248, 2021.

62. W. Cui, Z. Xue, and K.-P. Thai, "Performance comparison of an AI-based adaptive learning system in China," in *2018 Chinese Automation Congress (CAC)*, 2018.

63. A. Rahimi and D. Tafazoli, "The role of university teachers' 21st-century digital competence in their attitudes toward ICT integration in higher education: Extending the theory of planned behavior," *JALT CALL J.*, vol. 18, no. 2, pp. 238–263, 2022.

64. R. J. Passonneau, D. McNamara, S. Muresan, and D. Perin, "Preface: Special issue on multidisciplinary approaches to AI and education for reading and writing," *Int. J. Artif. Intell. Educ.*, vol. 27, no. 4, pp. 665–670, 2017.

65. S. Grassini, "Shaping the future of education: Exploring the potential and consequences of AI and ChatGPT in educational settings," *Educ. Sci.*, vol. 13, no. 7, p. 692, 2023.

66. I. Tuomi, "Beyond mastery: Toward a broader understanding of AI in education," *Int. J. Artif. Intell. Educ.*, vol. 34, no. 1, pp. 20–30, 2024.

67. A. R. Doshi and O. Hauser, "Generative artificial intelligence enhances creativity," *Sci. Adv.*, vol. 10, no. 28, p. eadn5290, 2023. https://ssrn.com/abstract=4535536 or http://dx.doi.org/10.2139/ssrn.4535536
68. E. Cherry and C. Latulipe, "Quantifying the creativity support of digital tools through the Creativity Support Index," *ACM Trans. Comput. Hum. Interact.*, vol. 21, no. 4, pp. 1–25, 2014.
69. K. I. Gero, V. Liu, and L. Chilton, "Sparks: Inspiration for science writing using language models," in *Designing Interactive Systems Conference*, 2022.
70. J. Koch, A. Lucero, L. Hegemann, and A. Oulasvirta, "May AI?: Design ideation with cooperative contextual bandits," in *Proceedings of the 2019 CHI Conference on Human Factors in Computing Systems*, 2019.
71. C.-P. Dai and F. Ke, "Educational applications of artificial intelligence in simulation-based learning: A systematic mapping review," *Comput. Educ. Artif. Intell.*, vol. 3, p. 100087, 2022.
72. A. F. Khalid, M. A. George, C. Eggen, A. Sritharan, F. Wali, and A. M. Viens, "Using simulation-based experiential learning to increase students' ability to analyze increasingly complex global health challenges: A mixed methods study," *bioRxiv*, 2023.
73. D. A. Cook, "How much evidence does it take? A cumulative meta-analysis of outcomes of simulation-based education," *Med. Educ.*, vol. 48, no. 8, pp. 750–760, 2014.
74. O. Chernikova et al., "Facilitating diagnostic competences in higher education – a meta-analysis in medical and teacher education," *Educ. Psychol. Rev.*, vol. 32, no. 1, pp. 157–196, 2020.
75. D. Duchatelet and V. Donche, "Assessing student learning during simulations in education: Methodological opportunities and challenges when applying a longitudinal case study design," *Stud. Educ. Eval.*, vol. 72, p. 101129, 2022.
76. H. Rico, M. A. de la Puente Pacheco, A. Pabon, and I. Portnoy, "Evaluating the impact of simulation-based instruction on critical thinking in the Colombian Caribbean: An experimental study," *Cogent Educ.*, vol. 10, no. 2, 2023.
77. W. Xu and F. Ouyang, "The application of AI technologies in STEM education: A systematic review from 2011 to 2021," *Int. J. STEM Educ.*, vol. 9, no. 1, 2022.
78. O. Chernikova, N. Heitzmann, M. Stadler, D. Holzberger, T. Seidel, and F. Fischer, "Simulation-based learning in higher education: A meta-analysis," *Rev. Educ. Res.*, vol. 90, no. 4, pp. 499–541, 2020.
79. B. George and O. Wooden, "Managing the strategic transformation of higher education through artificial intelligence," *Adm. Sci.*, vol. 13, no. 9, p. 196, 2023.
80. J. Lean, J. Moizer, C. Derham, L. Strachan, and Z. Bhuiyan, "Real world learning: Simulation and gaming," in *Applied Pedagogies for Higher Education*. Cham: Springer International Publishing, 2021, pp. 187–214.
81. S. Joksimovic, D. Ifenthaler, R. Marrone, M. De Laat, and G. Siemens, "Opportunities of artificial intelligence for supporting complex problem-solving: Findings from a scoping review," *Comput. Educ. Artif. Intell.*, vol. 4, p. 100138, 2023.
82. P. Jiang, X. Ruan, Z. Feng, Y. Jiang, and B. Xiong, "Research on online collaborative problem-solving in the last 10 years: Current status, hotspots, and outlook – a knowledge graph analysis based on CiteSpace," *Mathematics*, vol. 11, no. 10, p. 2353, 2023.
83. Meifitri, "Problem solving ability and communication skill through problem-based learning approach," in *Proceedings of the Eighth International Conference on Languages and Arts (ICLA-2019)*, 2020.
84. H. S. Sætra, "Generative AI: Here to stay, but for good?," *Technol. Soc.*, vol. 75, p. 102372, 2023.

85. S. L. Wismath and D. Orr, "Collaborative learning in problem solving: A case study in metacognitive learning," *Can. J. Scholarsh. Teach. Learn.*, vol. 6, no. 3, 2015.
86. R. Michel-Villarreal, E. Vilalta-Perdomo, D. E. Salinas-Navarro, R. Thierry-Aguilera, and F. S. Gerardou, "Challenges and opportunities of generative AI for higher education as explained by ChatGPT," *Educ. Sci.*, vol. 13, no. 9, p. 856, 2023.
87. S. Gökoğlu, "Challenges and limitations of generative AI in education," in *Transforming Education with Generative AI*. IGI Global, 2024, pp. 158–181.
88. R. Yilmaz and F. G. Karaoglan Yilmaz, "The effect of generative artificial intelligence (AI)-based tool use on students' computational thinking skills, programming self-efficacy and motivation," *Comput. Educ. Artif. Intell.*, vol. 4, p. 100147, 2023.
89. S. Habib, T. Vogel, X. Anli, and E. Thorne, "How does generative artificial intelligence impact student creativity?," *J. Creat.*, vol. 34, no. 1, p. 100072, 2024.
90. E. P. Torrance, "Creativity what research says to the teacher, series," *Natl. Educ. Assoc. Ser.*, p. 36, 1969. https://eric.ed.gov/?id=ED078435
91. A. M. A. Alabbasi, S. H. Paek, D. Kim, and B. Cramond, "What do educators need to know about the Torrance tests of creative thinking: A comprehensive review," *Front. Psychol.*, vol. 13, 2022.
92. A. Alhashim et al., "Work in progress: Assessing creativity of alternative uses task responses: A detailed procedure," in *2020 ASEE Virtual Annual Conference Content Access Proceedings*, 2020.
93. A. Chirico, V. P. Glaveanu, P. Cipresso, G. Riva, and A. Gaggioli, "Awe enhances creative thinking: An experimental study," *Creat. Res. J.*, vol. 30, no. 2, pp. 123–131, 2018.
94. P. Collard and J. Looney, "Nurturing creativity in education," *Eur. J. Educ.*, vol. 49, no. 3, pp. 348–364, 2014.
95. M. Csikszentmihalyi, "On runco's problem finding, problem solving, and creativity," *Creat. Res. J.*, vol. 9, no. 2, pp. 267–268, 1996. [64. M. A. Runco and S. Acar, "Divergent thinking as an indicator of creative potential," *Creat. Res. J.*, vol. 24, no. 1, pp. 66–75, 2012].
96. Y. Walter, "Embracing the future of artificial intelligence in the classroom: The relevance of AI literacy, prompt engineering, and critical thinking in modern education," *Int. J. Educ. Technol. High. Educ.*, vol. 21, no. 1, 2024.
97. J. M. Spector and S. Ma, "Inquiry and critical thinking skills for the next generation: From artificial intelligence back to human intelligence," *Smart Learn. Environ.*, vol. 6, no. 1, 2019.
98. X. Zou, P. Su, L. Li, and P. Fu, "AI-generated content tools and students' critical thinking: Insights from a Chinese University," *IFLA J.*, vol. 50, no. 2, pp. 228–241, 2023.
99. B. A. Hoyos, "Welcoming AI into the classroom," *IE Insights*, 5 May 2023.
100. A. J. Adetayo, "Artificial intelligence chatbots inacademic libraries: The rise of ChatGPT," *Library HiTech News*, vol. 40, no. 3, pp. 18–21, 2023.
101. S. C. Tan, W. Chen, and B. L. Chua, "Leveraging generative artificial intelligence based on large language models for collaborative learning," *Learn. Res. Pr.*, vol. 9, no. 2, pp. 125–134, 2023.
102. E. Hermann, "Leveraging artificial intelligence in marketing for social good – an ethical perspective," *J. Bus. Ethics*, vol. 179, no. 1, pp. 43–61, 2022.
103. A. Haleem, M. Javaid, M. Asim Qadri, R. Pratap Singh, and R. Suman, "Artificial intelligence (AI) applications for marketing: A literature-based study," *Int. J. Intell. Netw.*, vol. 3, pp. 119–132, 2022.

104. G. Kankam and I. T. Charnor, "Emotional intelligence and consumer decision-making styles: The mediating role of brand trust and brand loyalty," *Futur. Bus. J.*, vol. 9, no. 1, 2023.

105. L. Mousli, C. Larras, M. Bouchetara, and S. Iraten, "Personal and social skills' impact on marketing effectiveness," *Mark. Instytucji Nauk. Badaw.*, vol. 50, no. 4, pp. 137–164, 2023.

106. M. Nadeem, "Generative artificial intelligence [GAI]: Enhancing future marketing strategies with emotional intelligence [EI], and social skills," *Br. J. Market. Stud.*, vol. 12, pp. 1–15, 2024. 10.13140/RG.2.2.24421.99041.

107. N. Mabanza and L. de Wet, "Determining the usability effect of pedagogical interface agents on adult computer literacy training," in *E-Learning Paradigms and Applications*. Berlin, Heidelberg: Springer Berlin Heidelberg, 2014, pp. 145–183.

108. R. E. Mayer and C. S. DaPra, "An embodiment effect in computer-based learning with animated pedagogical agents," *J. Exp. Psychol. Appl.*, vol. 18, no. 3, pp. 239–252, 2012.

109. F. Wang, W. Li, H. Xie, and H. Liu, "Is pedagogical agent in multimedia learning good for learning? A meta-analysis," *Xin Li Ke Xue Jin Zhan*, vol. 25, no. 1, p. 12, 2017.

110. W. M. Lim, A. Gunasekara, J. L. Pallant, J. I. Pallant, and E. Pechenkina, "Generative AI and the future of education: Ragnarök or reformation? A paradoxical perspective from management educators," *Int. J. Manag. Educ.*, vol. 21, no. 2, p. 100790, 2023.

111. C. K. Y. Chan and W. Hu, "Students' voices on generative AI: Perceptions, benefits, and challenges in higher education," *Int. J. Educ. Technol. High. Educ.*, vol. 20, no. 1, 2023.

112. D. Leiker, A. R. Gyllen, I. Eldesouky, and M. Cukurova, "Generative AI for learning: Investigating the potential of synthetic learning videos," *arXiv [cs. CV]*, 2023.

113. A. P. Lawson, R. E. Mayer, N. Adamo-Villani, B. Benes, X. Lei, and J. Cheng, "Do learners recognize and relate to the emotions displayed by virtual instructors?," *Int. J. Artif. Intell. Educ.*, vol. 31, no. 1, pp. 134–153, 2021.

114. P. Pataranutaporn, J. Leong, V. Danry, A. P. Lawson, P. Maes, and M. Sra, "AI-generated virtual instructors based on liked or admired people can improve motivation and foster positive emotions for learning," in *2022 IEEE Frontiers in Education Conference (FIE)*, 2022.

115. R. Schlagowski, M. Volanti, K. Weitz, S. Mertes, J. Kuch, and E. André, "The feeling of being classified: Raising empathy and awareness for AI bias through perspective-taking in VR," *Front. Virtual Real.*, vol. 5, 2024.

116. T. C. Peck, S. Seinfeld, S. M. Aglioti, and M. Slater, "Putting yourself in the skin of a black avatar reduces implicit racial bias," *Conscious. Cogn.*, vol. 22, no. 3, pp. 779–787, 2013.

117. V. H. H. Chen, G. C. Ibasco, V. J. X. Leow, and J. Y. Y. Lew, "The effect of VR avatar embodiment on improving attitudes and closeness toward immigrants," *Front. Psychol.*, vol. 12, 2021.

118. D. Banakou, P. D. Hanumanthu, and M. Slater, "Virtual embodiment of white people in a black virtual body leads to a sustained reduction in their implicit racial bias," *Front. Hum. Neurosci.*, vol. 10, 2016.

119. Biswabhusan Behera, Mamta Gaur, and Mohammad Asif, *Impact of Artificial Intelligence on Skill Development Training in India*. River Publishers, 2023.

120. S. McKee and D. Gauch, "Implications of industry 4.0 on skills development," in *Education in the Asia-Pacific Region: Issues, Concerns and Prospects*. Singapore: Springer Singapore, 2020, pp. 279–288.

121. S. Morandini, F. Fraboni, M. De Angelis, G. Puzzo, D. Giusino, and L. Pietran-toni, "The impact of artificial intelligence on workers' skills: Upskilling and reskilling in organisations," *Inf. Sci.*, vol. 26, pp. 039–068, 2023.
122. A. Grájeda, J. Burgos, P. Córdova, and A. Sanjinés, "Assessing student-perceived impact of using artificial intelligence tools: Construction of a synthetic index of application in higher education," *Cogent Educ.*, vol. 11, no. 1, 2024.
123. A. Zirar, S. I. Ali, and N. Islam, "Worker and workplace artificial intelligence (AI) coexistence: Emerging themes and research agenda," *Technovation*, vol. 124, p. 102747, 2023.
124. M.-H. Huang, R. Rust, and V. Maksimovic, "The feeling economy: Managing in the next generation of artificial intelligence (AI)," *Calif. Manage. Rev.*, vol. 61, no. 4, pp. 43–65, 2019.
125. M.-H. Huang and R. T. Rust, "Artificial intelligence in service," *J. Serv. Res.*, vol. 21, no. 2, pp. 155–172, 2018.
126. J. Pane, E. Steiner, M. Baird, and L. Hamilton, *Continued Progress: Promising Evidence on Personalized Learning*. RAND Corporation, 2015.
127. V. S. Magomadov, "The application of artificial intelligence and big data analytics in personalized learning," *J. Phys. Conf. Ser.*, vol. 1691, no. 1, p. 012169, 2020.
128. A. Bhutoria, "Personalized education and Artificial Intelligence in the United States, China, and India: A systematic review using a human-in-the-loop model," *Comput. Educ. Artif. Intell.*, vol. 3, p. 100068, 2022.
129. M. C. Desmarais and R. S. J. d. Baker, "A review of recent advances in learner and skill modeling in intelligent learning environments," *User Model. User Adapt. Interact.*, vol. 22, no. 1–2, pp. 9–38, 2012.
130. S. Minn, "AI-assisted knowledge assessment techniques for adaptive learning environments," *Comput. Educ. Artif. Intell.*, vol. 3, p. 100050, 2022.
131. R. A. C. Dela Cruz, "Assessment of the adaptive learning system implementa-tion in selected private school: Basis for enrichment," *Cosmos Int. J. Art Higher Educ.*, vol. 12, no. 1, pp. 144–156, 2023.
132. J. McCormack, T. Gifford, and P. Hutchings, "Autonomy, authenticity, author-ship and intention in computer generated art," in *Computational Intelligence in Music, Sound, Art and Design*. Cham: Springer International Publishing, 2019, pp. 35–50.
133. J. A. Durlak, C. E. Domitrovich, R. P. Weissberg, and T. P. Gullotta, *Hand-book of Social and Emotional Learning: Research and Practice*. The Guilford Press, 2015.
134. M. H. Immordino-Yang and A. Damasio, "We feel, therefore we learn: The relevance of affective and social neuroscience to education," *Mind Brain Educ.*, vol. 1, no. 1, pp. 3–10, 2007.
135. P. Jarvis, *Learning to be a Person in Society*. London, England: Routledge, 2012.
136. G. Siemens, "Connectivism: A learning theory for the digital age," *Int. J. Instruct. Technol. Distance Learn.*, vol. 2, p. 9, 2005.

8

CASE STUDY

Streamlining Knowledge Acquisition through AI-Driven Summarization

Ashutosh Adhikari, Ananya Datta, and Ami Munshi

8.1 Introduction

In recent years, the growth of Generative AI (GenAI) has revolutionized information processing, particularly in the education sector. The ability to amalgamate bulk data and summarizing them is significant for students, educators, and researchers who are often swamped by the massive amount of academic material they must absorb and understand. The need for fast, accurate, and concise abstracts and summaries has never been more pressing. Publicly accessible but closed source proprietary language models like ChatGPT, Claude, and Gemini have demonstrated significant potential in automatic text summarization. These models, running on cloud-based platforms help streamline the learning and teaching processes. However, several challenges exist with using cloud-based large language models (LLMs). One major concern is privacy as there is risk associated with handling private and sensitive data, as there is no guarantee that user prompts and data are not being stored and used for further training ([1, 2]).

Additionally, these LLMs are subject to rate limits, which can reduce their usability, especially in environments requiring large-scale and continuous summarization tasks. There is also a question of optimization, as the outputs generated by these models might not always be tailored to specific needs of users, leading to underwhelming performance. To overcome these challenges, we are building an automatic text summarization [3] model which will summarize the research paper while retaining its most essential information. This approach allows for greater customization and optimization of the models. Furthermore, it eliminates interrupted access to summarization capabilities needed for educational purposes.

DOI: 10.1201/9781003422433-8

In the following section, we will present a literature review that explores the evolution of automatic text summarization (ATS) techniques, emphasizing the advancements brought by LLMs. We will detail our study's methodology, including experimental setup and models evaluated. We'll then present and analyze our experimental results, discussing key performance metrics. To conclude, we'll summarize our findings and highlight opportunities and challenges of using GenAI in the educational sphere. Finally, we'll accentuate on ethical implications and offer recommendations for educators and researchers.

8.2   Literature Review

Research on automatic text summarization has achieved milestones in the domain of natural language processing (NLP) which reflects its rapid advancements, guided by both theoretical and practical applications. The statistical and embedding techniques of language models were prominent early on to aid the task of summarization, with key developments such as term-frequency models [4], N-gram models [5], Word2Vec [6], and GloVe [7]. These models were simple and efficient but limited to extract grammatical and contextual meaning. Additionally, their performances were sensitive to stop words. To produce final summary text, extractive summarization models such as word counting [8] (TextRank [9], LexRank [10]), similarity-based models [11, 12], and classifiers [13] were built. Though, these extractive models diverge from the approach employed by human experts.

To overcome these challenges, LLMs [14] have marked a significant advancement in the realm of text summarization. LLMs are a fundamental component of GenAI, focusing on creating new content, for our case, text using deep learning models. Recent works in GenAI (refer to Table 8.1) have demonstrated its potential in various domains, including education and provide solutions to complex problems.

Several studies evaluated the use of LLMs in ATS to conclude that it surpasses human performance. Pre-training [15, 16] process of LLMs included models such as ELMo [17], RNN-based models [18], BERTSUM [19], and transformer-based encoder-decoder models [20, 21], which enabled more coherent summarization. Though the exclusive process of pre-training the LLM on an extensive dataset springs up concerns over its quality, these challenges can be improved by fine-tuning the LLM on the task of text summarization using techniques such as reinforcement learning with human feedback (RLHF) [22, 23], direct preference optimization (DPO) [24] and continual pre-training (CPT) [25].

The use of LLMs for ATS offers abundant benefits, including enhanced coherence and fluency [26], improved contextual understanding [27], the ability to handle diverse data [20], and scale effectively with increasing computational resources [28]. However, the large size of these models poses

TABLE 8.1 Recent Advances and Findings in GenAI

Cited as	Paper Title	Work Done
[36]	To Accept or Not to Accept? An IRT-TOE Framework to Understand Educators' Resistance to Generative AI in Higher Education	This study developed a theoretical model to empirically predict barriers preventing educators from adopting generative AI in higher education, using Innovation Resistance Theory and the Technology-Organization-Environment framework.
[37]	Generative AI Augmented Induction-Based Formal Verification	Formal verification is a mathematical-based proof method used to exhaustively verify the correctness of a design. In this paper, we demonstrate how GenAI can be used in induction-based formal verification to increase the verification throughput.
[38]	Revolutionizing Undergraduate Learning: CourseGPT and Its Generative AI Advancements	This paper introduces CourseGPT, a generative AI tool designed to support instructors and enhance the educational experiences of undergraduate students.
[39]	Generative Artificial Intelligence in Dentistry: Current Approaches and Future Challenges	In this review, they describe different generation modalities and discuss current and potential applications in Dentistry and challenges.
[40]	Comprehensive AI Assessment Framework: Enhancing Educational Evaluation with Ethical AI Integration	This paper presents a framework, an evolved version of the AI Assessment Scale (AIAS), targeted toward the ethical integration of AI into educational assessments.
[41]	Image Inpainting Models Are Effective Tools for Instruction-Guided Image Editing	This paper successfully builds a pipeline to show proper combinations of language models and image inpainting models (image generation) to achieve instruction-guided image editing.
[42]	zIA: A Genai-Powered Local Auntie Assists Tourists in Italy	In this article, they propose a GenAI-based chatbot for tourism assistance, to generate realistic and creative texts, adopting the friendly persona of the well-known Italian all-knowledgeable aunties, and to provide personalized information to tourists.
[43]	Adoption and Impact of Chat-GPT in Computer Science Education: A Case Study on a Database Administration Course	This study investigates the use of ChatGPT in computer science education, revealing that high-performing students utilize ChatGPT more effectively, potentially widening the gap between them and lower-performing peers. It highlights the need for methodological guidelines to optimize the use of GenAI tools like ChatGPT in education.

(Continued)

TABLE 8.1 (Continued)

Cited as	Paper Title	Work Done
[44]	Prompts First, Finally	This paper argues that our programming abstractions were headed to natural language.
[45]	Generative AI for RF Sensing in IoT Systems	This article includes a detailed analysis of the challenges of RF sensing and presents innovative GenAI-based solutions and proposes a unified framework for diverse RF-sensing tasks.
[46]	Teacher Agency in the Age of Generative AI: Toward a Framework of Hybrid Intelligence for Learning Design	This study aimed to analyze the way GenAI influences teacher's agency. The solution proposed was based on the combination of human intelligence and artificial intelligence. This combination also opens up new practices in learning design in which they support the extension of teachers' activity.

limitations such as high computational costs and energy consumption. To mitigate this issue, quantization [29] has emerged as a promising technique, which involves reducing the precision of the numbers used to represent the model parameters. It significantly decreases the model's memory footprint and computational requirement without substantially hindering its performance [30, 31]. Techniques like QLoRA [32], PRILoRA [33], GPTQ [34], AWQ [35], and GGML/GGUF combine quantization with optimization strategies to further enhance model compression and efficiency.

To evaluate the performance of text summarization models, several metrics and benchmark datasets are frequently used to ensure standardization and comprehensive assessment. Rouge [47] is the most common tool for ATS evaluation, to compare the overlap of N-grams, word sequences, and word pairs between the generated summary and reference summaries. ROUGE-N, ROUGE-L, and ROUGE-W are some of its variants which focus on the recall, and it does not directly consider the fluency and conciseness of a summary. Hence, to ensure high quality of the summaries, a summarization model that can be evaluated along four dimensions, namely, Fluency, Coherence, Consistency, and Relevance, was proposed [48]. Additionally, BERTScore [49], BLEU [50], METEOR [51], and Perplexity [52] are used for their capabilities of evaluating the generated text.

To benchmark datasets, long discourse scientific papers like Arxiv [53], PubMed [53], and Scisumm [54] can be used to help train and test summarization models, which can be used as ground-truth summaries [53] in their abstracts.

8.3 Methodology

The study on open-source large language models (LLMs) for text summarization was conducted in a Kaggle container environment equipped with the following hardware specifications: dual NVIDIA T4 GPUs and 30 GB of RAM. The LLMs under evaluation included the quantized versions of several notable models:

- The Mistral-7B [55] is a 7 billion parameter model using Grouped-Query Attention, Sliding-Window Attention, and a Byte-fallback BPE tokenizer, outperforming Llama 2 13B.
- Meta's Llama-3 [56], available in 8B and 70B, is optimized for dialogue, outperforming many chat models with supervised fine-tuning and RLHF.
- Microsoft's Phi-3-Mini-4K-Instruct [57], a 3.8B parameter lightweight model, excels in common sense, language understanding, math, and logical reasoning with supervised fine-tuning and preference optimization.
- Google's Gemma 7B [58], based on Gemini model research, is a text-to-text, decoder-only model adept at tasks like question answering and summarization, tailored for deployment in constrained computing environments.

To investigate the impact of model quantization on performance, two types of quantized models were selected: a minimally quantized model (8-bit quantization) and a maximally quantized model (2-bit quantization or 5-bit quantized). The performance variations between these quantized models were assessed to understand their implications on the summarization tasks. This study would indicate the difference of quality between these quantization levels.

To efficiently load and store these models in memory, the GGUF format was utilized. For benchmarking purposes, the ArXiV dataset [53] was employed. The ArXiv dataset was employed for summarization, operating under the assumption that human-generated abstracts represent the highest quality standard. The dataset, available in a large JSON format, includes fields such as ID, title, abstract, and categories. For efficient storage and processing, the JSON data was parsed into a DataFrame. To address issues with outdated records causing parsing problems, these entries were removed from the dataset. The current solution utilizes Langchain Document Loader to load PDFs, including the additional step of OCR processing to handle non-text PDFs. A state-of-the-art embedding model, specifically the fast embedding model, was used to build a vector store by generating sentence embeddings through the mx-bai embeddings [59]. This vector store facilitates similarity search to find relevant documents matching the vector query, effectively aiding in the summarization task. Furthermore, an essential step in the process involved removing abstracts to enable accurate scoring and evaluation of the summarization models.

Research papers were initially indexed in a vector store for summary generation. To facilitate processing with LLMs featuring shorter context windows, the following steps were implemented, as illustrated in Figure 8.1:

- Extract initial keywords from the paper's title.
- Utilize these keywords to retrieve relevant context from the vector store.
- Provide the title and retrieved context to the model to generate an initial summary.
- Use the generated summary to extract keywords again.
- Use these keywords to retrieve the corresponding context from the vector store.
- Feed the model with the title and retrieved context to generate a second summary.
- Refine the final summary by resubmitting it to the model.

An alternative approach to the conventional Retrieve and Generate (RAG) method [60] involves document chunking. This method divides the document into smaller, manageable sections, generates partial summaries for each segment, and subsequently aggregates these summaries to produce the final output. Implementing document chunking ensures efficient processing of lengthy documents while preserving the summarization quality.

A combination of similarity scoring metrics, including ROUGE-1, ROUGE-2, ROUGE-L [47], and BERTScore [61, 49] were used to evaluate the summarization performance.

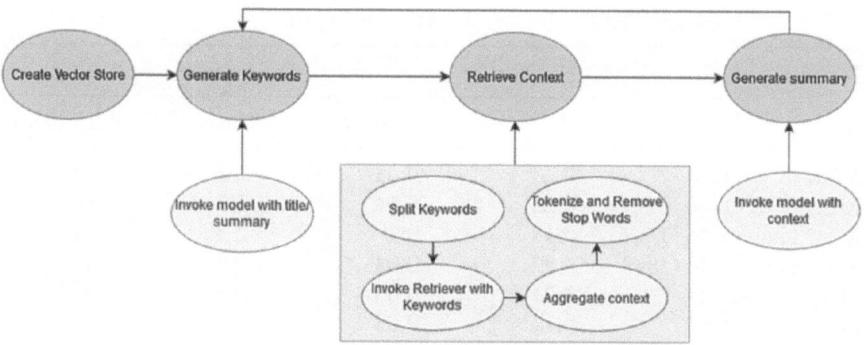

FIGURE 8.1   Workflow of summarization.

The results were calculated in terms of F1-score for each of these metrics. We also employed a LLM-based scoring method [62], which considers four metrics:

- **Relevance:** Assesses the quality of content selection from the source.
- **Coherence:** Measures the collective quality of sentences and the flow between them within the summary.
- **Consistency:** Evaluates the factual alignment between the summary and its source.
- **Fluency:** Analyzes the quality of the summary in terms of grammar, spelling, punctuation, word choice, and structure.

It is noted that while ROUGE and BERTScore metrics primarily focus on word matching between a reference and candidate summary, the LLM-based approach provides a more human expert-like evaluation by considering these broader dimensions of summarization quality. To address potential AI hallucinations, we also manually examined specific outliers in the scoring to ensure the accuracy and reliability of the generated scores.

8.4 Result

The experimental results are shown in Tables 8.2 and 8.3. Table 8.2 presents the F1 scores for various language models at different quantization levels. The ROUGE scores, while not exceptionally high, demonstrate effective performance even on limited hardware. Notably, Microsoft's Phi3 Mini 4K model stands out, achieving competitive scores despite its smaller size.

These scores indicate that models like Mistral 7B and Phi3 Mini 4K perform consistently well across different metrics and quantization levels. The results underscore the models' capability to achieve competitive performance

TABLE 8.2 Comparison of F1 Scores for Various LLM Models on ROUGE-1, ROUGE-2, ROUGE-L, and BertScore Metrics

Models	F1 Scores			
	ROUGE-1	ROUGE-2	ROUGE-L	BERTScore
Mistral 7B Q2_0	0.24	0.05	0.22	0.83
Mistral 7B Q8_0	0.25	0.06	0.22	0.83
Meta Llama3 8B Q2_K	0.15	0.2	0.13	0.13
Meta Llama3 8B Q8_0	0.22	0.04	0.19	0.8
Phi3 Mini 4K q4	0.21	0.03	0.19	0.82
Phi3 Mini 4K q8	0.21	0.03	0.19	0.83
Gemma 7b Q5_0	0.24	0.03	0.20	0.82
Gemma 7b Q8_0	0.24	0.30	0.20	0.82

TABLE 8.3 Comparison of the Metrics Computed by the LLM Scoring Method

Models	Parameters (Out of 5)			
	Fluency	Relevance	Coherence	Consistency
Mistral 7B Q2_0	3.85	3.71	3.57	3.43
Mistral 7B Q8_0	4.16	4.16	3.33	3.66
Meta Llama3 8B Q2_K	1.57	1.28	1.57	1.28
Meta Llama3 8B Q8_0	2.71	2.85	2.71	2.57
Phi3 Mini 4K q4	4.33	4.33	3.83	4.33
Phi3 Mini 4K q8	3.66	4.63	4.16	4.73
Gemma 7b Q5_0	2.87	2.62	2.62	3.25
Gemma 7b Q8_0	3.11	3.44	3.22	3.55

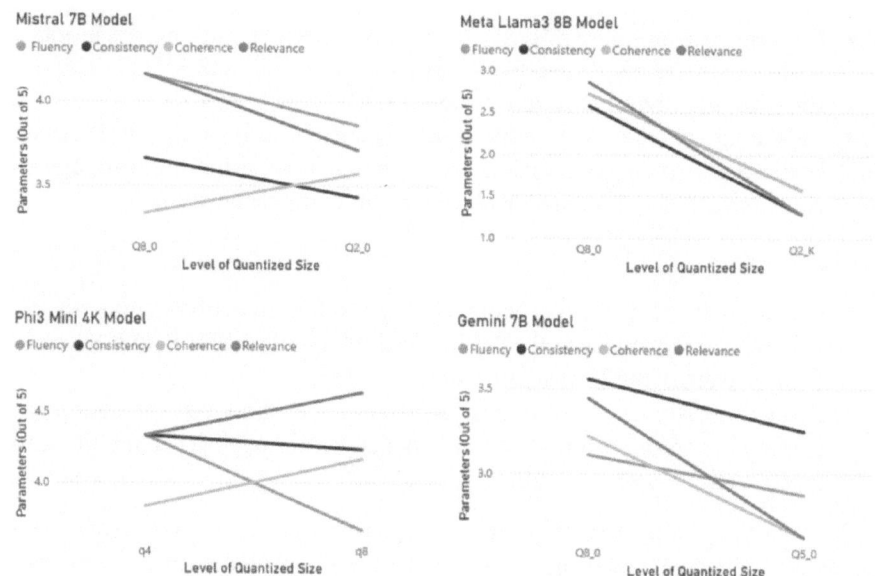

FIGURE 8.2 Trend of various parameters in each quantized model.

in natural language processing tasks despite variations in hardware constraints and model sizes.

From the values provided in Table 8.2 and Figure 8.2, several observations can be made about the performance of the LLMs across different evaluation metrics:

- Fluency:
  - Models like Phi3 Mini 4K q4 and q8, as well as Mistral 7B Q8_0, generally exhibit higher fluency scores (above 4.0), indicating their ability to generate summaries with good grammar, spelling, and overall linguistic quality.

- Meta Llama3 8B Q2_K shows the lowest fluency score (1.57), suggesting significant challenges in producing summaries that are linguistically smooth and coherent.

- Relevance:
  - Phi3 Mini 4K q8 and Mistral 7B Q8_0 achieve the highest relevance scores (above 4.0), indicating that their summaries contain content closely aligned with the input documents.
  - Meta Llama3 8B Q2_K again scores the lowest in relevance (1.28), indicating struggles in accurately selecting and presenting important content from the input.

- Coherence:
  - Coherence scores generally show moderate performance across models, with Phi3 Mini 4K q8 leading (4.16) and Meta Llama3 8B Q2_K again showing the lowest coherence score (1.57).
  - This suggests that while some models maintain a logical flow between sentences in their summaries, others struggle with maintaining coherence, potentially affecting readability and comprehensibility.

- Consistency:
  - Consistency scores vary widely, with models like Phi3 Mini 4K q8 achieving high consistency (4.73) and Meta Llama3 8B Q2_K again demonstrating the lowest consistency (1.28).
  - A low consistency score indicates discrepancies between the generated summary and the original content, which can impact the reliability and trustworthiness of the summary.

Overall, Microsoft Phi3 Mini 4K q8 appears to perform consistently well across all metrics, suggesting robust performance in generating fluent, relevant, coherent, and consistent summaries. On the other hand, Meta Llama3 8B Q2_K consistently shows the weakest performance, indicating areas for improvement in various aspects of summary generation.

By considering the effect of quantization we can make some observations on the different models.

Some observations using F1 scores from Table 8.2 are as follows:

- **Mistral 7B:** Both quantization levels (Q2_0 and Q8_0) show similar performance across ROUGE-1, ROUGE-2, ROUGE-L, and BERTScore metrics, with slight improvements in ROUGE-1 and ROUGE-2 scores for Q8 0.
- **Meta Llama3 8B:** Quantization has a noticeable impact on performance. Q2_K shows lower scores across all metrics than Q8_0, indicating that higher quantization (Q8_0) improves summarization quality significantly.

- **Phi3 Mini 4K:** The model shows consistent performance between q4 and q8 quantization levels across all metrics. There is no significant improvement or degradation with higher quantization, suggesting robustness in summarization quality. This could be a result of Phi's quantization-aware training procedures.
- **Gemma 7b:** Quantization from Q_5 0 to Q8_0 shows a mixed impact on performance. Q8 0 generally outperforms Q5 0 in ROUGE-2 and BERTScore, while showing varied results in ROUGE-1 and ROUGE-L.

Some observations using metrics from Table 8.3 are as follows:

- **Fluency:** Models generally improve in fluency with higher quantization levels, as seen in Mistral 7B Q8_0, Phi3 Mini 4K q4 and q8, and Gemma 7b Q8_0.
- **Relevance:** Similar to fluency, relevance tends to increase with higher quantization levels for Mistral 7B, Phi3 Mini 4K, and Gemma 7b models.
- **Coherence:** Coherence scores vary, but generally show improvement with higher quantization levels, particularly noticeable in Phi3 Mini 4K q8.
- **Consistency:** Consistency also improves with higher quantization levels, as evident in Phi3 Mini 4K q8 and Gemma 7b Q8_0.

8.5 Conclusion

This research successfully highlights the efficiency of quantized large language models in automatic text summarization, particularly in constrained computational environments. The study results showed that higher quantization levels generally lead to improved summarization quality across fluency, relevance, coherence, and consistency metrics for most models. Some quantized LLMs show clear improvements, specifically Microsoft's Phi3 Mini 4K, offering a promising path forward for deploying summarization models in practical, large-scale applications. Other models demonstrated mixed results depending on the metric evaluated. The choice of the quantization level should be balanced after considering specific requirements of the summarization task, as higher quantization may not always guarantee better performance and could increase computational costs.

This has significant implications for the education sector, where efficient and effective summarization tools can aid researchers in quickly digesting large volumes of academic literature.

8.6 Opportunities and Challenges of Using GenAI in Education

GenAI models provide considerable benefits in text summarization, addressing information processing difficulties across several domains. These models efficiently compress enormous amounts of text, improving the accessibility of complicated topics while guaranteeing consistent quality. Key advantages include customizable outputs, time and resource efficiency, assistance for quick decision-making, and multilingual capabilities. GenAI's flexibility to different material kinds and continual learning methods increase its usefulness. While intriguing, significant limits, such as AI bias, demand further investigation. Overall, GenAI is an effective tool for information synthesis in academic, educational, and professional settings, considerably increasing knowledge management and accessibility.

While GenAI presents numerous opportunities for text summarization, particularly in educational contexts, it also brings several challenges that need careful consideration. The risk of inaccuracies, misinterpretations, or omitting critical information by AI-generated summaries is the major obstacle. These GenAI models can preserve existing biases present in training data, leading to biased summaries which will skew interpretations and findings. One of the major challenges is navigating ethical considerations and data privacy regulations, especially when dealing with sensitive or proprietary information. In addition, sometimes AI models may struggle to fully grasp the nuanced context and subtleties of complex research papers, which can lead to over-simplified or misleading summaries. By implementing robust strategies to mitigate these issues, we can be certain that GenAI tools enhance educational outcomes while maintaining ethical standards.

8.7 Ethical Implications

We need to address the ethical implications of using GenAI in education. GenAI models can sometimes generate inaccurate or misleading summaries, potentially spreading misinformation if used without proper verification [63]. Educators and researchers should ensure the factual correctness of academic summaries since precision is paramount. These models could also inherit and amplify biases present in their training data, leading to biased summary, misrepresenting the original research. It is crucial to make sure the summarization process fairly shows all perspectives and findings of the research paper. There are concerns regarding the proper attribution of ideas and findings when using AI-generated summaries. It is important to cite the original authors and avoid any form of intellectual property infringement for the reason that automated summarization can blur the lines between original content and AI-generated text, leading to the risk of unintentional plagiarism. Often, research papers contain sensitive information. The GenAI systems should be able to handle these data securely, maintain the anonymity of study participants, and respect confidentiality agreements. Due to lack of transparency in how LLMs generate summaries, users should have a clear understanding of AI's decision-making process to trust its outputs. It is challenging to determine the responsibility of errors and biases in AI-powered summaries, but it is necessary to establish clear accountability for ethical use. Relying completely on AI on summarization could potentially deteriorate the practitioner's learning and comprehension skills. Instead, AI-generated summaries should be used as supplementary tools to assist and enhance the summarization process. It is essential to evaluate how these technologies affect the efficiency of the teacher–student relationship and overall educational environment.

8.8 Recommendations for Educators and Researchers

To use GenAI responsibly, we recommend the educators and researchers to ensure that AI-generated content is reviewed and validated by rechecking the facts and ideas to maintain accuracy and context [64]. The practitioners should clearly disclose when and how AI tools are used in the creation of educational content or research output to maintain transparency with students and peers. To identify and mitigate biases in AI-generated summaries or content, implement strategies to regularly audit and assess them. We recommend adhering to strict data privacy and security protocols when using AI tools, ensuring that student and research data are protected against unauthorized access and breaches. Ethical guidelines for the use of AI in education can be developed by educators and followed by students, ensuring that the technology is used to enhance learning rather than replacing critical thinking and creativity. Training can be taken on by educators and researchers to understand the capabilities and limitations of GenAI tools and use them effectively and responsibly. It is highly considerable to encourage students and researchers to critically evaluate AI-generated content and integrate it with their own analysis. In addition, equity and inclusion in educational and research settings can be promoted by ensuring that AI tools are accessible to all students, educators, and researchers.

References

1. H. Jo, "From concerns to benefits: A comprehensive study of ChatGPT usage in education," *Int. J. Educ. Technol. High. Educ.*, vol. 21, no. 1, June 2024.
2. K. Huang, F. Zhang, Y. Li, S. Wright, V. Kidambi, and V. Manral, "Security and privacy concerns in ChatGPT," in *Beyond AI*. Cham: Springer Nature Switzerland, 2023, pp. 297–328.
3. V. Gogulamudi, A. Yadav, and B. Vishnupriya, "Text summarizing using NLP," in *Recent Trends in Intensive Computing*. IOS Press, December 2021.
4. Z. Ke, Y. Shao, H. Lin, T. Konishi, G. Kim, and B. Liu, "Continual pre-training of language models," 2023. [Online]. https://arxiv.org/abs/2302.03241
5. A. Radford, J. Wu, R. Child, D. Luan, D. Amodei, and I. Sutskever, "Language models are unsupervised multitask learners," *OpenAI Blog*, vol. 1, no. 8, p. 9, 2019.

6. J. Devlin, M.-W. Chang, K. Lee, and K. Toutanova, "BERT: Pre-training of deep bidirectional transformers for language understanding," *arXiv preprint arXiv:1810.04805*, 2018.
7. T. Brown, B. Mann, N. Ryder et al., "Language models are few-shot learners," *Adv. Neural Inf. Process. Syst.*, vol. 33, pp. 1877–1901, 2020.
8. A. Gholami, S. Kim, Z. Dong, Z. Yao, M. W. Mahoney, and K. Keutzer, "A survey of quantization methods for efficient neural network inference," in *Low-Power Computer Vision*. Chapman and Hall/CRC, 2022, pp. 291–326.
9. B. Jacob, S. Kligys, B. Chen, M. Zhu, M. Tang, A. Howard, H. Adam, and D. Kalenichenko, "Quantization and training of neural networks for efficient integer-arithmetic-only inference," in *Proceedings of the IEEE Conference on Computer Vision and Pattern Recognition*, 2018, pp. 2704–2713.
10. S. Shen, Z. Dong, J. Ye, L. Ma, Z. Yao, A. Gholami, M. W. Mahoney, and K. Keutzer, "Q-BERT: Hessian based ultra low precision quantization of BERT," in *Proceedings of the AAAI Conference on Artificial Intelligence*, vol. 34, no. 5, 2020, pp. 8815–8821.
11. T. Dettmers, A. Pagnoni, A. Holtzman, and L. Zettlemoyer, "Qlora: Efficient fine-tuning of quantized LLMs," *Adv. Neural Inf. Process. Syst.*, vol. 36, 2024.
12. N. Benedek and L. Wolf, "Prilora: Pruned and rank-increasing low-rank adaptation," *arXiv preprint arXiv:2401.11316*, 2024.
13. E. Frantar, S. Ashkboos, T. Hoefler, and D. Alistarh, "Gptq: Accurate post-training quantization for generative pre-trained transformers," *arXiv preprint arXiv:2210.17323*, 2022.
14. J. Lin, J. Tang, H. Tang, S. Yang, W.-M. Chen, W.-C. Wang, G. Xiao, X. Dang, C. Gan, and S. Han, "AWQ: Activation-aware weight quantization for on-device LLM compression and acceleration," *Proc. Mach. Learn. Syst.*, vol. 6, pp. 87–100, 2024.
15. J.-E. Kalmus and A. Nikiforova, "To accept or not to accept? an IRT-TOE framework to understand educators' resistance to generative AI in higher education," 2024. [Online]. https://arxiv.org/abs/2407.20130
16. A. Kumar and D. N. Gadde, "Generative AI augmented induction-based formal verification," 2024. [Online]. https://arxiv.org/abs/2407.18965
17. A. M. Nazar, M. Y. Selim, A. Gaffar, and S. Ahmed, "Revolutionizing undergraduate learning: Coursegpt and its generative AI advancements," 2024. [Online]. https://arxiv.org/abs/2407.18310
18. F. Villena, C. Véliz, R. García-Huidobro, and S. Aguayo, "Generative artificial intelligence in dentistry: Current approaches and future challenges," 2024. [Online]. https://arxiv.org/abs/2407.17532
19. S. Kılınç, "Comprehensive AI assessment framework: Enhancing educational evaluation with ethical AI integration," 2024. [Online]. https://arxiv.org/abs/2407.16887
20. X. Ju, J. Zhuang, Z. Zhang, Y. Bian, Q. Xu, and Y. Shan, "Image inpainting models are effective tools for instruction-guided image editing," 2024. [Online]. https://arxiv.org/abs/2407.13139
21. A. Cassani, M. Ruberl, A. Salis, G. Giannese, and G. Boanelli, "zIA: A genai-powered local auntie assists tourists in Italy," 2024. [Online]. https://arxiv.org/abs/2407.11830
22. D. López-Fernández and R. Vergaz, "Adoption and impact of ChatGPT in computer science education: A case study on a database administration course," 2024. [Online]. https://arxiv.org/abs/2407.12145
23. B. N. Reeves, J. Prather, P. Denny, J. Leinonen, S. MacNeil, B. A. Becker, and A. Luxton-Reilly, "Prompts first, finally," 2024. [Online]. https://arxiv.org/abs/2407.09231

24. L. Wang, C. Zhang, Q. Zhao, H. Zou, S. Lasaulce, G. Valenzise, Z. He, and M. Debbah, "Generative AI for rf sensing in iot systems," 2024. [Online]. https://arxiv.org/abs/2407.07506

25. T. B. Frøsig and M. Romero, "Teacher agency in the age of generative AI: Towards a framework of hybrid intelligence for learning design," 2024. [Online]. https://arxiv.org/abs/2407.06655

26. B. Gong, W.-L. Chao, K. Grauman, and F. Sha, "Diverse sequential subset selection for supervised video summarization," *Adv. Neural Inf. Process. Syst.*, vol. 27, 2014.

27. C. Rioux, S. A. Hasan, and Y. Chali, "Fear the reaper: A system for automatic multi-document summarization with reinforcement learning," in *Proceedings of the 2014 Conference on Empirical Methods in Natural Language Processing (EMNLP)*, 2014, pp. 681–690.

28. T. Mikolov, K. Chen, G. Corrado, and J. Dean, "Efficient estimation of word representations in vector space," *arXiv preprint arXiv:1301.3781*, 2013.

29. J. Pennington, R. Socher, and C. D. Manning, "Glove: Global vectors for word representation," in *Proceedings of the 2014 Conference on Empirical Methods in Natural Language Processing (EMNLP)*, 2014, pp. 1532–1543.

30. V. Gupta and G. S. Lehal, "A survey of text summarization extractive techniques," *J. Emerg. Technol. Web Intell.*, vol. 2, no. 3, pp. 258–268, 2010.

31. R. Mihalcea and P. Tarau, "Textrank: Bringing order into text," in *Proceedings of the 2004 Conference on Empirical Methods in Natural Language Processing*, 2004, pp. 404–411.

32. G. Erkan and D. R. Radev, "Lexrank: Graph-based lexical centrality as salience in text summarization," *J. Artif. Intell. Res.*, vol. 22, pp. 457–479, 2004.

33. M. M. Haider, M. F. Hossin, H. R. Mahi, and H. Arif, "Automatic text summarization using gensim Word2Vec and k-means clustering algorithm," *2020 IEEE Region 10 Symposium (TENSYMP)*, pp. 283–286, 2020. [Online]. https://api.semanticscholar.org/CorpusID:226267454

34. Y. Zhang, Y. Xia, Y. Liu, and W. Wang, "Clustering sentences with density peaks for multi-document summarization," in *Proceedings of the 2015 Conference of the North American Chapter of the Association for Computational Linguistics: Human Language Technologies*, R. Mihalcea, J. Chai, and A. Sarkar, Eds. Denver, Colorado: Association for Computational Linguistics, May–June 2015, pp. 1262–1267. [Online]. https://aclanthology.org/N15–1136

35. S. Abdel-Salam and A. Rafea, "Performance study on extractive text summarization using BERT models," *Information*, vol. 13, no. 2, p. 67, 2022.

36. W. X. Zhao, K. Zhou, J. Li et al., "A survey of large language models," *arXiv preprint arXiv:2303.18223*, 2023.

37. M. T. R. Laskar, M. S. Bari, M. Rahman, M. A. H. Bhuiyan, S. Joty, and J. X. Huang, "A systematic study and comprehensive evaluation of ChatGPT on benchmark datasets," *arXiv preprint arXiv:2305.18486*, 2023.

38. H. Zheng and M. Lapata, "Sentence centrality revisited for unsupervised summarization," *arXiv preprint arXiv:1906.03508*, 2019.

39. V. Joshi, M. Peters, and M. Hopkins, "Extending a parser to distant domains using a few dozen partially annotated examples," *arXiv preprint arXiv:1805.06556*, 2018.

40. T. Mikolov, M. Karafiát, L. Burget, J. Cernocký, and S. Khudanpur, "Recurrent neural network based language model," *Interspeech*, vol. 2, no. 3, 2010, pp. 1045–1048.

41. Y. Liu and M. Lapata, "Text summarization with pretrained encoders," *arXiv preprint arXiv:1908.08345*, 2019.

42. J. Zhang, Y. Zhao, M. Saleh, and P. Liu, "Pegasus: Pre-training with extracted gap-sentences for abstractive summarization," in *International Conference on Machine Learning*, PMLR, 2020, pp. 11.328–11.339.

43. L. Basyal and M. Sanghvi, "Text summarization using large language models: A comparative study of MPT-7b-instruct, falcon-7b-instruct, and openAI Chat-GPT models," *arXiv preprint arXiv:2310.10449*, 2023.
44. L. Ouyang, J. Wu, X. Jiang et al., "Training language models to follow instructions with human feedback," *Adv. Neural Inf. Process. Syst.*, vol. 35, pp. 27.730–27.744, 2022.
45. T. Kaufmann, P. Weng, V. Bengs, and E. Hüllermeier, "A survey of reinforcement learning from human feedback," *arXiv preprint arXiv:2312.14925*, 2023.
46. R. Rafailov, A. Sharma, E. Mitchell, C. D. Manning, S. Ermon, and C. Finn, "Direct preference optimization: Your language model is secretly a reward model," *Adv. Neural Inf. Process. Syst.*, vol. 36, 2024.
47. C.-Y. Lin, "Rouge: A package for automatic evaluation of summaries," in *Text Summarization Branches Out*. Association for Computational Linguistics, 2004, pp. 74–81.
48. A. R. Fabbri, W. Kryściński, B. McCann, C. Xiong, R. Socher, and D. Radev, "Summeval: Re-evaluating summarization evaluation," 2021. [Online]. https://arxiv.org/abs/2007.12626
49. T. Zhang, V. Kishore, F. Wu, K. Q. Weinberger, and Y. Artzi, "BERTscore: Evaluating text generation with BERT," 2020. [Online]. https://arxiv.org/abs/1904.09675
50. K. Papineni, S. Roukos, T. Ward, and W.-J. Zhu, "Bleu: A method for automatic evaluation of machine translation," in *Proceedings of the 40th Annual Meeting of the Association for Computational Linguistics*, 2002, pp. 311–318.
51. S. Banerjee and A. Lavie, "Meteor: An automatic metric for mt evaluation with improved correlation with human judgments," in *Proceedings of the ACL Workshop on Intrinsic and Extrinsic Evaluation Measures for Machine Translation and/or Summarization*, 2005, pp. 65–72.
52. F. Bimbot, M. El-Bèze, S. Igounet, M. Jardino, K. Smaili, and I. Zitouni, "An alternative scheme for perplexity estimation and its assessment for the evaluation of language models," *Comput. Speech Lang.*, vol. 15, no. 1, pp. 1–13, 2001.
53. A. Cohan, F. Dernoncourt, D. S. Kim, T. Bui, S. Kim, W. Chang, and N. Goharian, "A discourse-aware attention model for abstractive summarization of long documents," *arXiv preprint arXiv:1804.05685*, 2018.
54. M. Yasunaga, J. Kasai, R. Zhang, A. R. Fabbri, I. Li, D. Friedman, and D. R. Radev, "ScisummNet: A large annotated corpus and content-impact models for scientific paper summarization with citation networks," in *Proceedings of the AAAI Conference on Artificial Intelligence*, vol. 33, no. 1, 2019, pp. 7386–7393.
55. A. Q. Jiang, A. Sablayrolles, A. Mensch, C. Bamford, D. S. Chaplot, D. de las Casas, F. Bressand, G. Lengyel, G. Lample, L. Saulnier, L. R. Lavaud, M.-A. Lachaux, P. Stock, T. L. Scao, T. Lavril, T. Wang, T. Lacroix, and W. E. Sayed, "Mistral 7b," 2023. [Online]. https://arxiv.org/abs/2310.06825
56. AI@Meta, "Llama 3 model card," 2024. [Online]. https://github.com/meta-llama/llama3/blob/main/MODEL_CARD.md
57. M. Abdin, S. A. Jacobs, A. A. Awan, J. Aneja, A. Awadallah, H. Awadalla, N. Bach, A. Bahree, A. Bakhtiari, H. Behl, and A. Benham, "Phi-3 technical report: A highly capable language model locally on your phone," *arXiv preprint arXiv:2404.14219*, 2024.
58. G. Team, T. Mesnard, C. Hardin, R. Dadashi, S. Bhupatiraju, and S. Pathak, L. Sifre, M. Rivière, M. S. Kale, J. Love, and P. Tafti, "Gemma: Open models based on gemini research and technology," *arXiv preprint arXiv:2403.08295*, 2024.
59. J. Lipp, "Open source strikes bread - new Fluffy embedding model – mixedbread.ai." https://www.mixedbread.ai/blog/mxbai-embed-large-v1 (accessed 29 June 2024).

60. P. Lewis, E. Perez, A. Piktus, F. Petroni, and V. Karpukhin, "Retrieval-augmented generation for knowledge-intensive NLP tasks," 2021. [Online]. https://arxiv.org/abs/2005.11401

61. T. Zhang, V. Kishore, F. Wu, K. Q. Weinberger, and Y. Artzi, "BERTscore: Evaluating text generation with BERT," in *International Conference on Learning Representations*, 2020.

62. A. R. Fabbri, W. Kryściński, B. Mccann, C. Xiong, R. Socher, and D. Radev, "Summeval: Re-evaluating summarization evaluation." [Online]. https://doi.org/10.1162/tacl

63. European Commission: Directorate-General for Education, Youth, Sport and Culture, *Ethical Guidelines on the Use of Artificial Intelligence (AI) and Data in Teaching and Learning for Educators*. Publications Office of the European Union, 2022. https://op.europa.eu/en/publication-detail/-/publication/d81a0d54-5348-11ed-92ed-01aa75ed71a1/language-en

64. D.-G. for Research and Innovation, "Living guidelines on the responsible use of generative AI in research," March 2024. [Online]. https://research-and-innovation.ec.europa.eu/document/download/2b6cf7e5-36ac-41cb-aab5-0d32050143dcen?filename=ecrtdai-guidelines.pdf

9

BUILDING TEACHER CAPACITY FOR EFFECTIVE INTEGRATION OF GenAI INTO CLASSROOM

A Framework for Teacher Education Programs

Harshith B. Nair

9.1 Introduction

Generative Artificial Intelligence (GenAI) is an advanced technology capable of producing new content, such as text, images, and music, based on the patterns and data it has been trained on (Alasadi & Baiz, 2023). This transformative potential extends to various fields, including education, where GenAI can revolutionize teaching and learning processes. By tailoring learning experiences, creating educational materials, providing feedback to students, and supporting teachers, GenAI offers innovative solutions to enhance the educational outcomes (Boscardin et al., 2024).

One of the key applications of GenAI in education is its ability to create interactive and adaptive learning environments that cater to individual student needs (Adiguzel et al., 2023). For instance, technologies like ChatGPT exemplify how GenAI can personalize education by adjusting to students' learning styles and progress (Tlili et al., 2023). However, the successful integration of GenAI into classrooms requires teachers to possess essential skills and knowledge to effectively utilize this technology. This need underscores the importance of teacher training programs that equip educators with the competencies to incorporate GenAI into their teaching practices (Wang et al., 2024).

GenAI holds significant promise for enhancing and personalizing learning experiences, fostering creativity, and improving administrative efficiency. However, to fully realize these benefits, teachers must be adequately prepared to integrate GenAI tools effectively into their classrooms. This chapter introduces a comprehensive framework aimed at building teacher capacity for the effective integration of GenAI, addressing both opportunities and challenges.

Teacher training programs should focus on several critical areas: enhancing teachers' technology self-efficacy, improving their pedagogical content

DOI: 10.1201/9781003422433-9

knowledge, and developing their ability to design GenAI-assisted teaching activities. Educators must understand the ethical and responsible use of GenAI tools in educational settings (Bahroun et al., 2023; Pack, 2024). Training modules within these programs should emphasize GenAI literacy, pedagogical strategies for GenAI integration, and ethical considerations to ensure responsible implementation (Wang et al., 2024).

This chapter believes that the attitude of educators toward digital resources are symbiotic (Nair & Karan, 2024) addresses the necessity for comprehensive teacher training programs to facilitate the integration of GenAI into educational settings. The proposed framework offers a structured approach to developing training modules that focus on GenAI literacy, pedagogical strategies, and ethical considerations. By delineating this framework, this chapter aims to assist educators in harnessing the full potential of GenAI to enhance teaching and learning outcomes. GenAI presents a transformative opportunity for education by providing innovative solutions to improve teaching and learning processes. However, effective integration in classrooms hinges on specialized training programs that equip teachers with the necessary skills and knowledge. The framework proposed in this chapter aims to guide the development of such training modules, ultimately building teacher capacity for the effective integration of GenAI into educational settings.

9.2 Literature Review

9.2.1 Impact of GenAI on Education

GenAI is revolutionizing education by creating interactive and adaptive learning environments that cater to individual student needs. Technologies like ChatGPT exemplify how GenAI can personalize education by adjusting to students' learning styles and progress (Tlili et al., 2023). Despite the transformative potential of GenAI, its integration into classrooms is contingent upon teachers being adequately prepared to leverage this technology effectively.

Research emphasizes the significance of understanding students' perceptions to create informed guidelines for the effective implementation of GenAI tools in higher education, ultimately enhancing teaching and learning experiences (Chan & Hu, 2023). Additionally, empirical studies on teachers' professional knowledge highlight the importance of developing Intelligent-TPACK for educators to ethically integrate AI-based tools into education (Celik, 2023). The potential applications of GenAI in education are vast, offering insights into how these tools can enhance learning experiences (Tlili et al., 2022; Zhang et al., 2022).

There is a notable gap in the literature concerning the impact of GenAI on school education, particularly from the perspectives of teachers and leaders. Most existing research focuses on higher education, with limited empirical studies examining how GenAI affects school education in terms of learning outcomes, student self-regulated learning skills, and the role of teachers. There is a pressing need for more empirical research to inform the development of guidelines and policies for the use of GenAI in educational contexts.

9.2.2 Teacher Needs and Challenges

The integration of GenAI into classrooms presents both opportunities and challenges for teachers. Comprehensive professional development programs are essential to build teacher capacity and confidence in using GenAI tools. Studies show that less than 20% of teachers feel adequately equipped to utilize AI technologies like ChatGPT in their classrooms (OECD, 2023). Providing hands-on training, resources, and strategies for integrating GenAI effectively is crucial (Yang, 2023).

Another significant challenge is addressing potential biases and ethical concerns associated with GenAI use in education. Teachers must be equipped to critically evaluate the outputs of GenAI systems, identify biases and ensure academic integrity and intellectual property rights are upheld. Additionally, developing students' critical thinking skills to assess the reliability and limitations of GenAI is essential (UNESCO, 2019).

Teachers also require support in adapting their instructional approaches to leverage the capabilities of GenAI while maintaining a focus on developing students' higher-order thinking skills, creativity, and human agency. Integrating GenAI should not compromise the holistic development of students, and teachers need guidance on striking the right balance (Establish a Teacher AI Literacy Development Program, 2024). The lack of clear policies and guidelines on the use of GenAI in educational settings poses a significant challenge. Establishing a robust regulatory framework to govern the ethical and responsible use of GenAI is crucial (UNESCO, 2019). The key challenges in implementing GenAI in educational settings are summarized in Table 9.1, which outlines the main barriers along with their descriptions and potential solutions.

9.2.3 Effective Teacher Education for GenAI Integration

To effectively integrate GenAI in the classroom, teacher education programs must adapt their curricula to equip educators with the necessary skills and knowledge. Existing models for integrating technology in the classroom provide valuable insights for incorporating GenAI training into pre-service and in-service programs.

Saimon et al. (2024) discussed the application of the 6E Learning by Design (LbD) model to support student teachers in integrating AI applications into their classrooms. Black et al. (2024) proposed a framework

TABLE 9.1 Representation of Challenges in GenAI Implementation

Challenge	Description	Potential Solution
Professional Development	Less than 20% of teachers feel equipped to use AI technologies	Hands-on training workshops
Technological Barriers	Lack of access to necessary technology and infrastructure	Investment in tech resources
Ethical Considerations	Concerns about data privacy, algorithmic bias, and academic integrity	Training on ethical use of GenAI

for approaching AI education in educator preparation programs, outlining critical strategies for preparing teachers to effectively integrate AI-powered instructional tools.

Successful approaches often involve a combination of hands-on workshops, case studies, and collaborative projects. For example, the TPACK (Technological Pedagogical Content Knowledge) framework emphasizes the interplay between content knowledge, pedagogical knowledge, and technological knowledge, which can be applied to GenAI integration (Koehler et al., 2013). Teacher education programs should provide opportunities for educators to experiment with GenAI tools, explore their pedagogical applications, and develop lesson plans that effectively leverage these technologies (Luckin et al., 2016).

The key components of effective teacher education programs for GenAI include the following:

1. **Pedagogical Approaches:** Training educators on designing learning experiences that actively engage students in critical thinking, problem solving, and collaboration using GenAI tools (Luckin & Cukurova, 2019). This may involve flipped classroom models, project-based learning (PBL), and personalized learning pathways.
2. **Ethical Considerations:** Addressing the ethical implications of using GenAI in the classroom, such as data privacy, algorithmic bias, and academic integrity. Educators should be equipped with strategies for promoting digital citizenship and responsible use of AI technologies (Jobin et al., 2019).
3. **Assessment Strategies:** Providing guidance on assessing student learning and evaluating the effectiveness of GenAI-based interventions. This may include formative assessments, performance-based tasks, and reflective practices (Redecker & Johannessen, 2013).

By incorporating these components into teacher education programs, educators will be better prepared to effectively integrate GenAI into the classroom, fostering student engagement, personalized learning, and critical thinking skills.

This chapter addresses the necessity for comprehensive teacher training programs to facilitate the integration of GenAI into educational settings. The proposed framework offers a structured approach to developing training modules that focus on GenAI literacy, pedagogical strategies, and ethical considerations. By delineating this framework, the chapter aims to assist educators in harnessing the full potential of GenAI to enhance teaching and learning outcomes. GenAI presents a transformative opportunity for education by providing innovative solutions to improve teaching and learning processes. However, effective integration in classrooms hinges on specialized training programs that equip teachers with the necessary skills and knowledge. The framework proposed in this chapter aims to guide the development of such training modules, ultimately building teacher capacity for the effective integration of GenAI into educational settings.

9.3 Course Design

The TPACK framework (Mishra & Koehler, 2006) and the social learning theory (SLT) (Bandura, 1977) will serve as the foundation for this course. The significance of collaborative learning is underscored by SLT, whereas TPACK concentrates on the convergence of technology, pedagogy, and content knowledge. Pre-service and in-service teachers will have more opportunity to collaborate on projects that promote TPACK development, exchange ideas, and learn from one another using this combined approach. This chapter hereby suggests a training program for educators. This course will be divided into three modules, each focusing on a specific aspect of GenAI in education.

9.3.1 Target Audience: K-12 Educators of All Subject Areas

9.3.1.1 Desired Instruction Time: Eight Weeks

9.3.1.1.1 Course Goals

1. Equip educators with a solid understanding of GenAI and its capabilities.
2. Explore diverse pedagogical applications of GenAI across different subjects.
3. Develop practical skills for integrating GenAI effectively into lesson plans.
4. Foster critical thinking and responsible technology use through GenAI activities.

9.3.2 Discipline-Specific Approaches

The course aims to enhance teacher capacity through discipline-appropriate approaches to GenAI literacy, ensuring pre-service educators develop practical skills for integrating GenAI across various subjects. Throughout the semester, the curriculum will emphasize discipline-specific strategies that prepare teachers to leverage GenAI effectively in their classrooms.

9.3.2.1   *Science*

AI Integration in Scientific Inquiry (TPK)

- **Approach:** Analyze how GenAI tools enhance scientific inquiry through data analysis, simulations, and visualization.
- **Implementation:** Engage pre-service teachers in using GenAI-driven simulations and predictive modeling to explore complex scientific concepts.
- **Pedagogy:** Incorporate inquiry-based learning methodologies where students utilize AI to hypothesize, experiment, and interpret results.

9.3.2.2   *Mathematics*

Enhancing Personalized Learning in Mathematics (TPK)

- **Approach:** Investigate GenAI's role in adapting mathematics instruction to individual student needs.
- **Application:** Utilize adaptive learning platforms powered by GenAI to personalize learning experiences, including real-time feedback and differentiated practice activities.
- **Pedagogy:** Integrate formative assessment techniques alongside AI tools to tailor instructional strategies for diverse learner profiles.

9.3.2.3   *Language Arts*

Developing Critical Literacy Skills through GenAI (TPK)

- **Approach:** Examine how GenAI impacts communication, literacy, and critical thinking skills.
- **Utilization:** Implement AI-powered tools for writing assistance and language translation, encouraging critical evaluation of AI-generated content.
- **Pedagogical Strategies:** Design activities that prompt students to analyze AI-generated texts for accuracy, bias, and relevance in literary contexts.

9.3.2.4   *Social Studies*

Exploring Societal Impacts with GenAI (TPK)

- **Approach:** Investigate GenAI's influence on historical research, data analysis, and civic engagement.
- **Integration:** Incorporate AI tools into PBL and simulations to deepen the understanding of historical events and societal issues.
- **Pedagogy:** Encourage critical reflection on the ethical and social implications of AI technologies in social studies contexts.

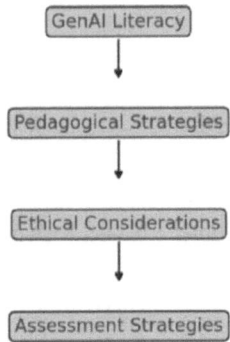

FIGURE 9.1 Flowchart representation of the course framework.

9.4 Framework Design and Implementation

The TPACK framework will guide the integration of GenAI literacy, combining social learning theories with discipline-specific applications. This approach aims to equip pre-service teachers with the necessary knowledge and skills to confidently integrate GenAI into their future classrooms. By leveraging strong pedagogical practices, educators can create meaningful, effective, and engaging learning experiences that prepare students for the challenges and opportunities of an AI-driven world. Figure 9.1 illustrates the course framework.

9.5 Course Structure

Table 9.2 presents the course structure along with the duration of the modules and their objectives.

9.5.1 Module 1: Demystifying GenAI (Two Weeks)

A. Focus: Technological Knowledge (TK) and Content Knowledge (CK)

TABLE 9.2 Representation of the Course Structure

Module	Duration	Objectives
Module 1: GenAI Basics	Two weeks	Understanding GenAI, its capabilities, and its basic applications
Module 2: Pedagogical Applications	Three weeks	Designing learning experiences with GenAI tools
Module 3: Ethical and Assessment Considerations	Three weeks	Addressing ethical issues, data privacy, and assessment strategies

B. Learning Outcomes (K, S, D):

1. Knowledge (K):

   - Define GenAI, its various forms (text, code, image, etc.), and its key applications in education (K)
   - Explain the basic principles of machine learning and neural networks underlying GenAI (K)
   - Identify and compare popular GenAI tools for different uses (text generation, code completion, and image creation) (K)

2. Skills (S):

   - Navigate and utilize user-friendly GenAI platforms with hands-on experience (S)
   - Distinguish between factual and fictional outputs of GenAI, fostering critical evaluation (S)

3. Dispositions (D):

   - Develop a critical perspective toward GenAI capabilities, acknowledging limitations (D)
   - Demonstrate curiosity and openness toward exploring new GenAI tools (D)

C. Activities:

Week one:

   - Interactive lecture with demonstrations of various GenAI forms (K, S)
   - "AI in Action!" Students explore pre-selected GenAI platforms generating text, code, and images (S)
   - Online quiz assessing basic GenAI knowledge (K)

Week two:

   - Guest speaker: Discussion of the ethical considerations of GenAI (K, D) by an AI researcher
   - Group discussion: Analyzing case studies of responsible and irresponsible uses of GenAI in education (K, D)
   - Hands-on activity: Debunking potential biases in GenAI outputs (S)

D. Resources:

   - Articles on types of GenAI and their educational applications
   - Tutorials on beginner-friendly GenAI platforms like Bard (Google AI), Jasper, or ShortlyAI
   - Sample case studies

9.5.2 *Module 2: Unleashing Learning with GenAI (Three Weeks)*

A. Focus: Technological Pedagogical and Content Knowledge (TPACK) and Learner Needs (SLT)

B. Learning Outcomes (K, S, D):

1. Knowledge (K):

- Identify and analyze learning objectives aligned with different GenAI applications in various subject areas (K)
- Explore diverse pedagogical approaches for utilizing GenAI tools in lesson plans (K)
- Understand how GenAI can support differentiated instruction and personalized learning (K)

2. Skills (S):

- Design engaging and age-appropriate lesson plans incorporating GenAI activities (S)
- Adapt existing curricula to leverage GenAI for deeper content understanding and skill development (S)

3. Dispositions (D):

- View GenAI as a tool to empower student creativity and critical thinking (D)
- Foster a collaborative learning environment where students explore GenAI responsibly (D)

C. Activities:

Week three:

- Subject-specific workshops: Educators collaborate to brainstorm GenAI-powered activities for their disciplines (K, S)
- "Beyond Textbooks!" Design a lesson plan utilizing a GenAI tool to enhance a specific learning objective (S)
- Peer feedback session on lesson plans, focusing on pedagogical effectiveness and student engagement (S)

Week four:

- Case studies: Analyzing successful GenAI implementation in classrooms across different subjects (K, D)
- "Personalizing Learning with AI": Exploring GenAI tools for adaptive learning and differentiated instruction (K, S)
- Short online quiz assessing the understanding of pedagogical uses of GenAI (K)

Week five:

- "Student Voice": Guest speaker: A student who has experienced GenAI in the classroom shares their perspective (D)
- Collaborative project: Design a student-led activity where GenAI is used for research or creative expression (S, D)
- Class reflection: Discussing the impact of GenAI on student engagement and learning outcomes (K, D)

D. Resources:

- Lesson plan templates with prompts for GenAI integration
- Curated list of case studies on effective use of GenAI in various subjects

9.5.3 Module 3: Assessment and the Evolving GenAI Classroom (Three Weeks)

A. Focus: TPACK and Skills (SLT)
B. Learning Outcomes (K, S, D):

1. Knowledge (K):

- Identify and evaluate effective assessment strategies for GenAI-based learning activities (K)
- Understand the limitations and potential pitfalls of GenAI in the classroom (K)

2. Skills (S):

- Implement GenAI tools effectively in their classrooms, managing student interaction (S)
- Develop rubrics and assessments for projects incorporating GenAI (S)
- Facilitate discussions on AI ethics and the responsible use of technology with students (S)

3. Dispositions (D):

- Cultivate a culture of innovation and exploration with GenAI in their classrooms (D)
- Reflect on the impact of GenAI on student learning and adapt practices accordingly (D)

C. Activities:

Week six:

- "Assessing the AI-Powered Classroom": Exploring various assessment methods for GenAI projects (e.g., presentations, portfolios, and rubrics) (K, S)

- Hands-on activity: Developing rubrics for evaluating student work generated using GenAI (S)
- Class discussion: Identifying and addressing potential challenges of using GenAI in assessments (K, D)

Week seven:

- Microteaching session: Educators present their GenAI-integrated lesson plans to peers (S)
- Peer feedback and discussion: Focusing on classroom management strategies and student engagement during GenAI activities (S, D)
- Short online survey: Assessing comfort level and confidence in using GenAI in the classroom (D)

Week eight:

- "The Future of GenAI in Education": Guest speaker: An AI education expert discusses trends and future directions (K, D)
- Course reflection: Completing a self-assessment on GenAI knowledge, skills, and dispositions (K, D)
- Action plan development: Identifying strategies for continued exploration and implementation of GenAI in their classrooms (D)

D. Resources:

- Sample rubrics for assessing GenAI-generated content and projects
- Articles on the future of AI in education
- Online resources for ongoing professional development on GenAI tools and best practices

9.5.4 Coursework

- **Weekly quizzes:** Assessing the understanding of key concepts and terminology related to GenAI (K)
- **Lesson plan design and implementation:** Developing and presenting a GenAI-integrated lesson plan (S)
- **Reflective essay:** Analyzing the potential and challenges of using GenAI in education, considering ethical implications (K, D)
- **Peer collaboration and presentations:** Active participation in class discussions, workshops, and microteaching sessions (S, D)

9.5.5 Assessment

- **Formative assessment:** Weekly quizzes, lesson plan feedback, and participation in class activities (K, S, D)
- **Summative assessment:** Lesson plan implementation, reflective essay, and self-assessment (K, S, D)

9.6 Discussion

The proposed framework for integrating GenAI into teacher education programs presents several strengths and weaknesses. Evaluating these aspects is crucial for understanding its potential impact and areas for improvement.

One of the strengths of the framework is its comprehensive coverage, addressing critical areas such as GenAI literacy, pedagogical strategies, and ethical considerations. This holistic approach ensures that educators develop a well-rounded understanding and application of GenAI tools. The framework's emphasis on both discipline-specific practices and practical implementation, through hands-on workshops, case studies, and collaborative projects, ensures that teachers acquire practical skills directly applicable in their classrooms. The focus on ethical considerations, including data privacy, algorithmic bias, and academic integrity, prepares educators to handle potential challenges responsibly, an essential aspect given the complexities of AI technologies. The integration of the TPACK framework and social learning theory ensures pedagogically sound training, fostering collaborative learning beneficial for both teachers and students.

However, the framework also has its weaknesses. One significant limitation is the lack of empirical evidence supporting its effectiveness. While the framework is theoretically robust, more empirical research is needed to validate its impact on actual classroom outcomes, which would enhance its credibility. Another concern is the resource-intensive nature of the framework's implementation. Significant resources, including trained facilitators, access to GenAI tools, and dedicated time for teachers to engage in the training, are required, potentially posing a barrier for some educational institutions. Scalability issues may arise when adapting the framework to diverse educational contexts and varying levels of technological infrastructure. Customizing the training to fit different school environments and teacher backgrounds could be complex.

A critical aspect to discuss is teacher readiness and self-efficacy. Assessing the current level of technology self-efficacy among teachers is crucial, and the framework should include pre-assessment tools to gauge teachers' initial confidence and skills in using GenAI. This will allow for tailored training that meets the specific needs of educators. Long-term support and continuous learning are also essential. Establishing ongoing support systems, such as peer learning communities and access to GenAI experts, will help sustain the integration of GenAI into classrooms. Continuous professional development opportunities should be part of the framework to ensure sustained growth and adaptation.

Incorporating mechanisms for evaluating the impact of GenAI integration on student learning outcomes and gathering student feedback will provide valuable insights for refining the framework. Policy and regulatory considerations are also important. Developing clear policies and guidelines at institutional and governmental levels will support the ethical and effective use of

GenAI in education, and advocacy for such policies should be integrated into the framework. Finally, while the framework provides a general approach, it should also offer subject-specific strategies for integrating GenAI. Different subjects may require unique applications of GenAI tools, and the training should reflect these nuances to be truly effective.

9.7 Conclusion

The proposed framework for integrating GenAI into teacher education programs marks a significant advancement in the effort to modernize educational practices. By providing a structured approach to equip teachers with the necessary skills and knowledge, this framework lays the groundwork for a more innovative and effective educational environment. Its holistic design, combining practical application with ethical considerations and pedagogical soundness, demonstrates a forward-thinking approach to professional development in education.

Looking ahead, several areas warrant further exploration to enhance the framework's impact and effectiveness. First, developing advanced metrics and methodologies to assess the long-term impact of GenAI training on teaching practices and student outcomes will be crucial. These metrics will provide deeper insights into the tangible benefits of GenAI integration and guide future refinements of the framework. Understanding these nuances will ensure that the framework is adaptable and relevant to a wide range of educational settings.

While the framework represents a significant step toward integrating GenAI into teacher education, ongoing research and development are essential. By continuously refining the framework based on empirical evidence and adapting it to diverse educational needs, we can maximize its potential to transform teaching and learning in the digital age.

References

Adiguzel, T., Kaya, M. H., & Cansu, F. K. (2023). Revolutionizing Education with AI: Exploring the Transformative Potential of ChatGPT. *Contemporary Educational Technology*, *15*(3), ep429. https://doi.org/10.30935/cedtech/13152

Alasadi, E. A., & Baiz, C. R. (2023). Generative AI in Education and Research: Opportunities, Concerns, and Solutions. *Journal of Chemical Education*, *100*(8), 2965–2971. https://doi.org/10.1021/acs.jchemed.3c00323

Bahroun, Z., Anane, C., Ahmed, V., & Zacca, A. (2023). Transforming Education: A Comprehensive Review of Generative Artificial Intelligence in Educational Settings through Bibliometric and Content Analysis. *Sustainability*, *15*(17), 12983. https://doi.org/10.3390/su151712983

Bandura, A., & Walters, R.H. (1977). *Social learning theory*, 1, 141–154. Englewood Cliffs, NJ: Prentice hall. http://www.asecib.ase.ro/mps/Bandura_SocialLearningTheory.pdf

Bickerstaff, A., Depriest, A., & Crouch Layne, C. (2024, June 24). *Establish a Teacher AI Literacy Development Program*. Federation of American Scientists. https://fas.org/sssspublication/teacher-ai-literacy-development/

Black, N. B., George, S., Eguchi, A., Dempsey, J. C., Langran, E., Fraga, L., Brunvand, S., & Howard, N. (2024). A Framework for Approaching AI Education in Educator Preparation Programs. *Proceedings of the AAAI Conference on Artificial Intelligence, 38*(21), 23069–23077. https://doi.org/10.1609/aaai.v38i21.30351

Boscardin, C. K., Gin, B., Golde, P. B., & Hauer, K. E. (2024). ChatGPT and Generative Artificial Intelligence for Medical Education: Potential Impact and Opportunity. *Academic Medicine, 99*(1), 22–27. https://doi.org/10.1097/ACM.0000000000005439

Celik, I. (2023). Towards Intelligent-TPACK: An Empirical Study on Teachers' Professional Knowledge to Ethically Integrate Artificial Intelligence (AI)-Based Tools into Education. *Computers in Human Behavior, 138*, 107468. https://doi.org/10.1016/j.chb.2022.107468

Chan, C. K. Y., & Hu, W. (2023). Students' Voices on Generative AI: Perceptions, Benefits, and Challenges in Higher Education. *International Journal of Educational Technology in Higher Education, 20*(1), 43. https://doi.org/10.1186/s41239-023-00411-8

Jobin, A., Ienca, M., & Vayena, E. (2019). The Global Landscape of AI Ethics Guidelines. *Nature Machine Intelligence, 1*, 389–399. https://api.semanticscholar.org/CorpusID:201827642

Koehler, M. J., Mishra, P., & Cain, W. (2013). What is Technological Pedagogical Content Knowledge (TPACK)? *Journal of Education, 193*(3), 13–19. https://doi.org/10.1177/002205741319300303

Luckin, R., & Cukurova, M. (2019). Designing Educational Technologies in the Age of AI: A Learning Sciences-Driven Approach. *British Journal of Educational Technology, 50*(6), 2824–2838. https://doi.org/10.1111/bjet.12861

Luckin, R., Holmes, W., Griffiths, M., & Forcier, L. B. (2016). *Intelligence Unleashed: An Argument for AI in Education* (1st ed.). Pearson Education.

Mishra, P., & Koehler, M. J. (2006). Technological Pedagogical Content Knowledge: A Framework for Teacher Knowledge. *Teachers College Record: The Voice of Scholarship in Education, 108*(6), 1017–1054. https://doi.org/10.1111/j.1467-9620.2006.00684.x

Nair, H. B., & Karan, S. P. (2024). Knowledge, Attitude and Usage of Information and Communication Technology (ICT) and Digital Resources in Pre-Service Teachers. *The New Educational Review, 75*(1), 228–243. https://doi.org/10.15804/tner.2024.75.1.18

Pack, A., & Maloney, J. (2024). Using Artificial Intelligence in TESOL: Some Ethical and Pedagogical Considerations. *TESOL Quarterly, 58*(2), 1007–1018. https://doi.org/10.1002/tesq.3320

Pons, A. (2023). *Generative AI in the Classroom: From Hype to Reality?* https://one.oecd.org/document/EDU/EDPC(2023)11/en/pdf

Redecker, C., & Johannessen, Ø. (2013). Changing Assessment – Towards a New Assessment Paradigm Using ICT. *European Journal of Education, 48*(1), 79–96. https://doi.org/10.1111/ejed.12018

Saimon, M., Mtenzi, F., Lavicza, Z., Fenyvesi, K., Arnold, M., & Diego-Mantecón, J. M. (2024). Applying the 6E Learning by Design Model to Support Student Teachers to Integrate Artificial Intelligence Applications in Their Classroom. *Education and Information Technologies.* https://doi.org/10.1007/s10639-024-12795-9

Tlili, A., Huang, R., Shehata, B., Liu, D., Zhao, J., Metwally, A. H. S., Wang, H., Denden, M., Bozkurt, A., Lee, L.-H., Beyoglu, D., Altinay, F., Sharma, R. C., Altinay, Z., Li, Z., Liu, J., Ahmad, F., Hu, Y., Salha, S., . . . Burgos, D. (2022). Is Metaverse in Education a Blessing or a Curse: A Combined Content and Bibliometric Analysis. *Smart Learning Environments, 9*(1), 24. https://doi.org/10.1186/s40561-022-00205-x

Tlili, A., Shehata, B., Adarkwah, M. A., Bozkurt, A., Hickey, D. T., Huang, R., & Agyemang, B. (2023). What if the Devil is My Guardian Angel: ChatGPT as a Case Study of Using Chatbots in Education. *Smart Learning Environments*, *10*(1), 15. https://doi.org/10.1186/s40561-023-00237-x

UNESCO. (2019). *National Commissions for UNESCO: Annual Report, 2019*. https://unesdoc.unesco.org/ark:/48223/pf0000373753

Wang, K., Ruan, Q., Zhang, X., Fu, C., & Duan, B. (2024). Pre-Service Teachers' GenAI Anxiety, Technology Self-Efficacy, and TPACK: Their Structural Relations with Behavioral Intention to Design GenAI-Assisted Teaching. *Behavioral Sciences*, *14*(5), 373. https://doi.org/10.3390/bs14050373

Yang, A. (2023). *Maximizing AI in the Classroom: Aligning IB ATL Skills with UNESCO's AI Education Guide*. Building Learning Aglity. https://alisonyang.com/ai-in-classroom-ib-unescos/

Zhang, X., Chen, Y., Hu, L., & Wang, Y. (2022). The Metaverse in Education: Definition, Framework, Features, Potential Applications, Challenges, and Future Research Topics. *Frontiers in Psychology*, *13*. https://doi.org/10.3389/fpsyg.2022.1016300

10

GenAI IN SPECIAL EDUCATION

A Case of Teaching and Learning GenAI for Design in Hong Kong Special Schools

Xi Liu, Newman Lau, and Tulio Maximo

10.1 Introduction

In recent years, the rapid development of Generative Artificial Intelligence (GenAI) has attracted significant interest in education (Sağdıç et al., 2024). Artificial intelligence (AI) has been widely applied in special education to diagnose, enhance learning, assess, and assist for decades (Hopcan et al., 2022). However, most AI discussions have focused on the concept broadly, with limited research explicitly examining the role of GenAI in special education (Barua et al., 2022; Hopcan et al., 2022; Knox et al., 2019; Kumar et al., 2023; Marino et al., 2023; Singh & Jain, 2024; Swargiary & Roy, 2024).

This study addresses this gap by exploring how GenAI can serve as an opportunity for special education. We begin by reviewing the concepts of special educational needs, special education, and special schools. Subsequently, we summarize the applications of GenAI in special education contexts.

Our literature review highlights several research gaps. Although some studies explore GenAI's use, such as providing personalized learning experiences and enhancing teaching efficiency (Sağdıç et al., 2024), there is a limited discussion on teaching students with special educational needs (SEN) to learn and use GenAI. GenAI education is emerging in secondary schools (Chiu, 2023a) but remains scarce in special schools. If this digital divide continues, it will undermine equality in education.

Thus, teaching and learning GenAI in special education is worth further exploration. Learning to draw and design with GenAI tools may be an effective entry point, as it fits the characteristics and interests of students with SEN (Osborne, 2003). This idea is proposed and elaborated in Section 10.4, followed by a case study in Section 10.5. The study involves teaching students at Hong Kong special schools to use text-to-image GenAI tools for game design. We examined the learning and design experiences of GenAI and

DOI: 10.1201/9781003422433-10

the perspectives of students, teachers, and social workers and the findings are discussed in Section 10.6.

Based on the literature review and case study findings, Section 10.7 discusses the potential and concerns of teaching GenAI in special schools. Section 10.8 provides recommendations for integrating GenAI education into special education. The final section concludes the study.

10.2 Special Educational Needs, Special Education, and Special Schools

Special educational needs (SEN) is an umbrella term encompassing various conditions and learning difficulties that may require additional support for children (UNESCO, 2017). SEN includes, but is not limited to, physical disabilities, developmental delays, sensory impairments, and behavioral or emotional disorders (Swargiary & Roy, 2024).

The terminology of SEN varies across contexts. For example, the Hong Kong Education Bureau (EDB) adopts the term "SEN." Table 10.1 provides an overview of nine types of SEN as classified by the Hong Kong EDB (2021). In the United Kingdom, the term "Special Educational Needs and Disabilities" (SEND) is widely used (GOV.UK, 2023). In addition, the term "special needs" is also used when not limited to educational context or child population.

Special needs education, or special education, refers to educational accommodations and support for students with SEN (UNESCO, 2017). This support includes adjusting teaching methods, adopting accessible equipment, and creating inclusive environments. Education for children with SEN is provided in three ways: special schools, special classes in ordinary schools, and integrated education in mainstream classes (Eurydice, 2023).

Hong Kong has 62 special schools receiving government aid. These schools can be divided into six categories (see Table 10.2). Schools for children with intellectual disabilities can be further classified into five types (EDB, 2023).

It is important to note that students in a single type of special school may have varying SEN, and individual students can present with multiple SEN conditions. For instance, Shatin Public School in Hong Kong, a special school for children with mild intellectual disabilities, reported in 2023 that there were 189 students with ASD, 15 with AD/HD, 9 with Down Syndrome, 13 with hearing impairments, 5 with visual impairments, and an additional 27 with other SEN conditions (Shatin Public School, 2023). Therefore, when conducting teaching and learning activities in special schools, teachers must consider the diverse learning needs of students and adjust support strategies accordingly.

TABLE 10.1 Overview of Nine Types of SEN

Types of SEN	Overview
Intellectual Disability	Intellectual Disability refers to neurodevelopmental conditions characterized by a concrete cognitive style, short attention spans, limited vocabulary, poor social skills, and coordination challenges affecting daily self-care.
Autism Spectrum Disorder	Autism Spectrum Disorder (ASD) is a neurodevelopmental condition. Individuals may find it challenging to connect and communicate with others, face difficulties in social interactions, and exhibit restricted and repetitive behaviors.
Attention Deficit/ Hyperactivity Disorder	Attention Deficit/Hyperactivity Disorder (ADHD) refers to a neurodevelopmental condition that affects behavior. The key symptoms include impulsivity, hyperactivity, and poor attention, making learning and social relationships more challenging.
Mental Illness	Mental Illness refers to health conditions that affect thinking, feeling, behavior, or bodily functioning. There are various types of mental illnesses.
Specific Learning Difficulties	Specific Learning Difficulties (SpLD) refer to challenges in reading, writing, math, and motor coordination. Students with SpLD have normal intelligence.
Physical Disability	Physical Disability refers to physical conditions limiting the mobility, dexterity, or stamina.
Visual Impairment	Visual Impairment is defined as vision in the better eye that cannot be restored to normal levels, even with glasses or surgery. It can be classified as mild, moderate, severe, or total blindness.
Hearing Impairment	Hearing Impairment refers to disorders in the auditory system that affect hearing ability. Hearing thresholds over 25dB HL are considered to be hearing impairments.
Speech and Language Impairment	Speech or Language Impairment refers to a series of communication difficulties, such as stuttering, voice impairment, and impaired articulation.

10.3 Applications of GenAI in Special Education

The rapid growth of AI has brought promising applications in special education (Barua et al., 2022; Drigas & Ioannidou, 2013; Fahimirad & Kotamjani, 2018; Marino et al., 2023). Among these, GenAI has gained significant attention. GenAI refers to machine learning models that can generate new text, images, audio, and video from the existing data (Han & Cai, 2023;

TABLE 10.2 Types and Number of Hong Kong Special Schools

School Types		Numbers of Schools
School for Children with Intellectual Disability (SID)	Schools for Children with Mild Intellectual Disability	12
	Schools for Children with Mild and Moderate Intellectual Disability	6
	Schools for Children with Moderate Intellectual Disability	14
	Schools for Children with Severe Intellectual Disability	10
	Schools for Children with Mixed Intellectual Disability	1
School for Children with Physical Disability (SPD)		7
School for Children with Visual Impairment (SVI)		2
School for Children with Hearing Impairment (SHI)		1
School for Social Development (SSD)		8
Hospital School (HS)		1

Hsu & Ching, 2023). Notable GenAI tools include chatbots like ChatGPT, Copilot, and Claude and text-to-image platforms like Midjourney, Stable Diffusion, and DALL-E. In addition, platforms like Sora, Runway, and Pika have text-to-video generation capabilities.

GenAI has multiple applications in special education (Chiu, 2023a; Marino et al., 2023). The four major applications are summarized as follows:

Enhancing Student Learning: GenAI can enrich the learning experiences by providing personalized, engaging, and interactive education tailored to students' needs (Chen et al., 2020; Kazi et al., 2022; Sağdıç et al., 2024). It helps students with SEN in developing skills and improving academic performance (Marino et al., 2023; Hopcan et al., 2022).

Supporting Teachers and Administration: GenAI can assist with teaching, assessment, and administrative tasks. AI systems can handle routine duties so teachers can focus on complex tasks (Marino et al., 2023). Teachers' top five uses of GenAI in K-12 education include creating assignments, generating tests, summarizing text, taking advice on teaching methods, and planning lessons (Laak & Aru, 2024).

Enhancing Assistive Technology: GenAI can benefit assistive technologies. Incorporating AI features can improve independence and quality of life for individuals with special needs (de Freitas et al., 2022). An example is the Be My Eyes app, which uses GPT-4 for image-to-text interpretation (Bendel, 2024). Users can take a photo and receive a description on the App. It offers 24/7 assistance to blind and low-vision individuals and reduces dependence on the help of others.

Medical Applications: GenAI can aid in diagnosing early disabilities and tracking behavioral patterns (Sağdıç et al., 2024). For example, GenAI-based models have been proposed for detecting ASD using electroencephalogram (EEG) signals and natural language text (Li et al., 2023; Mukherjee et al., 2023).

Despite its potential, the use of GenAI in special education also raised concerns and challenges (Bendel, 2024; Laak & Aru, 2024; Sağdıç et al., 2024). Teachers' concerns focus on students' over-reliance on GenAI, inaccurate information, and lack of GenAI training for teachers. There is debate about whether the complexity of GenAI tools poses challenges for students with SEN in using them effectively. Ethical issues like the digital divide, data privacy, and technology addiction also arise.

However, many concerns can be addressed by fostering AI literacy among teachers and students. AI literacy refers to the ability to evaluate, communicate, and use AI as a tool (Chiu et al., 2024; Long & Magerko, 2020). AI literacy, including GenAI education, is emerging in secondary schools. For example, Hong Kong EDB (2023) launched the "Module on Artificial Intelligence for Junior Secondary Level" in all local public schools. The CUHK Jockey Club AI for the Future Project (2024) published a curriculum on GenAI. These initiatives aim to educate students to understand the concept of AI, critically evaluate AI technologies, learn the use of GenAI, and reflect on ethical considerations.

AI literacy education is still at its early stages, and AI-based curricula are rarely provided in Hong Kong special schools (Liu et al., 2024). Teachers' and students' knowledge of AI and GenAI tools still needs to be improved. However, our research found that some students in special schools have mastered various digital literacy and design skills, which are considered prerequisites for AI literacy (Chiu et al., 2024). These findings support the promotion of AI literacy and GenAI education in special schools.

10.4 GenAI for Design in Special Education

The previous section summarizes the various applications of GenAI in special education, including teaching, learning, assistive technology, and medical detection. However, using GenAI to generate images or videos is rarely integrated into special education contexts.

Special education can greatly benefit from GenAI's capabilities of generating visual content. Art, design, and digital technology education play crucial roles in special education, as they align well with the needs of students with SEN. Unlike other subjects, art and design activities rely not solely on verbal communication or cognitive functions. Instead, they provide a common ground for students with SEN to effectively relate and interact with others (Osborne, 2003). Digital technologies, on the other hand, facilitate equal access to learning and the curriculum for all students (Florian & Hegarty, 2004).

In addition, many students with SEN show interest in courses related to digital literacy and design (Brown & Murray, 2001; Crowell, 2018). Courses like visual arts, craft-making, media design, and information and communication technology (ICT) can yield tangible outcomes, which give students a sense of achievement while developing their skills and literacy (Ofsted, 2011; Design & Technology Association, 2023).

Moreover, research indicates that some students in special schools are interested in pursuing careers in the art, design, and technology industries (Liu et al., 2023). In this context, teaching GenAI to special school students and introducing its use in design are highly beneficial.

In the next section, we will present a case study conducted at two special schools in Hong Kong, where we incorporated text-to-image GenAI learning into a six-session game design workshop. We examine students' learning and design experiences of GenAI and the perspectives of students, teachers, and social workers. By analyzing this case, the study explores the feasibility, potential, and concerns of integrating GenAI education into special schools. Ultimately, it provides recommendations for future GenAI teaching and learning efforts in special education settings.

10.5 Case Study: Teaching GenAI in Hong Kong Special Schools

This section presents a case study on teaching GenAI tools to students at special schools in Hong Kong for design purposes. In this study, the students act as GenAI learners and designers using GenAI tools.

10.5.1 Case Overview

The case demonstrates a collaborative project where students from two Hong Kong special schools worked with adult designers to create digital games for their fellow students. The project included six design workshop sessions at each school, featuring eight main design tasks: (1) empathizing with the player, (2) character design, (3) using GenAI for design, (4) game mechanism design, (5) background and user interface (UI) design, (6) logo design, (7) sound effects, and (8) user testing. The goal was to leverage the schools' existing hardware resources to design inclusive and engaging casual games.

The study received approval from the Institutional Review Board (IRB) of The Hong Kong Polytechnic University, and consent was obtained from students and their parents before participation. Our literature review indicates that the learning and use of GenAI by students with SEN remains underexplored. Due to ethical considerations surrounding new technologies for students with SEN, this study was conducted as a pilot on a small scale. Specifically, one of the eight design tasks in the second workshop was assigned to teach students on using text-to-image GenAI tools. The study aimed to qualitatively understand special school students' and stakeholders' experiences and perspectives in learning and using GenAI.

10.5.2 Contexts and Participants

We invited two schools, each catering to different SEN conditions, to join the project. The first school serves children with physical disabilities (SPD), some of whom may have additional special needs. The second school specializes in supporting children with intellectual disabilities (SID), including those with ASD or AD/HD. Involving diverse special schools aims to generate comprehensive findings that benefit the broader SEN community.

Seven secondary school students participated in the game design workshop, with four students from SID and three from SPD. Recruitment was based on school recommendations and required consent from students and their parents. Selection criteria focused on students' interest in art, design, and digital technology, regardless of their SEN conditions. Students attended the first workshop together at The Hong Kong Polytechnic University, while the remaining workshops, including the GenAI session, were held at their respective schools. Table 10.3 provides details on the participants and the workshops they attended. Although P7 was absent from session 2, we prepared a GenAI catch-up session for him. Therefore, his data was counted with an asterisk and analyzed.

In addition to student participants, three types of stakeholders played vital roles in the workshop: adult designers, school liaison teachers, and social workers. Two adult designers were responsible for planning and guiding the

TABLE 10.3 Information of Student Participants

ID	Gender	Schools	SEN Conditions	Interest	Attended Workshops
P1	Male	SID	Mild ID, ASD	Drawing, video production, and music	S1, S2, S3, S4, S6
P2	Male	SID	Mild ID	Digital game	S1, S2, S3, S4, S5, S6
P3	Female	SID	Mild ID, ASD	Drawing	S1, S2, S3, S4, S5, S6
P4	Male	SID	Mild ID, ASD	Drawing and piano	S1, S2, S3, S4, S5, S6
P5	Female	SPD	PD (progressive muscle weakness)	Gardening, handicrafts, and drawing	S1, S2, S3, S5, S6
P6	Male	SPD	PD (reduced coordination)	Sports, music, and drawing	S1, S2, S3, S4, S6
P7	Male	SPD	PD (highly spastic)	Design and technology (VR)	S2*, S3, S4, S5, S6

design workshop. The school liaison teachers created the workshop schedule and provided support as needed. Social workers contributed by offering connections, suggestions, and technical support.

10.5.3 Selected Text-to-Image GenAI Tools

In the GenAI workshop session, we introduced GenAI tools such as Stable Diffusion Online (Playground) and Canva. We selected these tools based on several key principles:

- **Geographic Availability:** The tool must be able to be used in Hong Kong.
- **Cost-Free:** The tool must be free of charge.
- **Ease of Use:** The tool should be user-friendly and have a simple interaction flow.
- **Responsible Content:** The tool should have a positive reputation and provide high-quality child-friendly content.
- **Preferred Chinese Language:** The tool should preferably be available in Traditional Chinese.

Stable Diffusion Online (Playground) was chosen as the main tool due to its simplicity. It does not require registration and has a simple task flow. However, it only supports English prompts, which can be a barrier as students in Hong Kong special schools prefer to use Traditional Chinese. Despite this, its simplicity led us to select it as the primary option.

Canva was selected because it offers a Traditional Chinese language option. However, a mobile phone number or email is required for registration. Moreover, it has a more complex task flow than Stable Diffusion Online (Playground). Therefore, we kept Canva as an alternate tool and provided instruction according to students' performance. Figure 10.1 compares the task flow of the two tools.

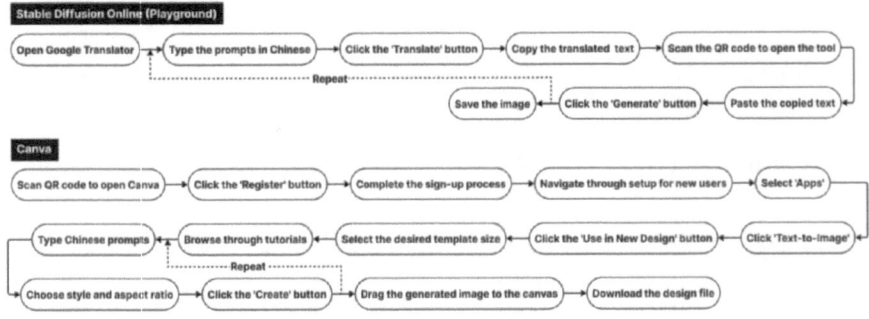

FIGURE 10.1 Stable Diffusion Online (Playground) and Canva's task flows.

10.5.4 GenAI Design Session

Each workshop took one hour, with the GenAI design session taking approximately 30 minutes. First, the adult designers presented examples of AI-generated images, such as a slideshow featuring four AI-generated cartoon cats and the prompts. Next, designers conducted a step-by-step live demonstration of using the GenAI tools. After that, students could try the tool themselves. Designers provided feedback and suggestions after students generated their images. Finally, designers encouraged students to present their generated images and conclude the session.

10.5.5 Data Collection and Analysis

We collected the following data and employed the corresponding techniques for analysis:

1. Video recordings: Videos were recorded during the workshops. We employed a qualitative approach to observe, code, and analyze students' behaviors and opinions in these videos. This data provided in-depth insights into students' performance during the GenAI learning sessions.
2. Generated images: We analyzed the images generated during the workshop to assess students' mastery of the text-to-image GenAI tool. It helped determine whether the students copied the design examples or generated novel images.
3. Questionnaires: Students completed a questionnaire to provide feedback on their game design workshop experience. Additionally, three liaison teachers and a social worker completed a separate questionnaire to share their perspectives.
4. Students' design choices: Although each school hosted only one GenAI-related workshop, students could continue using GenAI for their game design projects. Students were encouraged to design backgrounds and characters for the digital casual games using any method – hand-drawn, iPad-based apps, or GenAI tools. We analyzed whether students incorporated AI-generated elements into their game design projects.

Through triangulation of data from video recordings, questionnaires, and design artefacts, we comprehensively understood how students in special schools perceive, learn, and use GenAI for design.

10.6 Findings of Learning and Using GenAI for Design

10.6.1 Students' Challenges and Strengths in Learning Text-to-Image GenAI

We analyzed students' performance and visualized the GenAI learning process through the user journey map method (see Figure 10.2). Students'

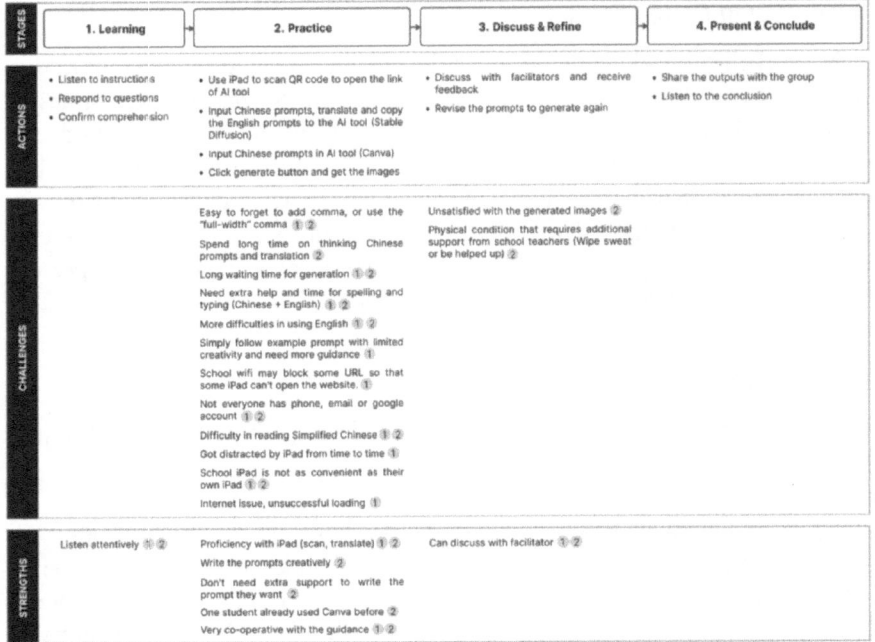

FIGURE 10.2 Students' GenAI learning journey referring to the: (1) SID group and (2) SPD group.

learning journey was divided into four main stages: (1) learning, (2) practice, (3) discuss and refine, and (4) present and conclude.

In the first stage, students gained a basic understanding of text-to-image GenAI and their potential effects. During the practice stage, despite step-by-step instructions, students encountered networking issues, typing and spelling difficulties, and a lack of creativity in prompting. Nevertheless, all students completed the image generation task, highlighting their strengths. In the third stage, students discussed with designers, revised the prompts, and regenerated their images. Finally, the designer guided the students in presenting their AI-generated images and summarizing their learning experiences.

In total, 14 challenges and 7 strengths were identified and grouped into three categories each.

Challenges

1. **Technical and Access Challenges:** Registration requirements for tools like Canva hindered in-class learning, as students could not use mobile phones during classes. Internet access issues and limited accessibility of GenAI services in Hong Kong further complicated the situation. Using non-personal

iPads often requires extra accessibility setup, which slows down the learning progress.

2. **Language Challenges:** Students were more comfortable with Traditional Chinese. Typing, spelling, and translating prompts into English added complexity. The frequent punctuation errors affected image generation.
3. **Creativity and Focus Challenges:** Students from SID copied examples directly at the beginning, limiting their creative exploration. Additionally, iPads and pop-up ads sometimes caused distractions.

Strengths

1. **Digital Literacy and Technology Proficiency:** Students showed strong digital skills, including proficiency in using iPads, scanning QR codes, and using Google Translate. Some students had prior experience with design platforms like Canva.
2. **Eagerness to Learn and Effective Communication:** Students followed instructions, sought help, and engaged in discussions to deepen their understanding and use of GenAI tools.
3. **Creativity Potential and Independence:** Students from SPD demonstrated creativity in writing prompts and showed independence and confidence, requiring minimal support.

10.6.2 Students' Design Experience with Text-to-Image GenAI

10.6.2.1 Students' First Attempts at Generating Images Using GenAI Tools

In addition to the learning journey analysis, Table 10.4 shows the analyses of students' initial attempts at AI-generated content (AIGC). The prompts and generated images were evaluated based on Benton et al.'s method for design examples and creativity (Benton et al., 2019). Relevance was judged by the ability to generate the corresponding images required by the task. The novelty was graded into three levels: (1) fixation – copying the example prompts only; (2) recycling – combining new keywords with the example prompts; and (3) novel – writing something unrelated to the example prompts.

The results showed that all students were able to generate images using the GenAI tools. However, most of the students asked for some help, such as confirming that they were doing it correctly or reminding them to add commas. The images generated by SPD students demonstrated greater creativity and detail as they created recycled or novel prompts. This result aligns with

TABLE 10.4 The Example Prompts and Students' First Prompts

ID	Example Prompts	Students' First Prompts	Relevant to Design Task	Fixate/ Recycle/Novel
P1	Cat, cartoon	Cat, cartoon	Yes	Fixate
P2	Cat, cartoon	Cat, cartoon	Yes	Fixate
P3	Cat, cartoon	Cat, cartoon	Yes	Fixate
P4	Cat, cartoon	Cat, cartoon	Yes	Fixate
P5	forest, game background, 2D cartoon	Forest, little girl, rainbow	Yes	Recycle
P6	forest, game background, 2D cartoon	Scary forest, dinosaur, colorful	Yes	Recycle
P7	forest, game background, 2D cartoon	Sea creature, 3D	Yes	Novel

FIGURE 10.3   Images generated during the GenAI workshop sessions.

Source: Photograph by the author.

the findings discussed in Section 10.6.1. Figure 10.3 shows images generated during the workshops. The first image on the left is from SPD, while the second and third images are from SID.

We observed that students from SPD expressed dissatisfaction with the first generated content. For example, P5 firmly stated she "does not like" the first image. P6 did not answer, but his shrug indicated his dissatisfaction. P7 sought advice on improving the image effect. Conversely, students from SID focused on following task instructions without strong opinions on the images.

We explained why the prompts could not generate the desired output and guided students to refine their prompts. We demonstrated another prompt example and provided tips for writing effective prompts. The effects of the next attempts improved significantly.

10.6.2.2 Students' Choices: GenAI versus Other Methods

Students were encouraged to design digital casual games using any method – hand-drawn, iPad-based apps (e.g., Procreate and 8bit Painter) or GenAI tools. We analyzed their design preferences and choices to determine whether they would use GenAI tools after the learning session.

First, we examined students' preferences between GenAI and other digital tools or hand drawing methods. P1 preferred hand drawing. P3 liked seeking inspiration from GenAI before drawing. P5 favored GenAI for its better effects, and P6 was comfortable with both approaches.

Next, we analyzed the game design artefacts to see if they incorporated AI-generated elements. Two students from SPD (P5 and P7) used AI-generated images. P6 did not use GenAI tools; instead, he used Procreate, an iPad-based application. All four SID students did not use any GenAI tools in their project. They chose hand drawing methods and 8bit Painter, an iPad-based pixel art application, for their game designs.

10.6.3 Students' Perspectives on GenAI

Students' perspectives on text-to-image GenAI include three aspects: (1) students' attitude toward learning GenAI, (2) the ranking of interest in GenAI design compared to other design tasks, and (3) the continuance intention to design with GenAI tools.

1. **Students' attitude toward learning GenAI:** All seven students enjoyed learning text-to-image GenAI tools. Six students chose "Like" it, and one chose "Strongly Like" it (see Table 10.5). Three students shared additional views: P5 thought it was a fun experience, P2 appreciated the fast generation process, and P6 found the tool easy to learn.
2. **Ranking of interest in GenAI design compared to other design tasks:** Students rated their interest in eight key design tasks from 0 to 5, and we calculated the average interest level for each task across the two schools. The results showed varying interest levels (see Table 10.6). Students from SPD ranked the GenAI design task as the most interesting, while students from SID ranked it as the second least interesting. This result aligns with the

TABLE 10.5 Self-Reported Attitudes toward Learning Text-to-Image GenAI

Schools	Strongly Dislike	Dislike	Neutral	Like	Strongly Like
SID	0	0	0	4	0
SPD	0	0	0	2	1

TABLE 10.6 Interest Level for Each Design Task

SPD		SID	
Design Tasks	*Interest Score*	*Design Tasks*	*Interest Score*
Using GenAI for design	4.33	Empathizing with the player	4.00
Character design	3.67	Character design	4.00
Game mechanism design	3.67	Sound effects	3.75
User testing	3.67	Game mechanism design	3.75
Logo design	3.67	Background and user interface (UI) design	3.75
Background and user interface (UI) design	3.33	Using GenAI for design	3.50
Empathizing with the player	3.00	User testing	3.50
Sound effects	2.67	Logo design	3.25

TABLE 10.7 Self-Reported Continuance Intention to Design with GenAI

Schools	Very Unlikely	Unlikely	Neutral	Likely	Very Likely
SID	0	0	2	2	0
SPD	0	0	1	0	2

challenges and design choices discussed in Sections 10.6.1 and 10.6.2. SID mainly enrolls students with intellectual disabilities and ASD. Although technology is important to their education, teachers encourage students to engage in social interactions and prevent addiction to electronics. Conversely, SPD supports students with physical disabilities, who rely more on assistive technologies like wheelchairs and digital devices daily. Thus, these students are generally more familiar with electronic devices, making them quick learners of new technology.

3. **Continuance intention to design with GenAI:** Students were open to the idea of designing with GenAI in the future, with students from SPD showing a higher willingness (see Table 10.7). Two students from SID chose "neutral," and one chose "likely." Two SPD students chose "likely," and one chose "neutral." P2 indicated the intention to use it when asked for their opinions, and P3 saw GenAI as an inspiration.

A conflict exists between students' design method preferences and their intention to continue using GenAI. For example, P5 preferred AI-generated output to hand drawing but remained neutral about future use. Additionally, inconsistencies appeared between students' attitudes and design choices. Although all students were interested in learning GenAI, only two from SPD integrated AIGC into their projects.

The Technology Acceptance Model (TAM) helps interpret the gap between intentions and actual behavior. According to TAM, perceived usefulness and ease of use impact users' intentions, which in turn affect their behavior (Ni & Cheung, 2023). While some students admired the speed of text-to-image generation, others were disappointed with the outputs. This implies that GenAI tools may not have produced superior results to enhance students' design outputs. To address this, future workshops could include comprehensive tutorials and an advanced GenAI curriculum. Additionally, several challenges identified during the learning process compromised their user experience. These challenges hinder students' further exploration of GenAI technology.

10.6.4 Teachers' and Social Worker's Perspectives toward GenAI Education

Three liaison teachers and a social worker who participated in the project were invited to share their perspectives on the design workshop and the students' learning experience with GenAI. All the participants provided positive feedback about the workshops. They observed that students engaged in the workshop sessions with enjoyment and interest. The teachers and social worker agreed that the students gained significant educational benefits, including the following:

1. Improved comprehension and practical experience with GenAI technology
2. Enhanced design knowledge and digital literacy
3. Strong market research capabilities
4. Better understanding of the game design process
5. Improved creativity, problem-solving, and communication skills

A teacher suggested to offer students long-term courses in their special school. With a regular schedule, student attendance can be ensured. Furthermore, the curriculum of the long-term course is more comprehensive, which provides students with sufficient time for learning and hands-on practice.

Overall, this feedback from the educators highlighted the valuable learning outcomes and positive impact of the GenAI design workshops.

10.7 Potential and Concerns of GenAI Education in Special Schools

The literature review highlighted various applications of GenAI in special education. In this case study, we explored teaching GenAI for design in special schools. This section discusses the potential and concerns of teaching and learning GenAI in this context.

10.7.1   Potential of Teaching and Learning GenAI

The rapid advances in GenAI technology hold promise for special education. Just a year after our case study, AI features in Canva have rapidly evolved, expanding to over 80 AI-powered applications. Its text-to-image application now includes image, graphic, and video generation. Features like background removal and sketch-to-digital image conversion were added to the tool. This indicates a commitment to refining GenAI tools for better user experience.

As GenAI becomes more prevalent in industries, teaching it in special education is increasingly valuable. Our research showed interest in art and technology among students with SEN, with some wishing to pursue related careers. Learning GenAI offers students alternative design options and inspiration. Equipping students with GenAI skills can prepare them for the future.

GenAI can promote inclusion and enhance students' autonomy and competence. Text-to-image or text-to-video GenAI tools empower students with physical disabilities, particularly those with fine motor challenges, to visualize ideas effortlessly. In our workshop, a student with high levels of spasticity generated graphics independently through AI technology. The use of GenAI increased his autonomy and competence by allowing him to participate equally in design tasks.

GenAI education can be integrated into interdisciplinary activities to cultivate various skills. First, GenAI tools that accept text input can train students to articulate their needs through clear and concise written expression. This training helps students to enhance their conceptual and communication skills. Second, GenAI can support language learning by encouraging engagement with English and Chinese prompts. This process increases opportunities to use English and adds a new motivation to language learning. Lastly, GenAI has the potential to stimulate creativity. Although some students in the case study copied design examples on their first attempts, they demonstrated creative potential when educators provided appropriate guidance.

Finally, because text-to-image or text-to-video GenAI produces visual content, it could effectively engage students with SEN, such as those with autism (Colorosa & Makela, 2014; Fleming & Mills, 1992). This approach can be used as a starting point for developing AI literacy in special schools. By learning and using GenAI tools, students can enhance their understanding, evaluation, and practical application of AI.

10.7.2 Concerns of Teaching and Learning GenAI

While the previous section discussed the potential of teaching and learning GenAI in special schools, concerns have also been raised.

First, although GenAI can empower some students, it may make others less confident. Students with different SEN conditions do not accept GenAI equally or learn at the same speed. Research shows that students with strong critical thinking, AI, and digital literacy skills benefit more from GenAI (Chiu, 2023). GenAI tools often rely on text input and require advanced thinking and writing skills, which may be difficult for some SEN populations. For example, in our case study, students from SID faced more challenges than students from SPD, struggling with spelling and punctuation when typing in prompts. Although all students enjoyed the GenAI sessions, those from SID preferred other design tasks. They chose hand-drawn and digital applications over GenAI to complete their game design project. This finding indicates that GenAI should be an optional aid, not a source of frustration. AI courses must be planned carefully to consider students' needs and strengths, avoiding negative feelings like anxiety.

Second, students may become overly reliant on GenAI and superstitious about its capabilities. If students lack critical thinking and AI literacy, they may trust the information provided by AI without questioning its accuracy (Laak & Aru, 2024). This concern is particularly relevant in special schools, where students with intellectual disabilities might struggle to evaluate information critically. In design scenarios, students might assume GenAI is superior because it can produce content quickly in various styles. During our workshop, student P5 initially preferred the AI-generated content over her own drawings. She seemed more confident in the AI's abilities than about her own skills. However, only when the designer guided P5 to think further did she realize the AIGC was not always superior to her artistic work. Therefore, it is significant to incorporate GenAI education into special schools, equipping students with a comprehensive understanding of GenAI and not over-relying on it.

Lastly, policies and regulations around GenAI still need to be completed. Issues such as how students can safely and compliantly use these tools need careful planning before implementing GenAI courses in special education. The United Nations Educational, Scientific and Cultural Organization (UNESCO) urged governments to regulate GenAI in education, including age limits and data protection (Wayne et al., 2023). Some GenAI platforms have age restrictions. For example, ChatGPT is not for users under 13, and those aged 13 to 18 need parental permission. Chinese GenAI tools, such as Wenxin Yiyan and Tongyi Qianwen, also require guardian consent for users under 18. However, strong measures for privacy protection are still lacking. If GenAI is promoted in special schools, student privacy and data security must be prioritized.

10.8 Recommendations for GenAI Education in Special Education

In the previous section, we discussed the potential and concerns of teaching students with SEN about GenAI. This section offers recommendations for teaching GenAI in special education.

10.8.1 Select GenAI Tools Based on Accessibility, Reliability, and Ease of Use

We summarized three key considerations for selecting suitable GenAI tools: accessibility, reliability, and ease of use.

1. **Accessibility:** This involves choosing tools that accommodate students with different SEN conditions and considering geographical, network, financial, and linguistic accessibility.

   - **Geographical Accessibility:** Ensure that the GenAI tools are available in the local region. For instance, OpenAI has not granted access to Hong Kong, which creates a barrier to using ChatGPT. Therefore, we must consider whether the tools are accessible within the school environment.
   - **Network Accessibility:** Tools must work smoothly within the school's internet setup. Some websites may be blocked or load slowly in this environment, so it is crucial to test in the school's network environment first.
   - **Financial Accessibility:** Choose affordable tools for the school or students. Some GenAI tools offer free trials, while others charge for advanced features. Consider budget constraints and necessary features in the curriculum.
   - **Linguistic Accessibility:** Select tools that support the local language. Many AI chatbots support multiple languages, but some text-to-image GenAI tools only accept English prompts. Language support is essential in Hong Kong, where Traditional Chinese is prevalent in special schools.

2. **Reliability:** This involves a solid reputation, privacy and data protection, and high-quality design.

   - **Solid Reputation:** Tools should be known for providing children with age-appropriate content and accurate information.
   - **Privacy and Data Protection:** Ensure that the tools have strong privacy policies to protect children's information.
   - **High-Quality Design:** Tools should have a clean interface without excessive ads. Avoid tools with distracting pop-ups.

3. **Ease of Use:** This involves a user-friendly registration process and interaction flow.

- **Registration Process:** Teachers must ensure students have access to all information required for registration during class. If mobile verification is restricted, prepare alternatives.
- **Interaction Flow:** The tool should have a simple, memorable, and learnable flow for students with SEN. If it is too complex, it may not be suitable for beginners.

10.8.2 Creating Learner-Centered Experiences Grounded in Autonomy, Competence, and Relatedness

Adopting a learner-centered mindset is crucial when planning GenAI educational content. The self-determination theory (SDT) provides insights for structuring learning activities. According to SDT, autonomy, competence, and relatedness are human beings' three basic psychological needs (Chiu, 2023b).

- Autonomy: Feeling control over one's independent actions and decisions.
- Competence: Experiencing mastery of necessary skills.
- Relatedness: Sensing connection with others and sharing a common goal.

Our case study found that combining GenAI learning with specific application scenarios enhances students' understanding and motivation. For example, we used GenAI to design game characters and backgrounds. GenAI tools were introduced as an alternative option to handdrawing and digital drawing. This approach aligned with the SDT principle of relatedness by making the learning content relevant to students' goals.

We also discovered that students are more inclined to use GenAI when it increases their efficiency and task effectiveness. One student used GenAI for game design because it helped him complete a challenging drawing task independently (autonomy). Another student felt that AIGC could generate effects they could not achieve alone (competence). This finding suggests that GenAI learning can meet students' needs for autonomy and competence, which are often interrelated (Chiu, 2023b). Therefore, the benefits of GenAI for students, such as skill development and autonomy, should be emphasized when conducting GenAI learning activities.

10.8.3 Developing the GenAI Curriculum in a Long-Term, Interdisciplinary, and Collaborative Way

We recommend planning a GenAI learning course with a long-term perspective. GenAI learning encompasses various applications and practical projects. A short-term introduction covers only superficial aspects and needs more depth. Long-term courses can systematically teach students about GenAI knowledge and hands-on practice. Scheduling is another consideration; ad hoc sessions are challenging for special schools due to individual schedule differences. In our workshops, student absenteeism was common. Long-term courses that are integrated into the school curriculum ensure better attendance.

In addition, we suggest project-based GenAI learning through interdisciplinary cooperation. GenAI involves multidisciplinary skills like critical thinking and digital literacy (Chiu, 2023a; Chiu et al., 2024). Therefore, GenAI learning can adopt a project-based learning (PBL) mode that integrates multidisciplinary content. For example, our game design project combined students' visual arts and ICT knowledge to achieve game design tasks. By adopting the project-based approach, teachers can integrate GenAI with other subjects' learning.

Finally, we encourage collaboration between schools and enterprises for GenAI education. The technology industry and higher education institutions are advanced in GenAI research and applications. Collaborating with them can ease pressures on teachers regarding curriculum development. Previous studies highlight insufficient AI knowledge and training for K-12 teachers (Laak & Aru, 2024). Involving companies and universities enriches teaching content and provides students with industry exposure. Such university-industry collaborative education programs are already being implemented at universities. For example, Aliyun released the PAI Artlab × 100 programme to establish in-depth education partnerships with 100 schools. Similarly, this model can be applied to special education.

10.9 Conclusion

In conclusion, this study explored GenAI's potential to enhance learning and design experiences in special education settings. The research first reviewed the key concepts of special educational needs, special education, and special schools. It then examined the main applications of GenAI that could be beneficial in this context. A need for GenAI education in special schools was identified.

Through a case study conducted in Hong Kong special schools, the study investigated students' learning experiences and perspectives on using text-to-image GenAI tools. Insights were gathered from students, teachers, and social workers involved in the process. The findings indicate that students and stakeholders in special schools expressed positive attitudes and openness toward learning and using GenAI. All participating students were able to learn how to use the text-to-image GenAI tools for design purposes.

The research also identified challenges and strengths during the GenAI learning process.

Drawing on the literature review and the empirical case study findings, the study discussed the potential for and concerns in teaching and learning GenAI in special schools. It concluded by providing recommendations for effectively integrating GenAI education into special education practices.

References

Barua, P. D., Vicnesh, J., Gururajan, R., Oh, S. L., Palmer, E., Azizan, M. M., Kadri, N. A., & Acharya, U. R. (2022). Artificial Intelligence Enabled Personalised Assistive Tools to Enhance Education of Children with Neurodevelopmental Disorders-A Review. *International Journal of Environmental Research and Public Health*, 19(3), 1192. https://doi.org/10.3390/ijerph19031192

Bendel, O. (2024). How Can Generative AI Enhance the Well-being of Blind? *Proceedings of the AAAI Symposium Series*, 3(1), 340–347. https://doi.org/10.1609/aaaiss.v3i1.31232

Benton, L., Varotsis, G., & Vasalou, A. (2019). Leading by Example: Exploring the Influence of Design Examples on Children's Creative Ideation. *International Journal of Human-Computer Studies*, 122, 174–183. https://doi.org/10.1016/j.ijhcs.2018.09.007

Brown, J., & Murray, D. (2001). Strategies for Enhancing Play Skills for Children with Autism Spectrum Disorder. *Education and Training in Mental Retardation and Developmental Disabilities*, 36(3), 312–317.

Chen, L., Chen, P., & Lin, Z. (2020). Artificial Intelligence in Education: A Review. *IEEE Access*, 8, 75264–75278. https://doi.org/10.1109/ACCESS.2020.2988510

Chiu, T. K. F. (2023a). The Impact of Generative AI (GenAI) on Practices, Policies and Research Direction in Education: A Case of ChatGPT and Midjourney. *Interactive Learning Environments*, 1–17. https://doi.org/10.1080/10494820.2023.2253861

Chiu, T. K. F. (2023b). Using Self-Determination Theory (SDT) to Explain Student Stem Interest and Identity Development. *Instructional Science*, 52(1), 89–107. https://doi.org/10.1007/s11251-023-09642-8

Chiu, T. K. F., Ahmad, Z., Ismailov, M., & Sanusi, I. T. (2024). What are Artificial Intelligence Literacy and Competency? A Comprehensive Framework to Support Them. *Computers and Education Open*, 6, 100171. https://doi.org/10.1016/j.caeo.2024.100171

Colorosa, S. R., & Makela, C. (2014). Integrative Literature Review: Styles of Learning for Autism Spectrum Disorders and Human Resource Development: Informing Performance Management. *International Journal of Business and Social Science*, 5(13), 1–12.

Crowell, C. (2018). Interaction Design of Full-Body Interactive Play Experiences for Children with Autism. *Proceedings of the 2018 Annual Symposium on Computer-Human Interaction in Play Companion Extended Abstracts*, 11–16. https://doi.org/10.1145/3270316.3270606

CUHK Jockey Club AI for the Future Project. (2024). *Generative AI Curriculum Introductory Brochure*. CUHK Jockey Club AI for the Future Project. https://cuhkjc-aiforfuture.hk/index.php/en/aibrochure/

de Freitas, M. P., Piai, V. A., Farias, R. H., Fernandes, A. M. R., de Moraes Rossetto, A. G., & Leithardt, V. R. Q. (2022). Artificial Intelligence of Things Applied to Assistive Technology: A Systematic Literature Review. *Sensors*, 22(21), Article 21. https://doi.org/10.3390/s22218531

Design & Technology Association. (2023). *Special Educational Needs*. https://www.designtechnology.org.uk/for-education/special-educational-needs/

Drigas, A. S., & Ioannidou, R.-E. (2013). A Review on Artificial Intelligence in Special Education. In M. D. Lytras, D. Ruan, R. D. Tennyson, P. Ordonez De Pablos, F. J. García Peñalvo, & L. Rusu (Eds.), *Information Systems, E-Learning, and Knowledge Management Research* (pp. 385–391). Springer. https://doi.org/10.1007/978-3-642-35879-1_46

Education Bureau. (2023). *Innovation and Technology Education*. https://www.edb.gov.hk/tc/curriculum-development/kla/technology-edu/resources/InnovationAnd-TechnologyEducation/resources.html

Eurydice. (2023). *Special Education Needs Provision within Mainstream Education*. https://eurydice.eacea.ec.europa.eu/national-education-systems/ireland/special-education-needs-provision-within-mainstream-education

Fahimirad, M., & Kotamjani, S. S. (2018). A Review on Application of Artificial Intelligence in Teaching and Learning in Educational Contexts. *International Journal of Learning and Development*, 8(4), Article 4. https://doi.org/10.5296/ijld.v8i4.14057

Fleming, N. D., & Mills, C. (1992). Not Another Inventory, Rather a Catalyst for Reflection. *To Improve the Academy*, 11(1), 137–155. https://doi.org/10.1002/j.2334-4822.1992.tb00213.x

Florian, L., & Hegarty, J. (2004). *ICT and Special Educational Needs: A Tool for Inclusion*. McGraw-Hill Education.

GOV.UK. (2023). *Children with Special Educational Needs and Disabilities (SEND): Overview*. https://www.gov.uk/children-with-special-educational-needs

Han, A., & Cai, Z. (2023). Design Implications of Generative AI Systems for Visual Storytelling for Young Learners. *Proceedings of the 22nd Annual ACM Interaction Design and Children Conference*, 470–474. https://doi.org/10.1145/3585088.3593867

Hong Kong Education Bureau. (2021). *Types of Special Educational Needs*. Integrated Education and Special Education Information Online. https://sense.edb.gov.hk/en/types-of-special-educational-needs/index.html

Hopcan, S., Polat, E., Ozturk, M. E., & Ozturk, L. (2022). Artificial Intelligence in Special Education: A Systematic Review. *Interactive Learning Environments*, 0(0), 1–19. https://doi.org/10.1080/10494820.2022.2067186

Hsu, Y.-C., & Ching, Y.-H. (2023). Generative Artificial Intelligence in Education, Part One: The Dynamic Frontier. *TechTrends*, 67, 603–607. https://doi.org/10.1007/s11528-023-00863-9

Kazi, K., Devi, S., Sreedhar, B., & Arulprakash, P. (2022). A Path Towards Child-Centric Artificial Intelligence Based Education. *International Journal of Early Childhood Special Education*, 14, 9915–9922. https://doi.org/10.9756/INT-JECSE/V14I3.1145

Knox, J., Wang, Y., & Gallagher, M. (Eds.). (2019). *Artificial Intelligence and Inclusive Education: Speculative Futures and Emerging Practices*. Springer. https://doi.org/10.1007/978-981-13-8161-4

Kumar, A., Nayyar, A., Sachan, R. K., & Jain, R. (Eds.). (2023). *AI-Assisted Special Education for Students With Exceptional Needs*. IGI Global. https://doi.org/10.4018/979-8-3693-0378-8

Laak, K. J., & Aru, J. (2024). Generative AI in K-12: Opportunities for Learning and Utility for Teachers. In A. M. Olney, I. A. Chounta, Z. Liu, O. C. Santos, & I. I. Bittencourt (Eds.), *Artificial Intelligence in Education. Posters and Late Breaking Results, Workshops and Tutorials, Industry and Innovation Tracks, Practitioners, Doctoral Consortium and Blue Sky. AIED 2024. Communications in*

Computer and Information Science (Vol. 2150). Springer. https://doi.org/10.1007/978-3-031-64315-6_49

Li, Y., Liao, I. Y., Zhong, N., Toshihiro, F., Wang, Y., & Wang, S. (2023). Generative AI Enables the Detection of Autism Using EEG Signals. In W. Jia, W. Kang, Z. Pan, X. Ben, Z. Bian, S. Yu, Z. He, & J. Wang (Eds.), *Biometric Recognition* (Vol. 14463, pp. 375–384). Springer Nature. https://doi.org/10.1007/978-981-99-8565-4_35

Liu, X., Lau, N., Chuin, A., Leung, W. K. R., Ho, A. H. S., Das, M., Liu, M., & Kwok, C. L. (2024). Understanding Students' Perspectives, Practices, and Challenges of Designing with AI in Special Schools. *Proceedings of the Eleventh International Symposium of Chinese CHI*, 197–209. https://doi.org/10.1145/3629606.3629625

Liu, X., Lau, N., Chuin, A., Reginia, W., Ho, A., Das, M., Liu, M., & Kwok, C. L. (2023). Enhancing Design Competencies for Students with Special Educational Needs for Future Career Development. *IASDR Conference Series*. https://dl.designresearchsociety.org/iasdr/iasdr2023/fullpapers/113

Long, D., & Magerko, B. (2020). What is AI Literacy? Competencies and Design Considerations. *Proceedings of the 2020 CHI Conference on Human Factors in Computing Systems*, 1–16. https://doi.org/10.1145/3313831.3376727

Marino, M. T., Vasquez, E., Dieker, L., Basham, J., & Blackorby, J. (2023). The Future of Artificial Intelligence in Special Education Technology. *Journal of Special Education Technology*, 38(3), 404–416. https://doi.org/10.1177/01626434231165977

Mukherjee, P., Sadhukhan, S., Godse, M., & Chakraborty, B. (2023). Detection of Autism Spectrum Disorder (ASD) from Natural Language Text using BERT and ChatGPT Models. *International Journal of Advanced Computer Science and Applications*, 14(10). https://doi.org/10.14569/IJACSA.2023.0141041

Ni, A., & Cheung, A. (2023). Understanding Secondary Students' Continuance Intention to Adopt AI-Powered Intelligent Tutoring System for English Learning. *Education and Information Technologies*, 28(3), 3191–3216. https://doi.org/10.1007/s10639-022-11305-z

Office for Standards in Education Children's Services and Skills (Ofsted). (2011). *Meeting Technological Challenges: Design and Technology in Schools 2007–10 (Ofsted Survey Report Reference No. 100121)*. Office for Standards in Education Children's Services and Skills.

Osborne, J. (2003). Art and the Child with Autism: Therapy or Education? *Early Child Development and Care*, 173(4), 411–423. https://doi.org/10.1080/0300443032000079096

Sağdıç, A., Elumar-Efe, E., & Sani-Bozkurt, S. (2024). GenAI, Robots, and Inclusive Special Education: Autism Spectrum Disorder in the Age of Generative AI. In R. C. Sharma & A. Bozkurt (Eds.), *Advances in Educational Technologies and Instructional Design* (pp. 309–326). IGI Global. https://doi.org/10.4018/979-8-3693-1351-0.ch015

Shatin Public School. (2023). *2022–2023 Annual Report*. https://www.shatinpublicschool.edu.hk/download/document/20231127151958677759812987 22598.pdf

Singh, S., & Jain, P. (2024). AI in Special Education: Emerging Trends and Challenges. In S. Misra, A. Jain, M. Kaushik, C. Banerjee, & Y. Singh (Eds.), *Advances in IT Personnel and Project Management* (pp. 56–75). IGI Global. https://doi.org/10.4018/979-8-3693-0790-8.ch005

Swargiary, K., & Roy, K. (2024). *AI Angels: Empowering Children with Special Needs through Artificial Intelligence*. Scholar Press.

UNESCO. (2017). *Inclusive Education and Effective Classroom Practices*. https://unesdoc.unesco.org/ark:/48223/pf0000248254/PDF/248254eng.pdf.multi

Wayne, H., Fengchun, M., & UNESCO. (2023). *Guidance for Generative AI in Education and Research*. UNESCO Publishing.

INDEX

Note: Page numbers in *italics* indicate figures, and page numbers in **bold** indicate tables in the text